Mairi Rennie is unusually placed to combine the insights of science with the intuitions of literature and music, together with her own subjective biological experience. She has a PhD and has been a lecturer in English literature in UK and USA. She believes literature is primarily concerned with human nature and its overt expression in action and relationship. This runs together with a deep understanding of the sciences which similarly attempt to explain human behaviour. The marriage of these two approaches allows unique and significant insights into the human psyche.

The author lives in the countryside and over many years has observed the behaviour of many animal species. She relates this to her own subjective biological experience as a human female and in particular to the powerful animal imperatives of motherhood. However as an accomplished musician, Mairi Rennie is also aware of a spiritual dimension to human life, the mysterious sources of inspiration, the dynamics of performance, and the communication of the deepest human sentiments.

The Apes
That Sing Their Souls

Mairi Rennie

The Apes
That Sing Their Souls

Vanguard Press

A CIP catalogue record for this title is
available from the British Library.

ISBN 978 184386 411 0

*Vanguard Press is an imprint of
Pegasus Elliot MacKenzie Publishers Ltd.*
www.pegasuspublishers.com

First Published in 2008

**Vanguard Press
Sheraton House Castle Park
Cambridge England**

Printed & Bound in Great Britain

Dedication

To Dearest Ann

Contents

Introduction   15

The Place of Homo Sapiens in the Cosmos   21

The story of the Species   38

Paradise and the Restless Spirit: Habitat   80

Fear of Famine: Diet and Exercise   101

Perception, Communication and Fantasy   115

EROS--Sex and the Family: Breeding Behaviour   139

PHILIA—'Brotherly' Love And Fellowship   165
The Self and other Homo sapiens

Aggression   204

The Self: Self Assertion, Surrender,
and the Life of the Spirit   245

Quo Vadis? A Purpose for the Planet?   290

O lyric love, half angel and half bird
And all a wonder and a wild desire --
Boldest of hearts that ever braved the sun,
Took sanctuary within the holier blue,
And sang a kindred soul out to his face,--
Yet human at the red ripe of the heart—

Robert Browning, *The Ring and the Book,* 1, 1391 – 1396

Introduction

What a piece of work is man! How noble in reason! how infinite in faculty! in form, in moving, how express and admirable! in action how like an angel! in apprehension how like a god! the beauty of the world! the paragon of animals! And yet, to me what is the quintessence of dust?

Shakespeare, *Hamlet*, II, ii, 323-29

A 100,000 Years Ago

Suppose biologists from another sphere visit 'Africa' some 100,000 years ago. They see smoke drifting upwards from a distant grove and imagine it is the result of a lightning strike or bush fire. On moving closer they see a fire deliberately kept burning by a large group of medium-sized apes. These apes are hominids; they stand and walk on two legs. This allows their upper limbs to move freely so that their hands are wonderfully nimble and expressive. Unlike other primates these animals lack body hair, and have moist, black skins.

The biologists begin to study these animals. They name them Homo sapiens. They watch how groups of some hundred and fifty individuals usually gather near water, and move along river-banks or the sea shore. The animals' senses fit them for their environment. They have good daytime sight, but a relatively poor sense of smell. Their naked skin is very sensitive, and they enjoy physical contact with their own family group. They are omnivorous and adventurous in their tastes. Their hearing is good within a limited range and they are alert to the slightest rustle or footfall, in a world full of the sounds of other wild creatures. These hominids kill for food, and are themselves killed and eaten by other carnivores. Survival depends on a deep understanding of the environment and closely bonded group living.

Bigger, stronger, and faster predators easily catch a lone Homo sapiens. The loneliness and fear felt by an isolated individual prompts the animal to find safety in the group, just as single sheep, horses, and dogs are frantic to find protection in a flock, herd or pack. Social animals have bonding mechanisms, and in Homo sapiens these are especially deep and meaningful. The animals communicate with great subtlety by physical expression, and sound signals, but have no language.

The observers notice that the apes' breeding behaviour is conditioned by the unusual fertility pattern of its females. Instead of coming 'into season', the females have a few fertile days each month, but these are not advertised by compelling mating hormones. Like bonobos, the animals copulate frequently, even when there is no chance of fertilization. Sex is therefore more for bonding than breeding, and Homo sapiens form strong pair bonds. These can be long standing, or at least long enough to secure the future of the offspring. The strength of the pair bond can bring great pleasure and emotional warmth, but betrayal and disappointment often arouse equivalent despair and jealous anger. Sometimes the bonding fails, leaving the young physically and emotionally vulnerable. Some other animals such as pandas or kangaroos give birth to infants so immature that gestation continues outside the womb, and to a lesser extent the same is true of man. The infant is highly dependent for many months. It takes many years for the young to reach physical maturity so that socialization is a long and complex process. The extended dependency of the Homo sapiens young requires a strong parental pair bond and a large, cooperative social group.

By closely observing Homo sapiens, the biologists notice a behaviour that hardly exists in other animals—a capacity for 'humanity'. Homo sapiens, like the animal it is, can be 'brutal' but also astonishingly affectionate and 'humane', as if it has a kindness gene. It seems to be able to understand the minds of others, and even experience their emotions. This ability to empathize underlies generous and kindly behaviour and the development of a sense of justice.

However, Homo sapiens all too easily reverts to its raw animal condition to become particularly cruel and aggressive, as if this is its emotional default setting. Humane behaviour is therefore like a higher development, and needs positive reinforcement.

A 100,000 Years Later—The Modern World

The female ape steered her car into a parking place and with her three young made her way into the superstore. There she mingled with others of her kind, experiencing moments of aggression, fear for her young, or pleasure in tracking down food. The young were particularly attracted to sweet foods coloured red or yellow, or crisp and salty foods--all tending to have a high fat content. At times they were extremely manipulative in trying to persuade the mother animal to provide them with what they wanted. The other apes went about their business, often in pairs or other family groupings. For the most part the apes moved about in close proximity with no interaction but there were occasional moments of greeting or annoyance. There had been times when shortages of a particular item led to competitive behaviour and even aggression.

A 100,000 earth years later the biologists return. To their amazement, the bi-pedal apes previously observed on the African plains have colonised the whole world with a huge and growing population. All other hominids, including the Neanderthals, are extinct. Homo sapiens in 100,000 years, or more particularly over the last 10,000 years, has walked the Earth, flown to the moon, built vast cities, and devised complex systems of law and trade. It has learned to communicate with extraordinary sophistication, not only with language but with music, painting, drama and other expressive arts. This success has distanced it so far from its biological origins it is a shock for the biologists to relate modern man to the wild creature that so recently had no language, no metal, and no agriculture.

At some time Homo sapiens developed an amazing ambition for progress. Other hominids learned to make tools but hardly improved them over millennia; for them there was virtually no cultural development. Man, on the other hand, developed mental capacities that drove it forward to imagine, invent and create. Such a potential may be thought of as 'sapientia', not so much wisdom but rather a particular restlessness, spirit of enterprise that presses the animal to seek change and betterment.

This ape's cooperative nature and sapientia has allowed it to dominate nature, but it never outgrows the underlying primitive instincts that it needed so recently to survive as a wild animal. These impulses are sometimes figured in the human imagination as 'the evil one' or the devil, prompting lust, greed, aggression and the assertion of self at the expense of others. There is a constant confrontation between this animal nature, and the moral, cooperative spirit. Beyond this, the biologists realise, human activity now seems to be coming into conflict with the Earth or Gaia. It is as if Gaia itself is moral, and reacting to man's greed and aggression.

Sapientia has brought enormous benefits to mankind, but it also generates discontent, an appetite for excitement and a compulsive need for mobility. This unusual animal characteristic is now becoming dangerous as it stimulates huge material demands, and a wasteful use of resources.

The visiting observers conclude that the species is at a point of crisis. Never before has its ability to cooperate, invent and rise above its animal nature been so important. If 6, 8, or even 9 billion Homo sapiens fail to control their greed and aggression, they will destroy themselves and the Earth as they know it. With great apprehension the biologists return to their sphere, unsure whether this wonderful animal will survive into the next millennium.

The Place of
Homo sapiens in the Cosmos

The space of the world is immense, before me and around me:
If I turn quickly, I am terrified, feeling space around me;
Like a man in a boat on very clear, deep water, space frightens and confounds
me.

I see myself isolated in a universe, and wonder
What effect I can have. My hands wave under
The heavens like specks of dust that are floating asunder.
.

I hold myself up, and feel a big wind blowing
Me like a gadfly into the dusk, without my knowing
Whither or why or even how I am going.

So much there is outside me, so infinitely
Small am I, what matter if minutely
I beat my way, to be lost immediately?

How shall I flatter myself that I can do
Anything in such immensity? I am too
Little to count in the wind that drifts me through.
D.H. Lawrence, 'Song of a man who is not loved'

Ape-people

Biologically Homo sapiens is a recently evolved sub-Saharan species of no particular importance in the vast timescale of life on Earth. However, modern Homo sapiens for the most part does not experience itself as just another ape species. This ape plays football, sings opera, performs heart surgery, and fights cruel wars. It covers its body with dress and adornments, populates enormous conurbations, organizes abundant food

21

supplies, transports itself in amazing machines, communicates like Michelangelo, Beethoven and Shakespeare, and has a moral sense and a spiritual awareness. Its abilities seem to set it apart, but modern genetics prove that all human beings—Einstein, Marilyn Monroe, the Queen of England, George Washington, Buddha, Jesus and all mankind—are hominid apes, only 1.6% genetically different from chimpanzees[1], and their other close primate relatives.

The Long Pre-history of Homo sapiens

A 100,000 years ago large bands of almost hairless brown-skinned apes moved across the African savannah from grove to grove, picking berries, digging roots, collecting leaves, scavenging and hunting food animals. They had no metal, no cereals, no dairy animals, and no set pattern to their existence, and for more than 60,000 years they had no speech. Even so they walked from Africa to Australia, and began to colonize all the more hospitable regions of the Earth.

Once speech developed it still took another 30,000 years for the animal to begin to live a settled life. Three hundred human generations goes back to the beginning of agriculture some 10,000 years ago, less than 10 % of Homo sapiens' existence as a species. 10,000 years is immeasurably ancient and beyond human record. 5,000 years is about the limit of the human historical imagination with the beginning of writing and some surviving buildings. Human history only comes into focus about 3,500 years ago, with real clarity developing only in the first millennium B.C.

The Sudden Impact of the Modern

After this animal-paced start Homo sapiens has rushed into technology in a brief minute of space-time. Its roaring, flashing activity criss-crosses the ball of the planet and tunnels under its surface. Oil, gas and water are sucked up from under the Earth's crust. Minerals are torn out of the rocks. Objects fly off into the atmosphere. The dark side of the globe is spattered with gatherings of lights. Transport webs breed across the Earth's crust and over the liquid expanses of ocean. This awesome technology has promoted a huge growth in the human population. One species provides food for another but Homo sapiens has long refused to accept itself as part of the food chain. It can protect itself and its group, so that it survives whether it is fit or not. For the individual and its group this is welcome, but for the natural mechanisms of the planet it is highly damaging. Fairly limited climate change could now easily precipitate human population chaos.

Driven by sapientia the man-made environment now alters so rapidly, that the life experience of one generation is very different from the next. The present generation has never known a time when moths were like snowflakes in the headlights, summer air hummed with insect life, or chilblains were an inevitable winter discomfort. They are unaware of the loss of countryside or the sudden collapse of a wildlife species; they cannot relate to their parents' hardships, any more than their parents can relate to those of the generations before them. The utopian efforts of one generation become the norm of the next. This is making huge demands on the planet's resources. Like aphids infesting and killing the plant on which they depend, Homo sapiens has become a plague across the Earth. Sapientia now has to change its focus from raw concepts of material improvement to an all-encompassing understanding of the interconnectedness of change.

Life on Earth as we know it may already be quivering on the cusp, possibly from natural causes or more possibly from human activity. The sheltering atmosphere could begin to disperse, radiation to intensify, the mix of gases to change, and the Earth's creatures begin to struggle for diminishing water supplies and other life essentials. Life itself could disappear and the planet again become a bare globe of rock orbiting the sun, but scarred forever with Homo sapiens' tracks and trash.

In the course of nature Homo sapiens will become extinct. Archaeologists of perhaps a different species will try to understand the suppurating landfill sites festering like abscesses in the Earth's crust and the huge dumps of debris left from its occupation. Homo sapiens' existence will be known only by fossilized remains—assuming there will be some future creature with the consciousness to understand these relics of man's existence. Tennyson faced this shocking possibility when it was first raised in the 1830s:

> Are God and nature then at strife
> That Nature lends such evil dreams ?
> So careful of the type [species] she seems
> So careless of the single life;

> "So careful of the type" but no.
> From scarped cliff and quarried stone
> She cries "A thousand types are gone:
> I care for nothing, all shall go."

> ...And he, shall he,

> Man, her last work, who seemed so fair...

> Be blown about the desert dust,
> Or sealed within the iron hills
> Tennyson, *In Memoriam,* lv 8-12; lvi 1-4, 19-20

The Prison of the Present

Living in this comfortable present, modern Homo sapiens has little awareness of the briefness and unimportance of its biological existence. Like all animals Homo sapiens lives principally in the present. How can Homo sapiens relate itself to the age of the Earth or the Universe when it takes a mental effort to recall a time when computers and mobile phones were rare? Skilled historians can interpret the past but modern western man is imaginatively detached even from comparatively recent times by its present huge technological success. It can hardly relate to a world, still within living memory, when cars were rare and electricity and running water were a luxury, never mind central heating, antibiotics, and air travel.

It takes great imaginative effort to picture a familiar place as it was a century ago, or a century ahead. Real people, with all the emotions and the bodily feelings we experience, must have chatted in our market place, drunk in our pub, watched their children play in our space in their 'eternal' present. Our future tenancy of their space was to them unimaginable, just as we cannot envisage the generations ahead inheriting our world and using it as their own. Man's perception of time is related to the animal's lifespan and metabolic rate.

The Vastness of the Cosmos

'Where wast thou when I laid the foundations of the Earth? ' God asks Job. The Old Testament writer seems to have a sense of the grandeur and mystery of the Earth in the huge expanse of time before the appearance of mankind. When Homo sapiens builds with what it calls 'limestone', it is handling the Earth's geological past, the fossilized remains of millions of tiny sea creatures that died millions and millions of years ago; coal, sand, granite, chalk are all products of distant events in Earth's history. The Earth is nearly five thousand million (five billion) years old and the universe was formed nearly fifteen thousand million (fifteen billion, 15,000,000,000) years ago. In comparison just one million years is far beyond man's experience or imagination; just a 100,000 years goes back towards the emergence of Homo sapiens, before the development of speech or man's migration out of Africa.[2]

If the age of the universe were a century, the modern world began a minute ago. The age of the Earth would be a third of that century, about thirty years. One billion years (one thousand million, 1,000,000,000) would be six years, or seventy two months, or 2016 days. One million years would be a thousandth of that time—two days. One 100,000 years would be a tenth of that time or about five hours. The last 10,000 years would be about half an hour, and historic time just fifteen minutes. The pyramids and Stonehenge were built in that last quarter of an hour. Christ lived and died about six minutes ago. The Renaissance began in Italy two minutes ago and the Industrial Revolution, which brought about the modern world we know, began in the last minute of the universe's century. To us the present seems secure and long lasting but it is just sixty seconds out of a hundred years, one moment out of more than 52 million.

Space is even more unimaginable with more than a hundred million galaxies. Our Milky Way galaxy alone has a hundred billion stars. The Sun is merely one of that hundred billion—a mere dot of dust in a whirl of matter, and the Earth a microscopic speck caught in its orbit. The whole mass is expanding and eventually the expansion might speed up so that gravity is overwhelmed and the universe explodes in a 'big rip'. The sun's nuclear furnace will eventually heat up, evaporate the oceans and leave the Earth like a shrivelled apple; or the sun itself might expand and engulf the planet. At present the galaxy is probably only half way through its history. Meanwhile tons of space dust, asteroid rocks and ice balls sometimes a kilometre wide, shower our near space every day. Fortunately Jupiter is much bigger than the Earth and its stronger gravity acts like a huge vacuum cleaner sucking in most of this space debris before it reaches Earth. Even the moon is protective. Direct impacts on the Earth are therefore rare; the last catastrophic one occurring 65 million years ago.

Back through uncountable sunrises, sunsets, summers, winters, the Earth has orbited the sun. The Earth's dry land has shifted, divided and re-formed over time. The land that was to become Europe was once near the equator. The huge landmass of Pangea once floated on molten magma, then began to fragment. As the land moved, sea beds crumpled up into chalk hills; vast estuaries dried up to become beds of sandstone. The segments of crust or tectonic plates at times have collided or crushed against each other. Sudden impacts must have been apocalyptic. Some 100,000,000 years ago the plates began to crush together, so that the land folded and rucked up into the chalk hills of southern England, and the mountain ranges of the Alps and the Himalayas. The plates still move centimetre by centimetre with periodic volcanic eruptions and seismic spasms. The Earth's crust stretches and suddenly snaps releasing the terrible energy of earthquakes and tsunamis and to this day steam still issues from the seabed and the ocean boils.

Uniquely in the solar system, and perhaps the wider universe, the Earth for this moment hosts a blooming of life. This is the result of a combination of unusual conditions. Unlike many solar systems ours has a single sun, so that the planetary orbits are unusually stable. The single moon's mass and orbit stabilizes the Earth's axis and generates its magnetic fields, which fend off cosmic rays harmful to life. Its effects on the ocean tides have also greatly aided evolution. The planet is at present enveloped in an atmosphere unusually benign to terrestrial life. The lower layers are unstable—swirling, surging, sucking up and showering down water vapour and parting to allow through the sun's radiation. Seventy per cent of the surface is covered with life-giving water. However, these hospitable conditions took many millions of years to develop, and are by no means permanent. Despite Jupiter and the moon, space debris has periodically collided with the planet over the millennia. This fall-out from space may have injected the Earth with the 'stardust' from which the first vestiges of life appeared as a spawn of biomass in the oceans, about a third of the way through the Earth's history. Since then, for over three billion years there has been a continual flux of life and death as life forms are forced to adapt or die.

Volcanic eruptions, reversals of the Earth's magnetic field, solar events or 'wobbles' of the planet's spin, axis or orbit affect the world climate. At times droughts have lasted for centuries; at times it has rained for a thousand years. Ice ages have lasted millennia and have hugely extended the polar regions. Snow and ice then reflect the sun's warmth back into space, further cooling the planet. Natural global warming thaws the ice fields releasing huge masses of melt water, raising the levels of the oceans but also allowing the land to lift as the weight of the ice slips away. As the oceans warm and melt, the dark water no longer reflects the sun's light away, but absorbs it, increasing the warming. The oceans also expand and raise water levels further. The present era is an interglacial at the end of the Pleistocene ('most recent') epoch which had been controlling the Earth's climate for 1,750, 000 years.

The balance of carbon dioxide and other gases in the atmosphere also changes. Carbon is like the 'blood' of the planet, circulating through all living things, fixed in rock, sunken in peat bogs and dissolved in the oceans. There may be a limit to how much CO_2 can be absorbed by the oceans. Already the extra CO_2 has increased the acidity of the oceans and this is damaging marine life—especially shelled creatures and corals. If the oceans become saturated, the extra CO_2 will be left in the atmosphere. Animal respiration and the processes of decay release carbon; plants absorb carbon and release oxygen to balance the system. Even without Homo sapiens' activities, the global climate is unstable, and quite small changes can have enormous runaway effects. The diversion of a river may, over the long term, alter flows of salt and fresh water, disturb ocean currents and change whole weather systems. Arctic melt water may dilute the salt of the northern Atlantic so that the Gulf Stream flows further south or ceases to flow altogether. Britain would then have a climate more like Alaska despite general global warming.

The Fragility of Life

There have already been catastrophic mass extinctions when life was almost obliterated. The Permian extinction of 250 million years ago was probably caused by volcanic activity in what is now Siberia. The energy released was the equivalent of a billion atomic bombs and over the following 8,000 years it melted methane deposits on the deep ocean floors and this heated the Earth by ten degrees centigrade, so destroying 95% of all living things. It took a 100,000 years for life to recover. All this happened long before the evolution of flowering plants some 100,000,000 years ago, or mammals, never mind man. The most recent mass extinction was 65,000,000 years ago as a result of the 10 kilometre wide Chicxulub asteroid crashing into the Earth near modern Mexico. The impact and its aftermath exterminated perhaps 70% of the Earth's species. The dinosaurs were perhaps the most significant casualties, becoming extinct after an existence of a 100,000,000 years.[3] The gap in nature that followed allowed mammals to establish themselves. Otherwise the Earth's present population might have been scaly reptiles and their descendants with little consciousness or memory, millennium after millennium. A few rat-like mammals might have clung to life at the margins of this reptilian kingdom.

The world climate is warming so that if this current trend continues, in the foreseeable future the Earth could be warmer than it has been since the evolution of man. There is some argument about a causal connection between this warming and Homo sapiens' activities, but certainly clearing forests, ploughing, burning, industrial pollution and burning fossil fuels releases huge amounts of carbon. Whether natural processes or human activities release carbon, if the oceans warm up, they will also begin to release their carbon increasing the 'greenhouse effect' which, in turn, will warm the Earth further. The whole could become a spiral of rising temperatures. Like the Sorcerer's Apprentice—a rash student experimenting with his master's spells—man is capable of unleashing forces beyond its imagination or comprehension. If the sea-surface temperature rises even by half a degree centigrade, the thermal energy generated is the equivalent of thousands of atomic bombs. This nuclear equivalent energy would then be released in ferocious hurricanes and there would be no learned Sorcerer to quell the tumult.

Climate Changes and Human History
Smaller climate changes may have precipitated events in human history. 10,000 years ago the earth had warmed after the last ice age and concomitantly agriculture began. The Roman Empire enjoyed a thousand years of warmer climate between 500 BC to 500AD. The voyages of the Norsemen occurred during two hundred years of unusual warmth between 900 to 1100 AD. Genghis Khan migrated westwards during a

particularly cold period. The Black Death took its terrible toll during a cold spell which lowered the immune systems of the European population. During Shakespeare's lifetime England endured a little ice age. Shakespeare describes a year of misery when it rained so that rivers flooded, crops were waterlogged and sheep drowned:

> ...the winds
>
> ...have sucked up from the sea
>
> Contagious fogs; which falling in the land
>
> Have every pelting river made so proud
>
> That they have overborne their continents;
>
> The ox hath therefore stretch'd his yoke in vain,
>
> The ploughman lost his sweat, and the green corn
>
> Hath rotted ere his youth attain'd a beard:
>
> The fold stands empty in the drowned field,
>
> The crows are fatted with the murrion flock;
>
> Shakespeare, *A Midsummer Night's Dream*, II, I, 88-97

Between 1650 and 1800, Europe was colder than it had been for ten thousand years. 1683-84 was a terrible winter with thick ice covering the land for two months, and the sea froze 5 kilometres into the English Channel. The eruption of Mount Laki in Iceland in the summer of 1783 devastated western Europe. A suffocating haze of poisonous gas trapped the summer heat, and blighted crops and livestock:

> The sun, at noon, looked as black as a clouded moon, and shed a rust-coloured ferruginous light on the ground and floors of rooms; but was particular lurid and blood-coloured at rising and setting. All the time the heat was so intense that butchers' meat could hardly be eaten on the day after it was killed; and the flies swarmed so in the lanes and hedges that they rendered the horses half frantic, and riding irksome.
>
> Gilbert White, *The Natural History of Selborne*, letter LXV

During the early nineteenth century the Thames froze almost every ten years so that there were 'frost fairs' on it. Between 1812 and 1820 there were six white Christmases in London. This was the London of Dickens' childhood and his writing has created the concept of the traditional white Christmas which lasts to this day. Snow is now rare in modern England, but in the national imagination Christmas comes 'in the bleak midwinter' when 'snow had fallen snow on snow'. The eruption of Tambora in the East Indies in 1815 meant there was no summer in 1816. The strange meteorological conditions helped to inspire Mary Shelley's *Frankenstein* and the lurid sunsets of Turner's land and seascapes. When Krakatoa erupted in 1883, the skies over the whole globe went red, and the temperature fell by a half degree centigrade. Throughout the twentieth century the climate has become warmer and may soon be warmer than it has been for 120,000 years, the time when Homo sapiens was an insignificant African ape, and the Neanderthals ruled Europe.

The Struggle for Survival

The vast interconnected engine of life passes on through the aeons. The struggle for existence means most creatures live on 'the edge', always competing for resources, avoiding injury, and struggling to pass on their genes. Fairly minor climate changes can bring about extinction. Without this continual dying there would be no adaptation and no new life. For nearly five billion years the teeming species have taken their fleeting chance to flourish while nature invents and re-invents itself.

Evolution is a slow process. It took some 2,000,000,000 years for life to emerge from the waters, with primitive plants and insects. Horseshoe crabs, sharks, the crocodilians, the Komodo dragon and cockroaches are amongst the most ancient creatures that still survive from that time, even pre-dating flowering plants. Homo sapiens has so far existed for about 200,000 years, 0.1% of the survival time of the cockroach. Many species become extinct quite quickly in terms of geological time; the lifespan of many mammalian species is less than a million years.[4]

Homo sapiens is now the sole survivor from a cluster of increasingly intelligent apes that populated the Earth over the last six million years. Some of these survived well over a million years; Homo sapiens has so far lasted less than a fifth of that time, and its survival for a million years is by no means assured. Until 10,000 years ago, the total Homo Sapiens population has some ten million—hardly more than the population of modern London.[5] This small population was vulnerable to any natural catastrophe like a tsunami, earthquake or volcanic eruption. The myths of lost Atlantis, Götterdammerung, Scandinavian legends such as Fimbulvinter and Ragnarok, Noah's Flood and Gilgamesh seem to be folk memories of calamitous near extinctions remembered from man's distant pre-history.

Death and Survival

Ironically, it is death that drives the will to survive. Individual death is essential for evolution; without death there would be immortal changelessness. Genes for fitness, intelligence, strength, and adaptability enhance survival chances, and so are likely to be passed on down the generations. Over time the species become more complex, intelligent, and more aware of themselves and their environment. The concept of the 'selfish gene' suggests the motive force of all living things is an impersonal drive for genes to reproduce themselves regardless of the individual's interests or needs. If this genetic force programmes the interaction of the individuals and species of the natural world, what drives this will to survive? The 'survival of the fittest' suggests that 'fitness' is itself the purpose, but why bother? A creature could simply exist by chance and die without angst or suffering. Life could drift aimlessly. Appetites could be satisfied with prey uncaring about their survival. There might even be a world where predation and death were unnecessary. There would be no need for hierarchies or defensive tactics, pain or fear. Life would be without motive, a kind of random waxing and waning according to chance. However, in such a system there would be no shaping force and the evolution of any advanced life-forms would be impossible. Is this 'will to survive' perhaps the creative force itself, with all its attendant fear and pain?

Homo sapiens, Higher Consciousness and Sapientia

As it is, most creatures are not capable of the full consciousness of Homo sapiens, but live instinctively, rather as the human body digests and makes the complex movements that allow it to walk or breathe. On a higher level there can be a kind of functioning awareness which is not altogether conscious. It is a common experience to discover one has driven several miles of familiar road quite safely on a kind of autopilot. Perhaps a great deal of animal mental activity is similarly conscious but unaware, almost sleep-walking through life, with moments of sharp awareness when necessary. Most animals spend long hours asleep and when awake, seem to be content to relax with no particular purpose or existential angst.

While other animals can be bored if denied their natural behaviour, human boredom is something different. Human lives require more conscious control with complex sequencing of tasks and social interactions, and the animal has the mental mechanisms to achieve this. Beyond everyday life, human creative thought can rise to a level of concentration and originality that is unique. In this it has a positive gearing, always looking for improvement, an easier way, a better future. The

Homo sapiens psyche is itself driven by a kind of ideational 'survival of the fittest'. This special hopefulness, or sapientia, is a search for betterment and progress which makes man an incurably optimistic creature. Life without hope is unbearable. Perhaps this is why the quest is such a standard feature of Homo sapiens' imagination. However, this quest for betterment has to be balanced to achieve contentment.

Other creatures simply live in the present and do not indulge false hopes, nor do they lose hope and suffer depression. Such passivity, means that they simply repeat their behaviours through the generations without imagining anything better. Even the Neanderthal hardly altered the design of its tools in 200,000 years; whereas Homo sapiens invents new tools almost every hour, travels all over the Earth, and has developed a sense of fashion which almost epitomizes the needs of its restless spirit. No other animal changes its self-presentation every season; there is no fashion for giraffes, dogs or even gorillas. This drive for progress has allowed Homo sapiens to multiply and rise above its animal limitations but this sapientia now presents a threat to the environment. It has precipitated 6 billion—and counting, restless animals, scrambling for the good life, whirling about the Earth more and more rapidly, and threatening to explode the whole system. This enormous creative energy can perhaps be sublimated towards non-physical objectives, or be otherwise redirected.

The Spiritual Impulse

Homo sapiens special search for betterment, its unique sapientia, has reached beyond its physical existence and in many individuals developed a spiritual impulse. Its awareness of cause and effect, its own helplessness in the face of huge natural forces, and its understanding of its mortality make it look for powers beyond the physical. Somehow out of all space and time the 'survival of the fittest' mechanism has brought this about.

The Evolution of Homo sapiens: Chance or Purpose?

The laws of nature are set very precisely for this evolution to take place. Stronger gravity would have limited evolution; weaker gravity would have allowed the stuff of life to drift off into space. If the system had worked at a different pace, with different rates of climate change a bigger more aggressive ape might have encountered Homo sapiens when it was comparatively undeveloped and eliminated it, just as the other hominid apes became extinct.

Homo sapiens seems to have had a charmed life. With its evolution a new kind of life-spirit seems to have entered into physical matter. This may perhaps suggest some creative purpose at work through the eternities of space and time, to purposefully bring into being such a creature.

> When I consider thy heavens, the work of thy fingers...
> What is man that thou art mindful of him?
> And the son of man that thou visitest him?
> For thou hast made him a little lower than the angels...
>
> *Psalm 8*, v.3-5

Or, in the vastness of the cosmos, it has to be possible that the Earth and its life could have developed by chance. After centuries of belief in a creator, such an agnostic or atheistic explanation for the cosmos is difficult to maintain, though that does not discredit it.

Ape-men: vandals to the rescue?

This strange ape has a gracious spirituality that may be able to protect the Earth by suppressing the primitive impulses of billions of years. What follows is an attempt to understand Homo sapiens as an animal, now capable of unimaginable technology which can devastate the planet and make it uninhabitable for itself and most other species; or it can accomplish the dream of universal peace and justice. To achieve such a dream, empathy and cooperation must be given the highest priority, above any technological advance. It may require something like a spiritual awakening to give this nobility of spirit the power and energy to achieve such a purpose.

---

[1] Jared Diamond, *The Rise and Fall of the Third Chimpanzee* (Hutchinson Radius: London) 1991, 18.

[2] Diamond 46.
Robin Mackie, *Ape-Man: The Story of Human Evolution* (BBC Worldwide Ltd: London) 2000, 176-77.

[3] Michael P. Ghiglieri, *The Dark Side of Man: Tracing the Origins of Male Violence* (Perseus: Reading,   Massachusetts) 1999, 59.
Diamond 280.

[4] Ghiglieri 59.

[5] Diamond 203-04, 214-15.

The Story of the Species

Outline Time Chart

8 million y.a. apes of Asia separated from apes of Africa

|

| |

Asia   Africa

gibbons orang-utans   gorillas chimpanzees bonobos

|

c.6 million y.a

AUSTRALOPITHECINES

australopithecine afarensis 3..5-1 million y.a. (bi-pedal)

all extinct

|

Palaeolithic or old stone age   2 million y.a HOMINIDS.

Homo habilis,   2million-1.6million   (tools)

The Pleistocene or 'most recent' age 1,750,0

Homo erectus   1.6 million- 250,000y.a (fire)

out of Africa 1,500,000 y.a. |

| |

(Europe) Heidelbergensis   (Africa) archaic Homo sapiens

300,000 y.a.   230-30,000 y.a

| |

(Europe) Neanderthals   (Africa) HOMO SAPIENS

230-30,000 y.a   200,000 y.a onwards

out of Africa 100,000 y.a.

[130,000-70,000 y.a. interglacial]

[*70,000 beginning of last ice age, cold increases* .....> > >]

40,000 y.a.Upper Palaeolithic or upper stone age (language)

30,000 y.a Neander6hals extinct

[*18,000 y.a. coldest point, gradual warming*...< < <]

12.000 y.a. Mesolithic

10,000 y.a. Neolithic or New Stone Age......agriculture

[*8,000 y.a. ending of last ice age .*]

6,000 y.a. bronze age

5,000 y.a. city life   5,000 y.a.writing—**5,000 y.a.**
    end of the 'pre-historic' and beginning of history

        Sumeria, Assyria, Babylon, Persia, (5,000- 2,500 y.a.)
                        Egypt (5,000-2,500 y.a)
3,500 y.a.   Stonehenge ,   pyramids

3,000 y.a. iron age

2,700-2,300 y.a.   Old testament etc   Homer   Greeks

2,500-1,500 y.a.   Romans
1,590 y.a. (410 AD)   Fall of Rome
  600 y.a.   Renaissance   printing—**500 y.a.**
  250 y.a.   Industrial Revolution
                        mass media-**50 y.a.**

                        information technology

The Story of the Species

...thou art the thing itself...; unaccommodated man

is no more but such a poor, bare, forked animal...

Shakespeare, *King Lear*, III, iv.109-111

THE AUSTRALOPITHECINES:*Developing Bi-pedalism 6million—2million years ago.*

After the extinction of the dinosaurs it took fifty million years for mammals to evolve to the point where the apes of Asia—the orang-utans and gibbons—separated from the apes of Africa. Then about six million years ago a new kind of ape split off from chimpanzees on the African branch.[6] These australopithecines (southern apes) gave rise to the stem species from which man was to evolve. Australopithecus afarensis (the southern ape from Afar in Ethiopia) began to walk upright some 3.5 million years ago.[7] This was a very important departure from the otherwise almost universal four-legged mammalian land locomotion. At first the bi-pedal movement would have been erratic and clumsy, but the skeleton would have slowly adapted as the upright stance produced an evolutionary advantage. The change was likely to have been a gradual response to a colder and drier climate which made the apes move on to the savannah as the forests receded.

Out on the open savannah the animals that stood upright could spot predators amongst the long grasses. The upright stance also kept more of the animal's body out of the direct rays of the sun, and most importantly freed its hands to collect and carry food. These apes were almost entirely vegetarian and as the savannah expanded, they had to cross the open grassland quickly to reach the groves where they might forage for the edible leaves and fruit that were their principal diet. Other modern apes can balance on two feet when necessary for a short time; for instance, lemurs sometimes 'skip' with excitement and proboscis monkeys have been observed wading through water on their hind legs. Homo sapiens often lived near water where its bi-pedal ability to wade would have been an advantage. On land the individuals that balanced more securely on two feet would have moved more efficiently. They would reach the groves safely while predators would catch their clumsier companions. Bi-pedal gait was therefore probably the response of an arboreal ape to the problem of moving quickly across sun-scorched open grassland where predators lurked.

Australopithecine afarensis was a small brown ape, just over a metre tall with a brain a quarter the size of a human brain. It was like a six year old child with a very small head. Afarensis used sticks and stones but could not envisage how to make tools. It seems to have been a social animal living in small groups, and was sexually dimorphic which suggests weak pair-bonding.[8] (Generally when males of a species have to compete for females, they are bigger than the females. They also have gender features such as manes or antlers that help their competitiveness. Where there are strong pair-bonds there is less competition, and the sexes are similar in size.) From this line of terrestrial primates came australopithecus africanus, and probably the other bipedal apes or hominids, and ultimately, Homo sapiens.

For four million years when these apes lived and died in Africa there was intense evolutionary activity with eight or even as many as sixteen similar species arising, existing for some million years at a time and then becoming extinct,[9] as the climate fluctuated. It was as if nature was experimenting with a new 'recipe' for living creatures. Many such species left no fossil record and may for ever remain undiscovered. Furthermore, the links between known species are inevitably hypothetical. From a tooth here and a femur there, scientists make careful deductions and postulate theories. These ape populations were probably always fairly small, and mostly died where their bodies shrivelled into dust, or became part of the general food chain. Much has to be made from very little, but human ingenuity meets the challenge and tells a story of bi-pedal gait, freed hands, tool making, an increasingly carnivorous diet, brain enlargement, adaptability, control of fire, social intelligence, a cooperative spirit, changes to the mouth and larynx, and a system of symbolic communication. In an extraordinarily brief time Homo sapiens has freed itself from its biological limits imposed by its ancestors to reach literally for the moon.

THE HOMINIDS: Full Bi-pedalism
2 million years ago to present:

In Africa a new genus 'Homo' (man) split off from the australopthecines about 2,000,000 years ago.[10] The australopithecines continued a parallel evolution for another million years but then slipped into extinction. The Pleistocene or 'most recent' geological epoch began about 1,750,000 years ago, soon after the evolution of the first hominids. Its repeated glaciations and interglacials caused huge variations in the global climate. Over the last 800,000 years there have been some eight glaciations when the Earth's temperature fell by fifteen degrees centigrade, locking up vast quantities of carbon in the frozen oceans as their levels fell by 150 metres exposing land bridges where once there had been deep water.[11] This reduced rainfall so that grasslands became deserts, and forests became savannah. Living things moved, adapted or died. Then interglacials brought back the warmth and the rain, the seas rose and the forests returned. We are currently living in an interglacial that began some 15,000 years ago.

Homo habilis: the Beginning of Tool Usage.
The Palaeolithic or Old Stone Age.
2 million-1.6 million years ago

The first animal of the hominid branch was Homo habilis (skilful or handy 'man') existing between 2 million and 1.6 million years ago in the Olduvai area of Africa.[12] (Some authorities classify habilis as an australopithecine). Habilis was a small upright ape, and like the known australopithecines about a metre tall, and also sexually dimorphic. The brain of this small hominid was double the size of the australopithecines but still less than half the size of a Homo sapiens brain.[13] It was like a little hairy pygmy with a small head. Habilis was long thought to be the first animal to make—rather than just use—tools, though this is now sometimes disputed. Chimpanzees use sticks to raid ants' nests; capuchin monkeys use rocks to crack nuts, and seas otters smash shellfish open with stones. Groups of animals may even adopt particular habits in using such materials and pass on a kind of rudimentary culture. However, no animal adapts a stick or stone as purposefully as the hominids. This requires very different mental skills—an awareness of cause and effect, an ability to sequence the elements of a complex process, imagination, and a sense of purpose. Chimpanzees and other primates can copy, but cannot generate and sequence complicated processes. Whether Homo habilis, or some other lost species, was the first toolmaker, this extraordinary new behaviour marks the beginning of the Palaeolithic or old stone age nearly two million years before the advent of Homo sapiens.

Evidence from the fossilized skull of habilis suggests the first signs of Broca's Area, the area of the brain concerned with the generation of language and perhaps originally a side-effect of the lateralizing brain which aided manual dexterity. [14] (Orang-utans also show some evidence of handedness). Habilis was mainly vegetarian but also an opportunistic carnivore, scavenging carrion and the kills of other animals. A vegetarian diet requires more food to generate energy, and therefore as the animal began to eat meat, it freed itself from continually foraging for food. Its digestive system may then have begun to adapt to meat eating. Where other carnivores just tear into dead animals with their its teeth, habilis could also use primitive stone tools—choppers, cutters with flaked edges and so on—to smash and cut the carcases it recognized as potential food.[15] After an ice age that lasted a 100,000 years Homo habilis began to become extinct. It had existed for 400,000 years, twice as long as Homo sapiens to date.[16]

Homo erectus (1.6 million-250,000 years ago): The Use of Fire and the Migration out of Africa

As habilis disappeared, Homo erectus emerged. It was a larger animal and adapted to the warming African climate; it was black-skinned, nearly two metres tall, slim and athletic. It lived in groups of some 150 individuals, much larger than most ape groups. With a brain three-quarters the size of a Homo sapiens brain, its head would still have looked small on its tall body. The face was coarse-featured with a low forehead and heavy jaw. The lean body dispersed heat but the animal possibly developed a new cooling system and sweated from its near-naked skin. This had important implications for respiration control, as the animal no longer needed to pant to cool down. Erectus may have begun to make shelters. It discovered how to use fire, but was unable to control it at will or light a new fire. This hominid discovered how to find and cook tubers and other foods thus extending and varying its food resources.[17] All food eaten before Homo erectus would have been raw. No other animal in the long history of the planet had ever used fire with intention. It is inconceivable that gorillas or chimpanzees could keep a fire burning—never mind lions, giraffes or elephants. Frightening away predators, living in colder climates, cooking, working metal, and eventually steam technology and industrialization were to follow from this new skill.

Erectus needed to relate to its larger social group and this required extra brain power. Relationships within the group were subtle and complex beyond anything previously known among animals. Erectus might have felt compassion [18] and cared for weaker members of the group, and so began to redefine the evolutionary process. At this point when the animal's eyes began to develop whites round the pupils which in a dark-skinned face were literally 'eye-catching'. The larger brain, capable of such an intense social life, was the result of its more carnivorous diet. It began to share food. This exchange of favours bonded the group and was the beginning of reciprocal altruism. The ability to use fire to tenderize food meant its dentition and jaw could adapt. The smaller teeth and jaw allowed the mouth parts to become more nimble which in turn helped towards the possibility of spoken communication. The animal also had something of a Broca's area which indicates an ability to communicate beyond the call system of apes, though probably nothing like fully developed human speech.[19] With its comparatively large brain and its meat-eating allowing more leisure, it could relax, dream, and perhaps share its imaginings.

Erectus became an intentional hunter as well as a scavenger.[20] It had the intelligence to realise that footprints indicated the whereabouts of prey, and that clouds meant there might be rain. Although cooking was possible, meat was often eaten raw. Meat is a more compact source of calories than plant food and selection began to occur for meat-eating. Meat is also more digestible than plant food so the animal's gut began to become smaller and more streamlined, saving valuable energy for the expanding brain[21] which required something like a sixth of the daily intake of calories

Erectus was less sexually dimorphic than habilis suggesting a stronger pair bond. Sex might at times have been a passionate rather than a merely bestial act. The animal's upright stance narrowed the pelvis which meant its large-brained young had to be born in an immature state like modern humans. Erectus infants therefore needed close and affectionate nurturing over a long period, hence the need for the strong pair bonding of its parents.[22] Its life span was extended beyond the forty years normally expected for a creature of its size and the females unusually became infertile later in life. This allowed for a supportive post-menopausal generation of females, who with their male partners were extra carers for the young and the custodians of an invaluable residue of wisdom and prior experience— like the folk loric 'wise woman'. Wise old males ('senex', Latin for old man.) in later Homo sapiens societies became the seniors, señor , signiors or senators.

The bigger brain was already becoming lateralized, with the right and left hemispheres developing specialist areas for logic, spatial awareness, emotion and communication. This bigger brain allowed the animal to make better tools. It made cleavers, picks and hand-axes.[23] In some regions few stone tools have been found because erectus used biodegradable materials like bamboo for its tools. There is no evidence that erectus had discovered how to throw weapons and kill at a distance. For the million years and more of the animal's existence there was very little change in its tool design and use. Erectus made its tools rather as a bird builds its species-specific nest. In the process of making its quite complex tools it had to have some awareness of design which suggests some ability for abstract thought. Erectus was apparently able to envisage how a blade could be made from a particular lump of stone. The animal was developing an understanding of how a cause had an effect, and how a particular action had consequences. Erectus also had the beginning of an ability to put itself in the position of someone making a tool, and follow the process. It would then be able to imitate it. Only the higher primates have any such understanding. This was the beginning of learning, culture and also self-awareness, a hominid characteristic of enormous importance.

Homo erectus—Out of Africa 1.5 million years ago

For over three million years all australopithecines and hominids, like all other apes, evolved in Africa. Erectus lived there for its first 100,000 years, a time span almost as long as the history of Homo sapiens so far. Then erectus began to move out of Africa 1.5 million years ago and spent the rest of its million year existence wandering the Earth, perhaps driven by climate change, population growth and diminishing food supplies.[24] Moving further generation by generation, erectus walked into the vast spaces of the Eurasian land mass, following the coastlines and colonizing land from the Atlantic to the China Sea. It was the first hominid ever to enter Europe; it reached Spain 800,000 years ago.[25] To have wandered so far suggests a curiosity to seek new experience. It was evidently not rooted to a home base but an adaptable animal with an appetite to try new food sources and able to survive in environments for which it was not programmed by nature. Erectus is now popularly known as 'Java or Peking man' from the specimens found far away from its African birthplace.

Several other hominid species evolved, possibly from erectus, in both Eurasia and Africa. Newly discovered fossils of a small hominid on the island of Flores in Indonesia suggest a descendant of erectus may have been isolated for millennia on the island and became miniaturized. This animal was about a metre tall, and described in the media as a 'hobbit'. Eventually after a successful existence of more than a million years erectus itself began to become extinct about 250,000 years ago. Small numbers may have survived in Asia and might therefore have been alive during the time of the Neanderthals and early Homo sapiens.[26]

Europe and Africa: Homo heidelbergensis 700,000—300,000 years ago

One possible descendant of erectus was Heidelberg 'man'. Homo heidelbergensis inhabited Africa and Europe from about 700,000 to 300,000 years ago. It was a large animal, about two metres tall, with a brain three quarters the size of that of Homo sapiens. Heidelbergensis had the concept of owning a favourite tool rather than using a tool and dropping it like a young child when something else caught its attention.[27] This indicates forethought and preparedness. This hominid was a skilful hunter rather than a scavenger and made hand-axes, spears and flint cleavers with which it killed and butchered big game animals. It built shelters, used fire and even applied herbs for healing. There was some awareness of mortality as they sometimes hid their dead in caves, though there is also evidence of ritual cannibalism. This suggests group endeavours and cooperation which would require organization and therefore complex communication and social intelligence.[28]

A 700,000 year-old hand axe has been found in East Anglia, thus proving heidelbergensis early in its history reached this part of Europe. A 500,000 year-old heidelbergensis specimen has been found in Boxgrove in southern England. The climate had then warmed, and during the interglacial African species like hippopotamuses and rhinoceroses had extended their range northwards. Heidelbergensis participated in this migration. There were huge climatic changes during the 400,000 years of heidelbergensis' existence and the hominid for a considerable time was resourceful enough to adapt successfully to its changing environment.

Archaic Homo sapiens c. 300,000 years ago

As heidelbergensis began to become extinct, several species of archaic Homo sapiens were already evolving in Europe and Africa. There were certainly proto-human beings in South Africa 150—120,000 years ago.[29] Several species of hominid ape were populating the more hospitable areas of the Earth before the advent of modern Homo sapiens. Perhaps they encountered each other from time to time. A few very ancient primitive carvings date back to about 300,000 years ago.[30] There was no developed speech and virtually no culture, but there was high animal intelligence above what can be observed in present-day chimpanzees. If these proto Homo sapiens survived now, modern man would probably not recognise them as its own kind. These animals for all their intelligence would not pass for 'human' at a restaurant or a concert, and would more than likely be confined by their modern descendants in a zoo or some place of asylum. There have been tales of a three metre tall gigantepithecus, a real King Kong, in distant Asia. Is it possible that the rumoured sightings of 'Big-foot', the Abominable Snowman, or the Yeti are dim folk memories of these other hominids, or do they perhaps indeed still exist—the last survivors from man's pre-history?

Europe and Eurasia: The Neanderthals 230,000— 30,000 years ago: Kings of the Ice Age

Some of the European archaic Homo sapiens had broad, prominent noses as an adaptation to a cold climate, allowing in-drawn air to be warmed before it reached the inner organs.[31] They had a thick skin with a high pain threshold, and were unlikely to sweat. From these non-African proto-humans came the Neanderthals about 230,000 years ago during a period of glaciation when the ice reached as far south as Spain. The land that was to become central England was under ice three kilometres thick. The Neanderthals were the first hominids fully to evolve in a colder climate. Their probably whitish skins[32] and stocky build—under two metres tall, and twenty or so pounds heavier than a comparable Homo sapiens—were also adaptations to the cold. They had a lifespan of about forty years.

Compared with Homo sapiens the Neanderthal brain was bigger but lacked developed frontal lobes. The animal was probably capable of sequencing ideas along a single pathway but it was unable to abstract and make cross-references. It could plan an ambush and perhaps anticipate a birth, but beyond that it could not make contingency plans in case of changing circumstances. It could plan to collect firewood but could not at the same time have in mind that a change in the weather might make a deer hunt more productive. One situation could not easily be compared with another by cross-referencing; a location where a particular plant grows did not suggest to them that in a similar location elsewhere, the same plant might be found.

The animal made very slow cultural progress over its 200,000 years of existence, suggesting a limited capacity to imitate and learn by example. It simply kept making the same tools century after century, millennium after millennium, as if it had no sense of betterment or impulse for invention. Neanderthals made shelters and some kind of clothing from fur and hides, but had no concept of needles and sewing. They were probably right-handed. They were social animals living in groups of about forty individuals. The animal has been characterized as coarse, brutal and stupid but although it lived in harsh conditions, it could be gentle, affectionate, and must have smiled and laughed. There are some examples of Neanderthal ornaments and art dating from fifty thousand years ago—bones and an elephant tooth with zigzag markings, in the later stages even copied from nearby Homo sapiens.[33] Perhaps it made music with drums and other rhythmic instruments. It also began to domesticate dogs. Dogs scavenged food from the middens of Homo erectus and therefore would have been attracted to groups of Neanderthals in the same way.

This hominid had advanced enough to control fire. It made flaked stone tools and sharpened wooden spears with which it stabbed its prey, but it never discovered how to wound or kill at a distance by throwing a spear. Prey were driven over cliffs, or into swamps where the Neanderthals would close in on them for the kill like a pack of dogs. Many Neanderthal remains show evidence of terrible injuries to the upper body, suggesting daring and dangerous hunting missions which must often have meant cornering or trapping large, frightened animals and killing them at close quarters.[34] Healed fractures on some remains suggest that injured hunters were rescued and the weak or disabled cared for by the rest of the group. This is evidence of compassion, social bonding, and an ability to project a hope for future recovery. The sometimes careful interment of their dead shows that these animals had an awareness of the meaning of death, and probably some awe and reverence for the mysterious changed state of one of its group.

The Neanderthal in its day was the most intelligent animal that had ever existed on the Earth. It has been thought that the high larynx and conformation of the throat would have made it impossible for a Neanderthal to articulate the range of complex sounds required for human speech. However, new findings challenge this. Almost certainly Neanderthals used some kind of proto-language.[35] It was the ice age king from the Atlantic to Afghanistan and may have cohabited with the last of erectus or heidelbergensis and various intermediate hominid species frequenting the same range.

Meanwhile in Africa….. Homo sapiens, c.200,000---140,000 years ago

A long ice age triggered a period of intense evolutionary activity and Homo sapiens was one of the last large animals to evolve. Mitochondria are genetic material within the cell and only passed on through the mother's genes. The mitochondrial evidence suggests that Homo sapiens ('wise' or 'intelligent' man) originated in central Africa about 200,000 years ago but there are still arguments about the statistics that support this hypothesis. Although there were many females in the original Homo sapiens population the progeny of only one individual survived. The whole of mankind are the descendants of this one 'Eve' and carry her mitochondria.[36] . The evolutionary process from Homo habilis, perhaps through erectus and heidelbergensis, to Homo sapiens had taken about two million years.

Early Homo sapiens or 'wild' man was a brown-skinned African ape of moderate size with an especially large brain which was nourished by meat. The ape was hairless except for a covering of long hair on the head perhaps to protect it against the African sun as it walked upright.[37] There was a mane which ringed the face in the adult male as a device to intimidate rivals and predators, and impress prospective mates, rather like the fleshy cheek 'flaps' of male orang-utans. Otherwise there were tufts of hair under the armpits and round the genitals of adults which trapped individual odours to aid personal recognition, and exude erotic pheromones. There was light body hair on some individuals, especially males, but the pelt had otherwise disappeared to leave a smooth skin.

When over-heated the skin oozed sweat from every pore, bathing the creature in cooling moisture—an unusual animal cooling system. Like Homo erectus, Homo sapiens did not need to pant to keep cool, and this allowed finer control of the diaphragm and respiratory system. It is extremely difficult to talk while panting or breathing heavily so this adaptation helped to make speech possible. The diaphragm was also strengthened to hold the organs in place against gravity, and this also helped develop the breath control needed for speech.

The upright stance full-frontally exposed the vulnerable belly. The shoulders were held apart by straight 'collar bones' or clavicles so that the chest was broadened and the female breasts became fatty pads advertising gender. The fatty buttocks provided extra weight at the centre of gravity perhaps to balance the upright stance. From the side view the animal was strangely flat, with the head held high above the ground on the vertical spine. This upright stance meant that the animal was prone to spinal injuries and circulatory problems. However, the circulation of the blood vertically up and down a column, rather than horizontally may have helped keep the brain cool. Scents are at their strongest near the ground so the vertical body meant that the human sense of smell was disadvantaged. Its small nose allowed the face to be more expressive, but also reduced the acuity of its sense of smell. The face was broad, flat and forward-facing so that its expressions were immediately apparent, and social encounters were literally 'face to face'. With no muzzle, and little or no hair its complex musculature could be easily seen. The eyes were particularly noticeable with whites outlining the pupils, and were extremely important for social interactions. The open face and unusual facial mobility allowed a wide range of expression and response between individuals. Eye contact, the eyebrow 'flash', smiling, grimacing, frowning, became far more meaningful in human society than in the social groups of other apes

The animal was of lighter build than the Neanderthals and had a more finely shaped head. It was moderately sexually dimorphic, and formed fairly strong pair bonds within which to rear its highly dependent young. In nature it had a life-span of about sixty years and like erectus, the females became infertile in middle age. It probably lived in large interrelated groups of about a 100 or 150 individuals.

In the ordinary way of things, these apes would have remained a small population in their particular area of Africa like gorillas and chimpanzees, controlled by their natural predators and adverse environmental factors. Homo sapiens faced such predators as the giant short-faced bear, a huge creature now extinct. Predation would have been an everyday occurrence and this animal already had a unique imaginative awareness of its personal danger. To this day many Homo sapiens have an innate fear of snakes or spiders and other creatures which in the original African habitat would have had poisonous bites and stings. Other animals also instinctively avoid predators but they probably do not have the imagination to envisage being killed and eaten. Homo sapiens however, constantly rehearse predation terrors and fears of cannibalism in horror movies like *King Kong*, *Jaws*, age old folk tales like the *Cyclops*, *Three Little Pigs*, *Hansel and Gretel*, *Little Red-Riding Hood*, and individual nightmares of 'maneaters' such as tigers and sharks.

Like its other ape relatives, over the millennia Homo sapiens often faced the possibility of extinction and may at times have been an endangered species. All Homo sapiens have their origins in this tiny seed population which might so easily have disappeared for ever thousands of years ago. However, after keeping to its native range in Africa for perhaps a hundred thousand years —half of its existence to date, its numbers grew. It began to migrate into the south of Africa.

The survival of the fittest mechanism works slowly in terms of human time; one estimate suggests it takes 10,000 years, or three hundred generations to effect any significant biological change in an animal with a lifespan of man. Another estimate calculates it takes a million years to make a 3% change, and Homo sapiens has existed only about a tenth of that time.[38] Modern man is therefore biologically almost the same as the ape that evolved in Africa over a 100,000 years ago. However, man's cultural nature changed rapidly; it had developed the precious ability to imitate and think creatively. This implies an ability to look ahead, hope and strive for a better way, a better place, a better time—human sapientia. Other animals tend to make the best of their situation. They will move towards the sun or shade, or seek water, perhaps with a feeling of something like the Homo sapiens' emotion of hope. However, they do not seem to have the ability or psychological energy to imagine ways of adapting their environment and its products to their use. Homo sapiens is not so much 'wise' as positive thinking and creative, a creature of 'sapientia'.

Homo sapiens discovered how to make use of stones, bone, antlers, branches, clay and fibrous stems to extend its natural abilities to hit, throw, tear and hold. It polished and ground its tools to achieve a fine finish. It knew how to throw a spear, and invented the altatl or spear thrower to improve its natural abilities.[39] For the first time an animal could kill at a distance. In time it would use slings, catapults, bows and arrows, learn to train birds of prey to kill for it at a distance, and eventually would invent the gun. This was a new kind of intelligence, something far removed from the nest-building of a bird or the repetitive functions of earlier hominids. For Homo sapiens once an idea was discovered, often by chance or serendipity, other individuals did not have to re-discover it for themselves but could immediately learn by example, so short circuiting individual trial and error. This learning required a social setting. Curiosity, innovation and the exchange of ideas were by-products of Homo sapiens' intense cooperation and companionship. Beyond that there was an extraordinary ability to imagine and plan how to achieve something new, an understanding of cause and effect, and an enormous drive to make improvement. This was the real beginning of culture, something new and potentially explosive in the natural world.

A unit of information has been called a meme.[40] Unlike genes, memes can spread horizontally across a culture independent of heredity, as well as vertically through the generations. In man there has been a unique gene-meme co-evolution. Genes programmed the animal's physical form; memes shaped its cultural development. Other animals do not learn easily from imitation, but have to be 'trained' by repetition, and reward. Some higher animals do watch and learn, but the process is slow and limited in comparison with human learning. As the brain evolved, its capacity to store memes grew. Individual after individual, generation after generation, the species has built on the memes already accumulated, so that it has jumped from knowing how to fashion a stone scraper to space travel and the internet in a mere moment of evolutionary time. The cultural evolution of previous hominids in comparison was almost static, the same repetitive tool-making continuing for hundreds of thousands of years.

'Wild' man controlled fire and made hearths. Cooking allowed a new range of foods and made the animal more able to cope with necessary changes in diet in times of shortage. About 70,000 years ago it learned to light up darkness with burning moss soaked in animal fat. No creature in the long history of the Earth had ever mastered darkness in this way before. Like other animals it could make shelters, but with more invention. Other hominids had built circular stone shelters where caves or other natural refuges were not available. The human group developed shelter-building skills and would gather round the hearth (rather significantly, the Latin for hearth is 'focus') to share food and indulge its compulsive need to socialize. Homo sapiens owed its survival to its intense social life, making for cooperation, empathy and cultural development. This allowed the animal to survive among other animals that were bigger, stronger, swifter and better adapted to their particular niche in nature. Its powerful social bonding and capacity for empathy made it care for weaker members of its social group, and even after death, dispose of the bodies sympathetically. This may have had a practical aspect. Humans have a natural aversion to decomposing dead bodies because corpses are instinctively recognised as a source of infection.

There is evidence that brain size is related to the size of the social group. The Homo sapiens group was bigger than the groups of other ape species, except for Homo erectus. The other apes groom each other to reinforce social bonds, but grooming in the larger human group would take 40% of the group's time. Some other bonding mechanism was needed, such as 'vocal' grooming and sharing food. The need to establish bonds promoted a subtle sound system of communication which over the millennia developed into speech.

The sharing of food is a very unusual animal behaviour, occasionally observed in chimpanzees. However, even in infancy Homo sapiens have an innate impulse to share. Other animals and even other primates eat food where they find it, eating their fill with no regard for others, except their own dependent young. Group-living animals and many other creatures establish a hierarchy where the strongest and fittest animals eat their fill first. Dominance is enforced even if weaker members of the group starve as a consequence hence the drive to hold a place in the hierarchy. In the pitiless scheme of nature at least the species would survive even if the weaker individuals died off. Although hierarchy remained an important aspect of Homo sapiens society, this animal often brought food back to a central area and shared with others of its group. Group feeding is still a hugely important part of Homo sapiens social life.

Early Homo sapiens was very sensitive to its status and above everything driven to hold its place in the group hierarchy. This obviously led to rivalry and conflict. An individual had to judge where it stood in the hierarchy, and how the others in the group perceived it. There was also a developing contrary altruistic impulse. Each individual had to judge whether it was prudent to behave generously to another individual, and whether that generosity would be repaid. This reciprocal altruism seems to be encoded as an extraordinary sense of natural justice. Even very young children have a strong sense of what is 'fair'. In time the sense of justice became internalised as 'conscience' and a moral intuition.

Social sensitivity was at a premium.[41] The more successful individuals were those that socialized best and these males were likely to accomplish more matings, often with females that had similar qualities. A cerebral selection process began to operate. The better socializers were able to empathize better, and understand what it is to be in the position of another individual. From this came the social intelligence necessary for a complex social life. This, in turn, developed the larger and more complex brain. 'Wild' man has sometimes been characterized in cartoons and other media as brutal and vicious—-hair-pulling, club-wielding, growling and shrieking. Yet 'wild' man shared modern man's genes and would have had the same capacity for tenderness, humour, wonder and empathy.

Whole industries are now built on human interest stories; the success of 'chat shows' and new developments like 'reality' and 'voyeur' TV illustrate an insatiable appetite for such material. The detection of scheming and lying is an important survival skill essential to the reciprocal altruism by which man lives. Stories and gossip work out endlessly how to avoid betrayal and recognize loyalty. To succeed in such 'reality' shows or in life itself requires an acute sensitivity to tell-tale cues in the demeanour of companions. This imitates the original human condition where survival itself no doubt depended on trusting, helping, deceiving and manipulating others. Other 'reality' shows present participants with various challenges to test courage and personal qualities and establish a hierarchy. Failures are voted out. There may be disappointment or even shame, but that is nothing compared with combats of the past where failure often meant certain death. Challenge, success and failure are essential experiences whether in life or in play.

Out of Africa:
The Human Diaspora:100,000 years ago.
The Pleistocene epoch entered another interglacial about 130,000 years ago which lasted 60,000 years. During the interglacial the fauna and flora of the earth were wonderfully prolific and vegetable and fruit sources were abundant. The warmth allowed elephants and other African animals to range across Europe as far as the north of England. About half-way through this interglacial Homo sapiens followed these creatures of Africa northwards up the Nile valley into the lands of the eastern Mediterranean. [42]Then 70,000 years ago the Earth began to cool

into the latest glaciation. The species also wandered east along the shorelines of east Africa, and India until it reached Australia 60,000 years ago. By then the climate had begun to cool again. The animal's skin colour and certain features slowly changed according to the prevailing environment as the population dispersed. By about 20,000 years ago it is probable that there were already different racial types—a skin-deep adaptation of little significance to the species as a whole.

At the rate of perhaps thirty miles a year this remarkable ape dispersed across the huge land mass ahead of it. It must also have found a means of crossing water by logs, rafts or even boats, held together with wooden dowels and ropes as there was no metal. As the ice returned, the sea levels fell, exposing land bridges into new territory. Homo sapiens' ancient cousin, the Neanderthal, by then some 200,000 years old, already inhabited some of these areas. Erectus might also still have existed in Asia and perhaps some other archaic Homo sapiens. The energy, adaptability, and courage of modern Homo sapiens' journeying must surely have been extraordinary, especially as the cold was becoming more intense.

The Upper Palaeolithic:
The Development of Language—40,000 years ago.

Homo habilis had begun the Palaeolithic age when it made the first stone tools two million years ago; with Homo sapiens' acquisition of language the Upper Palaeolithic period began 40,000 years ago. The development of language may have been a gradual development or a comparatively sudden breakthrough. The physical apparatus must have developed first. The human face and mouth parts are capable of fine control, developing as complementary to the dexterity of the human hand. The human respiratory tract also has features that allowed for extraordinarily subtle control of the breath and shaping of sounds. The diaphragm is strengthened and the larynx is lower in the throat than in other hominids. The modern human infant is born with the higher larynx of its hominid ancestors but it drops by the age of two years and the development of human speech.

Homo sapiens had had the physical attributes that make speech possible for tens of thousands of years. The mental capacity developed more gradually. The best communicators were likely to breed more and gradually the ability to communicate verbally was therefore genetically encoded. A meme or copiable idea might be more easily remembered and communicated if it could be represented in a shortened form—an abstraction or a symbol standing for the whole process. As memes accumulated in the human collective consciousness, some kind of shorthand would be necessary to avoid overload. It was at least 50.000 years (1,500 generations, more than half the animal's existence) before fully symbolic language developed and became hard-wired into the human psyche as a template or universal grammar for the use of language.[43] Language requires so much structuring and concentration, it would be impossible for an individual to acquire it without some neural adaptation. The human brain has therefore developed a template for language acquisition. Just as the infant first crawls and then becomes bipedal soon after its first birthday, it is born programmed to speak and day by day progresses in a predictable sequence from babble to fully developed language over its first five years. It can tune into its mother's language in the womb—literally its mother tongue, and by the first year it has usually learned the vowel sounds of its native language.

It has been suggested that there may have been a single ancestral language which has been called Nostradic.[44] This language may have gradually diversified as the animal dispersed. However, man had already migrated out of Africa into almost every continent on earth before symbolic language developed so that it is also possible that there may have been several ancestral languages developing independently.

Homo sapiens had already colonized Australia before speech developed. As it began to speak it moved into Europe about 40,000—35,000 years ago. Despite the increasing cold, man reached Siberia 40,000 years ago. It had certainly reached the Americas 11,000 years ago, or possibly much earlier, by the ice corridor between Asia and America to the north, or even by marine exploration. Recent genetic findings suggest several waves of population moving into the Americas from Asia and even from across the Atlantic. It then took a mere thousand years for Homo sapiens to traverse the whole American continent.[45] Homo sapiens reached the land at the other edge of the Europe between 12,000 and 8.000 years ago, and crossed into the land that was to become known as Britain. By then the ice was melting and the water was filling the channel between England and France.

With the development of language man became an altogether different animal from any creature that had evolved before. Earlier hominids were certainly conscious and perhaps had some mute awareness of themselves and some incipient symbolism.[46] Inspired by Shakespeare's 'Caliban', Robert Browning's poem "Caliban upon Setebos" imagines the workings of a primitive mind. Caliban, a sub-human hominid, describes how he wallows in a pit of mud amongst squirming things, looking out of his cave to the sea glittering in the intense sunlight. He begins fearfully to mutter to himself about Setebos, his concept of a god who terrifies him. Like a young child he speaks about himself in the third person as if having no sense of an inner self or 'me'. A child might say, 'Sam want drink' rather than 'I want a drink', and Caliban says 'Will sprawl...flat on his belly' rather than 'I will sprawl...flat on my belly'. He speaks as if he is seeing himself from outside rather than describing inner experience:

> Will sprawl, now that the heat of day is best,
> Flat on his belly, in the pit's much mire,
> With elbows wide, fist clenched to prop his chin.
> And while he kicks both feet in the cool slush,
> And feels about his spine small eft-things course,
> Run in and out each arm, and make him laugh:
> And while above his head a pompion*-plant,
> Coating the cave-top as a brow the eye,
> Creeps down to touch and tickle hair and beard,
> And now a flower drops with bee inside,
> And now a fruit to snap at, catch and crunch,--
> He looks out o'er yon sea which sunbeams cross
> And recross till they weave a spider-web
> (Meshes of fire, some great fish breaks at times)
> And talks to his own self, howe'er he please,
> Touching that other, whom his dam called God.

(*pumpkin)

Robert Browning, 'Caliban upon Setebos', 1-16

Man, on the other hand, became self-conscious, aware of its own consciousness and capable of self-reflexive thought.[47] There is an inner awareness of 'me' participating in a world of other 'mes', who also have inner experience of themselves – 'cogito ergo sum' (I think, therefore I am). With language, the inner experience of emotions could be externalized and used as a tool for consciousness, language constructed man's view of reality. Human groups also developed a collective consciousness. With language, memory was sharpened, concepts shared, empathy heightened and at some point came the realisation of a cause and effect relationship between events. This awareness of cause and effect was to transform the life of the planet. The future could be envisaged; for instance, it was consciously understood that a bird would hatch from an egg and that sexual intercourse would generate offspring. This is far removed from reflexes, conditioned by repeated associations with reward or punishment. Homo sapiens developed the ability to make fully conscious connections between events separated in time and space, without repeated occurrences. A certain herb is found to heal a rash; another is found to 'cause' vomiting. This knowledge can then be used in different places and at different times with the expectation of the same results.

Early on its journey Homo sapiens met its ancient cousin, the Neanderthal, in the near east corridor between Africa and Eurasia. There the two ape species lived side by side for many millennia, perhaps even sharing living space from time to time. William Golding imagines the first sighting of Homo sapiens by a small group of Neanderthals in his novel *The Inheritors*. Golding betrays his Caucasian bias in depicting his Homo sapiens as white-skinned and the Neanderthals as dark. The reverse was probably the case; the European Neanderthals were almost certainly lighter-skinned than the African Homo sapiens. Golding's Neanderthals are aware of the extraordinary alertness of the new men:

> At last they [the Neanderthals] saw the new people face to face and in sunlight. They were incomprehensibly strange.

> The eyes of the face … were dark and busy....Lok [Neanderthal] saw the ears of the new men. They were tiny and screwed tightly into the sides of their heads.

> Their play was complicated and engrossing. There was no animal on the mountains or the plain, no lithe and able creatures of the bushes or forest that had the subtlety and imagination to invent games like these, nor the

These two great hominid apes may have shared food; they may have hunted each other. Across the almost unpopulated countryside they may have sought each other and enjoyed the stimulus of meeting; they may have shunned and feared each other. They occupied similar natural habitat and the same ecological niche, though Homo sapiens preferred uplands and the Neanderthals—as their name suggests ('thal', German for 'valley') —preferred valleys. (A small population of Homo erectus might also have survived in Asia). Genetic analysis suggests no mixing of genes between the two species. [48] Then mysteriously the Neanderthal population collapsed some 30,000 years ago, only about halfway through its natural span of existence.

The Neanderthals were cold-adapted and survived 40,000 years of the increasing cold, but had been extinct for 12,000 years by the time the glaciation reached its coldest 18,000 years ago. For thousands of years these hominids, and perhaps others that have never been identified, had roamed the planet together. Species by species they became extinct.

How would the various hominid species have related to each other had more of them survived? The Neanderthals were much stronger than Homo sapiens, and if the two species had cooperated together it could have been advantageous for them both. The Neanderthals must have understood a good deal of sapiens' language, and been able to labour intelligently for its nimbler thinking cousin. Man might have been able to communicate directly with the thinking mind of another species. Shakespeare, Browning, William Golding and other writers have given voices to their sub-humans and imagined them in relationships with Homo sapiens. Perhaps like perennial adolescents, these hominids would delight us with their cleverness, amuse us with their quaint ways but also frighten us with their animal impulsiveness and aggression. If erectus, heidelbergensis, and the Neanderthals had survived to become a normal part of the modern world, modern man might understand itself as part of the hominid species continuum and not a creature set apart with a claim to special rights.

Some of the last Neanderthals retreated to what is now the Rock of Gibraltar and whatever the cause, the Neanderthals eventually succumbed leaving the huge uncharted spaces of the Middle East, Europe and the whole world beyond to 'wild' man, the only surviving hominid of the many that had gone before.

Upper Palaeolithic (stone age) Culture 40,000—10,000 years ago

The first European Homo sapiens are known as Cro-Magnons after the place in France where their remains were first found.[49] These Homo sapiens were able to communicate with speech by the time of their arrival in Europe 40,000 to 35,000 years ago. In jeans and tee-shirts or tuxedos and evening dress, they would be 'us'. They were extremely skilful in making stone tools and weapons, and controlling fire. They were able to make shelters, including tents, essential for survival as the ice-age continued. They had extraordinary knowledge of their environment, knowing how to source food, medicinal herbs and materials necessary for clothing and domestic use. Rather like modern aboriginal peoples they would seem to have almost supernatural abilities to track prey, understand the weather and to access special powers of the mind.

The ice-age deepened and it must have seemed that the cold would last for ever. At about this time the animal began to develop wall or parietal art of extraordinary beauty and insight. From the first, some 30,000 years ago, the wall art demonstrated a fully developed sense of form and colour. The famous cave paintings of Lescaux are 17,000 years old. These cave paintings must have had some ritualistic purpose; perhaps the caves were secret places of initiation. It was possible to light these dark recesses enough for the paintings, whatever their purpose. Similar parietal art has been found in Brazil, Africa and Australia, in populations that have no relationship with each other. [50]It is as if there is something universal in the human psyche at that time that drove a need to externalize a record of the magical beasts of the upper world.

Sculpture, musical instruments—drums, harps, horns and eventually bag-pipes—bone implements, and the bow and arrow followed in a fast-moving cascade of invention and creativity. No account can be made of items made of more perishable materials. Shelters ingeniously built of mammoth bones 30,000 to 15,000 years ago have been found in north Eastern Europe. Individuals began to enjoy ornaments and bodily decoration. There are female fertility figures 30,000 years old; the Wittendorf Venus is more than 25.000 years old. There is a burial dating from 28,000 years ago where the corpse's grave clothes were decorated with thousands of beads.[51] This suggests some spare energy and time, perhaps as the result of social stratification. Trade expanded across a distance of some two hundred miles. There is evidence of occasional social aggregations of perhaps five hundred individuals forming regional tribal groups.[52]

From about 18,000 years ago the Earth began to warm again and entered the present interglacial. The Neanderthals were extinct while the world population of Homo sapiens had reached about ten million.[53] . For 90% of the animal's existence it had travelled over its expanding range, measuring distance by landmarks, recalling the past by word of mouth and experiencing time as an undivided sequence of light, dark, cold and heat. There was no metal, no writing, no systems of measurement, no money, no roads, no plough and no wheel. However, speech and man's special qualities of social sensitivity, creativity, enquiry and innovation—sapientia—were beginning to bring about enormous changes in lifestyle.

Agriculture, c. 10,000 years ago (8,000 B. C.): The Neolithic (new stone) Age.

In the plains of some great rivers, populations began to settle. As the result of some mysterious synchronous cause—perhaps the warming climate—in populations as far apart, and out as of touch as the Americas and the Fertile Crescent, settled agriculture developed. At this point the Upper Palaeolithic era ended. There was a brief period of transition of about 2,000 years known as the Mesolithic or middle stone age and by about 10,000 years ago Homo sapiens entered the Neolithic or new stone age. These humans were culturally quite sophisticated, but nevertheless still dependent on stone, wood and bone for their technology. Cloth was woven slowly on wooden frames, pottery was sun-baked, and simple lamps filled with animal fat lit the darkness.

The development of agriculture was probably not a sudden process. Querns have been found in the Fertile Crescent dating back 18,000 years indicating that Homo sapiens was grinding some sort of grain in the Middle East at this time. The animal had discovered a kind of grass seed that could be stored or crushed and the resultant powder mixed with water to make a compact and palatable source of energy-rich carbohydrate. Some accidental fermentation then provided yeasts that made possible leavened bread and drinks like beer. Bread was an improvement on collecting berries, fruits, roots and nuts.

However, Homo sapiens was designed to be a hunter-gatherer, and in some ways a settled way of life distorted its cooperative nature, and the 'liberté, egalité, and fraternité' of its way of life as a 'noble savage'. As agriculture intensified, this required social stratification and more complex social organization. For the first time, a leader had to dominate a large population, most of whom had no relationship with him (or her). The primal group bonds of human society began to be distorted. Women lost status as they were pregnant more often because food supplies were more reliable, and this restricted their independent life. Although food supplies were more reliable, the diet was less varied, and there is evidence of widespread malnutrition. Diseases also took tenacious hold amongst the close-packed populations killing hundreds in a way that was impossible with small groups of wandering hunter-gatherers. Clearing ground by burning, chopping down forests, and opening the soil for crops also started to alter the carbon balance in the Earth's atmosphere.

Humans had often followed migrating herds such as reindeer or caribou to make survival less uncertain. The Ridgeway path across southern England is perhaps 11,000 years old and may originally have been a route for migrating animals as they moved across ice-age Europe from Bristol to Berlin. For more settled communities the domestication of animals was crucial. This was more than the symbiosis otherwise observed occasionally in nature. It was deliberate and controlled in a completely new way. Man was capable not only of emotional bonds with other species but also had the imagination to envisage how to adapt the other animal's potential for its purposes. However, surprisingly few animals can be successfully domesticated. Deer are too nervous and wild cats are too independent; foxes, squirrels, and badgers just not amenable to man's control.[54] Domesticated animals must not be too territorial, or have too strong a migratory instinct and they must breed successfully in captivity. It has to be possible for man to supply their food easily, and they must be pack animals that will accept man as their pack leader.

Wolves and their cousins, the dogs, were probably the first species to live with man. Species of dogs had existed for perhaps an unimaginable 40,000,000 years before the advent of Homo sapiens. These animals for almost all of their existence had roamed in packs, subject only to natural forces and their own pack organization. Only in the last million years has the dog encountered the hominid apes that it has befriended. Man soon learned that dogs could be used for hunting, tracking, herding, attack, protection and even entertainment. Aurochs, cattle, sheep, goats, pigs, and above all horses became the domesticated creatures of the Eurasian land mass. The Americas and Africa were not so fortunate, their equivalent species having either never existed or for some reason—most probably over-hunting by man before their usefulness was understood—had become extinct.[55]

The domestication of the horse transformed human life. There are other beasts of burden—donkeys, oxen, buffaloes, camels— but the horse has power, nobility, and spirit. For thousands of years man and horse have worked together in war and peace. The knight, the chevalier or cavalier, the horseman, the cowboy have a glamour that runs through folklore to the modern media where the Western has entertained audiences for nearly a century. With the help of the horse, Homo sapiens was able to move large loads and travel long distances which would otherwise have been far beyond its physical capacity. For thousands of years Homo sapiens depended on the horse; with the coming of the railways only some 200 years ago did that dependence diminish.

Technological development was increasingly rapid. The cumulative collective learning experiences of a thousand generations brought more cultural change in 30,000 years than in all the rest of the Earth's history. Memes were replicated in the hundreds and thousands of individual minds making up the human community, like a benign virus colonizing body cells. Change followed change, new questions, new discoveries and new memes. Some 10,000 years ago man became the only animal to begin to master its environment. All other creatures from the beginning of Earth's story have had to adapt to their circumstances or succumb. No rabbit, hedgehog or water vole, for instance, can tell the time, wash clothes or row a boat. The White Rabbit, Mrs Tiggywinkle, Ratty and so many other imagined animal characters blur this unbridgeable difference; it needs to be emphatically re-stated.

The first small towns began to grow on the ancient trade routes in the Middle East. Ripples of civilization moved across what is now modern Iraq, Syria and Iran, then down the Nile to Egypt from 8,000 B.C. onwards. In this way human ingenuity confronted the uncertainties of nature, and civilization—literally 'city life'—began. Jericho with perhaps a population of 2,500 dates back 8,000 years, to about 6,500 B.C.[56] It still took about 2,000 years before man learned to work copper and discovered its alloy, bronze.

Towards the end of the neolithic period in northern Europe (c.3,500 years ago) sacred sites were marked by stone circles all over Britain from the Hebrides to southern England and across the Channel into northern France and beyond. The most notable of these is of course Stonehenge on Salisbury Plain. These circles are connected with the movement of the sun and moon. Stonehenge marks the solstices, and for a northern people dependent on the seasons, the winter solstice was particularly significant as it promised a return of light and warmth. Even in our time of electric light and central heating, the turning point of the year is still significant. These inventive northern Neolithic people were however still illiterate and so have left no written record of their clearly well-developed culture.

The Bronze Age 6,000 years ago, (4,000 BC): The First Use of Metal

It is now impossible to imagine life without metal. No animals, not even the earlier hominids, ever made use of metal, and for over a 100,000 years of Homo sapiens' history tools had been made from stone, wood, and bone. Bronze made metal tools possible and transformed Homo sapiens' abilities. About 7,000 B.C. there were the first experiments with copper ores such as malachite in Anatolia. These were different kinds of 'stone' which could be bent and twisted. Little by little, the human animal explored their properties, first using the ores as pigments to colour pottery. On their own, copper and tin are too soft to be useful, but by mixing 10% of tin into the molten copper, a harder, stronger metal results. The first bronze castings were made about 4,000 B.C. in the near east, and the Stone Age began to pass into history. Never before had the nature of a substance been so changed; the smithcraft almost like magic made stone-like lumps into gleaming metal. Gold too had been discovered and was prized for its permanent lustre, never rusting or tarnishing. It was already used for ornamentation and objects of special value and significance.

At the point where the bronze age superseded the Neolithic, about 5,500 years ago (3,500 B.C.), there was a surge of invention—-the plough, wheel, swords, bricks, weaving looms, glass-blowing, candles, wine and beer (the distillation of spirits was not possible until 700 years ago when the process was discovered, rather ironically, by Arab chemists), carpentry, and writing. Gradually over some 3,000 years Bronze Age technology spread from the Mediterranean to northern Europe.

Writing had began as a method for keeping accounts on clay tablets 5.000-6,000 years ago (3,000-4,000 B.C.). This momentous advancement allowed information to be reliably stored and transmitted and Homo sapiens was no longer 'prehistoric'. Many different forms of writing later developed using many different materials—clay, wax, wood, animal skin, stone, papyrus, paper. Ink was invented about 4,500 years ago. During this period all sorts of invasions, journeying and mythical events seem to have taken place. The Aryans moved westwards, and Jews developed their sense of being a 'Chosen People'. For 500 years such stories were elaborated and mythologized then collected and written down about 2,800 years ago in hugely influential texts such as *The Iliad, The Odyssey,* and perhaps the early books of the *Old Testament.* The literate civilizations of the Mediterranean began to lay the foundations of Western culture.

The Beginning of City Life
The small settlements on the trade routes began to expand. About 3,000 B.C (5,000 years ago) in ancient Sumer (now part of modern Iraq) close to the great rivers, Tigris and Euphrates, Ur and Uruk grew to accommodate populations of some 50,000. For the next 3,000 years in that area political power passed from the Sumerians, to the Assyrians, to the Babylonians, the Persians, the Greeks and the Romans, while further south and west the Egyptian civilisation lasted throughout the same three thousand years. Irrigation, and the mathematics to calculate the flooding pattern of the Nile made the Egyptians extraordinary engineers

73

able to construct pyramids and great temples. To the east other inventive civilisations developed in the Indus, Yellow River and Yangtze valleys.

The Iron Age: c.1000 B.C.

Man learnt to extract iron ore and work the metal as wrought iron for several centuries. Then improved furnaces allowed iron to be melted to the point that it could be poured into stone moulds. Such iron-age smithcraft may be the source of the legend of the young King Arthur drawing his sword, Excalibur, out of stone. The Hellenic empire expanded under Alexander across the Mediterranean, then the Romans slowly advanced their empire from Portugal to Syria, and Libya to Scotland.

For millennia the phases of the moon and course of the sun measured time and barter served for trade. As civilizations developed they had to make more sophisticated calculations, so more precise systems to organise time, and to exchange goods had to be devised. Sundials tracked the movements of the sun during the day, or time was measured by flows of water, oil or sand. (Clocks required sophisticated metal working and engineering which were not possible until the last few hundred years.) Various calendars were used in the different civilisations, dividing time into sections, usually with reference to the moon. The Roman calendar devised by Julius Caesar became the basis for the calendar of the west. Then the months were also divided into manageable units or weeks. Coinage began to replace the system of bartering about 700 B.C.

Parallel to these mathematical and technological advances were philosophical and spiritual developments. These seem to cluster between 700-350 BC across human populations from China to Israel, from India to Greece:—Isaiah (c.700 BC), Lao-tze (c.600 B.C), Jeremiah (c,600B.C.), Ezekiel (c.600 B.C.), Buddha (563-

74

483 B.C.), Confucius (551-478 B.C.), the Upanishads (Hinduism c.500 B.C.), Socrates (470-399 B.C.) and Plato (427-347B.C.)—those few short centuries have shaped the religious and philosophical development of man.

Yeshua of Nazareth was born one summer shortly before the death of Herod in 4 B.C. Greek was still widely spoken and written, and so unsurprisingly the story of Yeshua and his followers was first set down in Greek 'Yeshua' became 'Jesus', and 'Messiah' therefore became 'Christ'.. The Jews constantly challenged the Romans, and in 70 A.D. the Romans took Jerusalem by force and destroyed Herod's temple, leaving only the 'Wailing Wall'. In 132 A.D., after a further rebellion, the remaining Jews were driven out of their 'Promised Land'.

The Americas

For some 8,000 years or more the American Indians had lived as hunter-gatherers. City life began in the Americas with the Olmecs about 3,000 years ago (1,000 B.C.), parallel to the iron age cities of the Mediterranean. The Mayas of central America, 300B.C. –900A.D., and the Zapotec culture in Oaxaca both developed during that first millennium. The Zapotecs had a 260 day calendar, built the Pyramid of the Sun, and practised human sacrifice. The city of Teotihuacán had a population of 200,000. Toltecs followed the Zapotecs in Mexico from 900-1,100 AD. The Aztecs came next with their Lake Island city of Tenochtitlan and a population of 250,000; its remains are now lost under Mexico City. Labour was plentiful and cheap, so there was never the incentive to invent the labour-saving wheel. The Spanish destroyed the Aztec culture in 1521 and a decade later also destroyed the Incas of Peru, whose city life had rivalled that of ancient Rome. The northern Europeans were by then beginning to colonize the American continent further to the north where no city life had developed, and the Indians continued to live as nomadic tribes.

The Rise of the West: 1—2,000 AD

Christianity spread rapidly inside the Roman Empire. Rome fell in 410 A.D., leaving Constantinople the capital of what remained of the Roman Empire in the east. However, Christianity was well-seeded in what had been the western Empire. Then Mohammed was born in 570 A.D. and founded the third great religion derived from Abraham. Islam soon overran the Holy Land, and swept into North Africa and southern Spain. Finally in 1453 Constantinople fell to the Turks and the Roman Empire was finished after nearly two thousand years.

However, although the Empire had fallen, within a thousand years its influence was already being revived with the Renaissance which moved western culture into a new mode, accelerated by the fall of Constantinople and the flight of its scholars and artists to the west. Printing had first begun in China, but reached Europe in the fifteenth century. The western phonetic alphabets allowed a system of moveable type, and the new printing technology had massive impact. About a century later came the Reformation, emphasizing individual freedom and responsibility. The sixteenth century Copernican, the eighteenth century Industrial, and the nineteenth century Darwinian revolutions followed, transforming and superseding age-old ideas. Instead of devoting time, energy and resources to monuments and places of worship, the industrialized societies directed their efforts to machinery, bridges and other practical feats of engineering. Over the last two centuries the speed of change has accelerated beyond anything previously known. Writing began about five thousand years ago; printing—five hundred years ago; mass media—fifty years ago; and now information technology makes the 'global village' a reality with worldwide instantaneous communication.

This animal can now see its planet from space. Its conception of the past is also changing. Historical events can now be 'replayed' as never before. Now for the first time it is possible to bring back the past to virtual life. Photographs preserve images, and recordings capture voices. Films allow the old to relive their youth, and the dead to move and speak again. With information technology Homo sapiens is at the point of a revolution as big as any ever experienced, and can now even read its own genetic code.

---

[6] Jared Diamond, *The Rise and Fall of Third Chimpanzee*, Hutchinson Radius, London 1991, 20, 28.

Roger Lewin, *In the Age of Mankind: A Smithsonian Book of Human Evolution*, Smithsonian Books, Washington D.C. 1988,, 48.

[7] Lewin, 50, 59.
Robin McKie, *Ape-Man. The Story of Human Evolution*, BBC Worldwide Ltd, London, 2000, 12.

[8] Lewin, 64., Diamond 60-62.

[9] Michael P. Ghiglieri, *The Dark Side of Man: Tracing the Origins of Male Violence*, Perseus Books, Reading, Massachusetts, 59.
Lewin 88.

[10] McKie 59.

[11] ed. Richard Overy, *The Times History of the World, New Edition*, Times Books, London 1999, 34.

[12] McKie 59.

[13] McKie 59.

[14] Lewin 180.

[15] McKie 65-67, Lewin 106

[16] McKie 50-51, 59.

[17] McKie 76-79, 110.

[18] McKie 90. ·

[19] McKie 82-83, Ghiglieri 60-61.

[20] McKie 108-09.

[21] McKie 111-14.

[22] McKie 88- 89, 114.

[23] McKie 103.

[24] McKie 106-07, Diamond 31.

[25] McKie 106-07, 118-19, 133.

[26] McKie, 51, 119, Diamond 31.

[27] McKie 129-33.

[28] McKie 119-21, 133, 138-39.

[29] Lewin 114, 129.

[30] Lewin 186.

[31] Lewin 118. McKie 152.

[32] McKie 148-49, Lewin 145.

[33] Lewin 186,
Ian Tattersall, *The Last Neanderthal,*   Macmillan: New York, 1995, 162.

[34] McKie 157.

[35] Lewin 184-85.

[36] McKie 170-72, Ghiglieri 67-68.

[37] McKie 22-23, Tattersall 43

[38], 115. Diamond 20.

[39] Lewin 148.

[40] Susan Blackmore, *The Meme Machine*, Oxford University Press: Oxford and New York, 1999, 63., 132.

[41] McKie 199.

[42] McKie 203.

[43] Diamond 145-46, Ghiglieri 60-61.

[44] Lewin 186.

[45] Diamond 305-08.

[46] McKie 85. Ghiglieri 60-61.

[47] Lewin 180. 229. McKie 201.

[48] Diamond 45, McKie 187.

[49] McKie 167.

[50] McKie 194-95.

[51] Diamond 41, Lewin 197, McKie 195.

[52] Lewin 151.

[53] Diamond 203-04.

[54] Diamond 215-16.

[55] Diamond 304-08. Lewin 167-69.

[56] Lewin 221.

Paradise and the Restless Spirit: Habitat

Southward through Eden went a river large.

...   for blissful Paradise

Of God the garden was, by him in th' East

Of Eden planted...

...

...   murmuring waters fall

Down slope hills, dispersed, or in a lake,

That to the fringed bank with myrtle crowned,

Her crystal mirror holds, unite their streams.

The birds their choir apply; airs, vernal airs,

Breathing the smell of field and grove, attune

The trembling leaves, while universal Pan

Knit with the Graces and the Hours in dance

Led on th' eternal spring...

Milton, *Paradise Lost* IV, 209—268

Homo sapiens is an African ape. The ability to make clothing, construct shelters, and control fire has allowed it to extend its range far beyond its natural habitat. It can live in a wide range of temperatures, environments, and population densities. Homo sapiens living at high altitude in time will overcome their altitude sickness; skin and eye colour adapt to the sun's radiation, but there are natural limitations. Humans cannot live on the peak of Everest; they cannot live under water. Some environments are generally experienced as ugly and impoverished—dry, barren, crowded, dirty, desolate, cold, or depressing. These feelings are the urging of nature for the human species to search out its ideal life location which is a peaceful, warm, sylvan environment with clear, running water idealized as some mythical heaven like the Elysian Fields. Milton's description of the Paradise Garden 'East of Eden' probably derived from his visit, as a northern European, to Vallombrosa in Tuscany: it is eternally spring in the lush woodland, fertile with fragrant flowers and fruits, where birds sing and contented flocks graze.

Paradise and the Love of water

> If I were called in
> To construct a religion
> I should make use of water...
>
> Philip Larkin, 'Water' 1-3, *Whitsun Wedding*

> "He leadeth me beside the still waters...
>
> *Psalm 23*

Homo sapiens loves water. Paradise is imagined as a warm, fragrant garden with fountains and streams, or perhaps an island with palm-fringed beaches and sandy shores, but somewhere in this dream is water. Water is, of course, a life-essential but beyond this Homo sapiens, unusually for an ape, has an extraordinary psychological delight in water.

Not only is man powerfully attracted to water, it also has physical features that suggest it has been an aquatic ape. Its layer of subcutaneous fat is a better underwater insulation than fur and also aids buoyancy. The fingers and toes are slightly webbed, especially between the thumbs and first finger. The animal needs at least four litres (eight pints) of water a day, especially in a hot climate like its African homeland. It exudes liquid from pores all over the naked skin to keep itself cool and refreshes its sweat-laden skin in pools or showers of water. Human tears and sweat would be wasteful unless water was the animal's natural habitat; the hair follicles and their format on the almost bare skin suggest a sleekness compatible with a watery lifestyle, and moreover human infants have a natural buoyancy and swimming response during the first weeks of life. In recent times some expectant mothers have opted to deliver in special birthing pools, perhaps responding to the promptings of a long forgotten instinct.

Bi-pedal locomotion helps the human animal to wade in water, its supple spine allows it to swim efficiently, and the shape of its nose allows it to avoid inhaling water, unlike other primates. An ability consciously to control breathing allows swimming and diving. Under water the human body immediately adapts its breathing and circulation. This ability to control the breath might later have been a factor in the motor development of speech. The hard teeth enamel and use of stone tools is similar to creatures like coastal populations of Capuchin monkeys and sea otters which live on shellfish. Oily fish are important in a healthy diet, and this suggests a natural habitat close to the sea. When Homo sapiens left its homeland it probably followed the course of the Nile or walked along the east coast of Africa to begin its journey into the world beyond. Perhaps most significantly, Homo sapiens dream of water as the essential element in its ideal habitat. Water gives Venice its beauty, and the world's most beautiful cities are either on rivers or harbours beside the sea. A glance at holiday brochures illustrates the overwhelming desire for beaches, rivers, waterfalls and pools.

Hot dry deserts, cold frozen wastes, flat featureless plains, have their appeal but given a choice (and other matters such as security being equal) the creature seeks water for recreation and solace. The most privileged populations who can arrange their perfect living conditions, choose to live near water, or have lakes, waterfalls and pools constructed for their enjoyment. The green-blue swimming pools, Jacuzzis, and commercial waterparks are urban man's substitute for lake, stream and sea. Even the multiple luxury bathrooms of modern housing suggest a love of water. These are perhaps the echoes of that primeval habitat of waterfalls and rivers where those aquatic ape ancestors sported in the original paradise garden.

Temperature and Light

Man is most comfortable in a daytime temperature of about 75 degrees Fahrenheit, 25 degrees Celsius. Colder and hotter temperatures can be stimulating and enjoyable, but like a particular genus of plants, man has an optimum temperature range of 60-80 F degrees—the setting for most indoor climate control or air-conditioning systems. As man migrated to colder or hotter climates, it has to some extent adjusted and acclimatized, but the species in its nakedness is still naturally adapted to its original sub-tropical climate.

Colder areas with long dark winters and weaker summer sunlight required an adaptation of skin tone, eye and hair colour. Brown is the natural eye colour of Homo sapiens—an African species; the gene for blue eyes is recessive. Dark skins are protective in strong sunlight, whereas lighter skin colouring allows the best use of reduced levels of light. Geographic isolation and possibly the human propensity to choose partners of the same type, consolidated these colour differences. These differences are comparatively recent—perhaps developing only about 20,000 years ago. They are not an aspect of the animal's evolution as a species; the differences are more like different breeds of dogs which have been developed by man's deliberate selection. All races of Homo sapiens are the same species and can successfully interbreed from the poles to the equator.

Animals that inhabit harsh climates have special coping strategies. Some species hibernate; some migrate; some have special winter or summer fur or plumage. Homo sapiens has uniquely adapted by inventing non-biological ways of keeping its body temperature stable. It can control fire, and make coverings for its naked body. However, in addition to temperature, like most creatures Homo sapiens also has a sensitivity to fluctuating day lengths and seasonal variations, and these are not so easily controlled.

Night and Day

Homo sapiens is a diurnal creature, needing about eight hours of sleep during darkness. Most individuals suffer some sort of malaise if this basic circadian rhythm is disrupted by shift working, modern air travel, or other stress. The balance between wakefulness and sleep, as might be expected, matches the day length in Africa where Homo sapiens had its origin. The human animal has poor night vision. It therefore has an instinct to hide away somewhere quiet and safe before nightfall, prompted by a fear of the dark when it is vulnerable to nocturnal predators. It naturally seeks a home base where it can sleep safely—a cave, roundhouse or other shelter shared with kin and other familiars. This retreat is often surrounded by some protective barrier like a wall or stockade, and beyond is the empty wilderness. The modern house and garden remains a version of this, preferably set apart in its own space. In modern cities and suburbs Homo sapiens live unnaturally close to unrelated neighbours and this often generates a sense of insecurity and intrusion which can express itself in disproportionate aggression.

The night is associated with anxiety, ambushes, eerie sounds and a sense that the individual is unable to control its environment; it is also associated with mystery, especially when the moon is high. Some individuals are psychologically excited by the full moon even now, though before electric light the effect of the moon must have been literally 'mind-blowing' to the susceptible. This was a time when ancient rites were performed, seeds were sown and crops planted, and stealthy groups set off on hunting expeditions. The moon's phases helped measure the passage of time and often became the basis of early calendars. It also waxed and waned in rhythm with the Homo sapiens' female fertility pattern, which in conjunction with the moon's effects on water, associates it with fruitfulness.

As an African ape, man is not a creature native to darker and colder latitudes and the more extreme changes in seasons and day length. The animal loves sunshine and long periods without it can lead to mood alteration now diagnosed as Seasonal Affective Disorder. This syndrome is the animal's response to conditions to which it is not ideally adapted. Even working or living in rooms like basements without windows is generally experienced as depressing. The effect of winter darkness when firelight, oil-soaked moss or rush lights were the only sources of light can hardly be imagined. Something of this dark, dangerous atmosphere pervades the old sagas and northern folk tales. Some accounts of winter in northern latitudes suggest human populations became almost dormant, sleeping and hardly moving outside the home base for several months. Over the last century artificial lighting has allowed man to overcome the darkness and modern tourism allows some fortunate individuals to migrate for winter warmth and light, or even buy a 'place in the sun'.

Light and Warmth: The Coming o f Spring

Cold and dark is unnatural to Homo sapiens; it longs for warmth and light. This longing is built into the calendars of northern inhabitants, and perhaps those of similar latitudes in the southern hemisphere, with festivals of light for the darkest days—Santa Lucia, Christmas, Uphellya, Yule etc.-- and springtime awakenings like Easter and May Day. April literally means 'opening' and is much celebrated in northern literature. Just as certain cells in the eyes of birds trigger spring mating behaviour, so mammals, including Homo sapiens, respond to the changing season:

> When April with its sweet showers
> The dryness of March has drenched to the root
> And filled every stem with so much juice,
> That the rush of sap engenders the flower;
> When the west wind with its balmy breath
> Has stimulated in every wood and heath
> New growth, and the spring sun
> Is halfway through the sign of Aries
> And little birds are in full song
> And sleep all night with their eyes open
> (They're so excited by their instincts);
>
> Geoffrey Chaucer ,'The Prologue', 1-12,
> *The Canterbury Tales*, modern version by M Rennie

> Oh to be in England now that April's there…
> Robert Browning, 'Home Thoughts from Abroad' 1.

The spring 'opening' can however be distressing to individuals beset by sadness.

> April is the cruellest month, breeding
> Lilacs out of the dead land, mixing
> Memory and desire, stirring
> Dull roots with spring rain.
>
> T.S. Eliot, 'The Burial of the Dead' 1-4,
> *The Waste Land,*

Relationship with the natural world

While sunshine lifts the spirits and warmth is experienced as pleasant, like other African species such as lions, Homo sapiens will seek shade in the heat of the day. An expansive view from a hillside or cliff top also seems to be deeply felt need, perhaps as a safety mechanism to allow foreknowledge of attack, but inwardly felt as an exaltation of the spirit. Pleasure is experienced in the colour and fragrance of blossoms, and the shapes, colours, textures and tastes of fruits. Like other creatures, man is unconsciously an agent for the plants it gathers; its enjoyment of fruit, seeds, and roots encourages it unwittingly to disperse seeds, prune plants, and spread vegetable matter like compost.

Pleasure gardens, city parks, modest personal gardens all try to create oases of colour, fragrance, sun and shade, to answer these deeply felt needs.

> In Xanadu did Kubla Khan
> A stately pleasure-dome decree:
> Where Alph, the sacred river, ran
> Through caverns measureless to man
> Down to a sunless sea..
> So twice five miles of fertile ground
> With walls and towers were girdled round:
> And here were gardens bright with sinuous rills,
> Where blossomed many an incense-bearing tree;
> And here were forests ancient as the hills,
> Enfolding sunny spots of greenery.
>
> Coleridge , 'Kubla Khan' 1-10

In terms of basic survival man could be at ease on the surface of the moon, assuming food and other necessities were provided, but the lack of vegetation and water make an existence in such circumstances bleak and depressing to the imagination. Sprawling urban development without distinctive features is experienced as depressing and aesthetically barren. Housing areas need recognizable zones, often identified by landmarks, which equate to villages or even the tribal areas of the original habitat. Architectural design and community planning strongly affect human behaviour. Striking evidence from urban planning experiments in the 1960s in Britain shows how a functionally adequate environment may nevertheless promote vandalism, crime and depression. The hated tower blocks hardly lasted a generation.

Wild creatures need to be hyper-aware of their environment to monitor food sources and the whereabouts of predators and felt emotions seem to be associated with this. What does a watchful bird feel as it sings, flies or feeds? The watchfulness looks almost like a constant state of panic, insecurity or desperation for food; but birds simply have a different metabolic rate and are completely fixated on the avoidance of predators and the search for nourishment. Many observers have intuited states of pleasure in nature: after all these creatures live in the present and have no awareness of future pain or death.

> Through primrose tufts, in that green bower,
> The periwinkle trailed its wreath;
> And 'tis my faith that every flower
> Enjoys the air it breathes.
>
> The birds around me hopped and played,
> Their thoughts I cannot measure:--
> But the least motion that they made,
> It seemed a thrill of pleasure.
>
> The budding twigs spread out their fan,
> To catch the breezy air;
> And I must think, do all I can,
> That there was pleasure there.
>> Wordsworth, 'Lines Written in Early Spring,
>> 1798,' ll. 9-20,

Higher animals are often playful and express pleasure in living. Undoubtedly humans have a considerable capacity for enjoyment, sympathy and awe as they experience their place in the natural world. Like other creatures, Homo sapiens is prompted by pleasurable emotions to seek conditions which once best suited its chances for survival. The aesthetic pleasure of an expansive view or the sounds and scents of woodlands, meadows and shores often became an almost clairvoyant rapport with the natural world. Pleasure, as much as fear, can be the mechanism for keeping a creature alert and in tune with its environment.

Among others the Bushmen, Australian aborigines, and the Native Americans have a heritage of miraculous understanding of the natural world. 'Wild' man must have been even more hyper sensitive and responsive to its environment. It hunted with stealth and teamwork; it used its group experience to find resources. The search for food and avoidance of predation would depend on responding to the slightest changes and movements. It is difficult to imagine the world as it would have been, without engine noise, light pollution, roads, or cities—just endless forest, rivers, oceans, full of wildlife, deep, deep stillness and nights of silent darkness or a wilderness resonating with the howls, calls and cries of other animals. Homo sapiens was completely at home in this world for more than a 100,000 years.

Urban Man: From the Countryside to the City
Homo sapiens has found enjoyment in many different environments—deep forests, empty deserts, snowy wastes but only comparatively recently has it gathered together in bustling cities. Although there were substantial cities in the ancient world, this is only 10,000 years ago, and it is only over the last two or three centuries that huge populations have left the

countryside for cities. For the first time in the history of mankind, the majority of the species is urbanised.

In the past, invasion, drought and famine drove populations towards cities where they hoped to find sanctuary or organized food supplies. Cities allowed better group defence against the perils of predation or the other vicissitudes of existence. More recently huge populations have been drawn to cities as refugees from the dullness, poverty, and the often feudal restrictions of their lives in the countryside. Villages are hotbeds of gossip, passed on for generations. Only by leaving can an individual make a new start. However, the price of such movement can be high, and poverty on a city pavement can be even starker than rural penury. Nevertheless, the dream of fortune and the anonymity of urban life has made rural inhabitants leave the countryside in their millions. The huge variety of experience makes the risk seem worthwhile. As Dr Samuel Johnson said over two hundred years ago: "A man who is tired of London, is tired of life". City life offers stimulus to a creature that once had to forage for its food and constantly expect predation.

The Dangers of Alienation from the Natural World

Populations long habituated to crowded cities become unused and almost unaware of their need for nature and may feel the countryside is dangerous, or even ugly. From savannah to concrete jungle, urban Homo sapiens can physically live without the natural world. For urban man, Ceres—goddess of the Earth-- is as good as dead. Human ingenuity can probably devise substitutes for the natural mechanisms that until now have sustained the species. To produce abundant cheap food and extract raw materials to satisfy its desires, it can eradicate troublesome insects and plants careless of the wild life that depend on them. Its huge machines can clear forests in a fraction of the time taken by American settlers or Neolithic Europeans.

Damming rivers, draining marshland, quarrying, and building—houses, factories, roads, airports—it irrevocably changes habitat. The natural world tries to survive, following its age-old strategies in the face of this huge intrusion. Never before has there been such power in the hands of one animal species; the full implications of this as yet are hardly understood.

Nature in the Modern Urban World

As a creature of the natural world, Homo sapiens despite its modern disconnectedness, is spiritually rooted in nature and needs to relate to the natural world from which it came. Many Homo sapiens still naturally seek country spaces, the sea, rivers, woodland or hills, and engagement with surrounding wildlife. With the mobility of the car, city-dwellers can increasingly travel to the countryside and experience it as a kind of theme park or playground. Romantic and unrealistic though this may be, it suggests urban man cannot entirely suppress the longing for its natural habitat. This need for the natural world is also often expressed in a widespread delight in keeping pet animals and decorating homes with houseplants and flowers. Urban residents seem unconsciously to be attempting to recreate a tame 'natural' habitat for themselves. Homo sapiens frequently anthropomorphize other creatures, especially pet cats, dogs, and other companion animals. Originally, perhaps animals were domesticated for some evolutionary advantage, but the pleasure of relating to animals is a pervasive but now seemingly purposeless emotion. Perhaps it is an overflow of the human familial or personal bonding mechanism. It is known that relating to animals can relieve stress and depression, as if Homo sapiens is healed by this touch of nature. Certain animals, dogs in particular, seem to express affection but this is probably their response to their human 'pack leader' on whom the animal depends for food and protection. The human then interprets the dog's loyalty as affection and responds accordingly.

The Growing Concern for the Environment

Care for the environment is deeply felt by a growing minority. The demise of other species is emotionally upsetting to many even though it happens on the other side of the world and there are no direct personal consequences. The loss of the dodo is felt to this day as a wound in the fabric of the environment. The anticipation of an earth entirely devoted to human needs, to agribusiness and commerce, with urban landscapes and no forests or countryside is debilitating to the imagination and spirit. Ultimately it could lead to six billion or more depressed and psychologically imprisoned Homo sapiens. Unless man learns to live in harmony with the wilderness, materialistic over-indulgence could devastate the natural world, leaving the wilderness unable to regenerate until Homo sapiens itself becomes extinct. It has been calculated that if bees were extinct, man would be unable to survive even a decade. The threat of global warming now adds a whole new dimension to man's relationship with the natural world.

Wandering in the Wilderness

Wildness and wilderness are treasured amenities, vital to many human spirits even though often experienced only in the imagination. There seems to be a need to fit humanity into the context of the natural world with all its teeming diversity and feel the 'otherness' of it.

> What would the world be, once bereft
> Of wet and wilderness? Let them be left,
> O let them be left, wildness and wet;
> Long live the weeds and the wilderness yet.
>
> Gerard Manley Hopkins, 'Inversnaid' 13-16.

Wilderness is often equated with freedom despite its threats and unknown dangers. Odysseus, King Arthur and his knights, many other mythical heroes, and the wanderers of the American West have played this out endlessly, often having the hero ride off alone to find further adventures. For more than 90,000 years the human population wandered across the uncharted earth; this gypsy life is the natural state of man, rather than the settled life of modern cities, and may explain man's constant need for travel.

The Need for Stimulus
When Milton wrote *Paradise Lost*, he had the problem of giving some sort of purpose to the lives of Adam and Eve. They are depicted as performing some light but rather pointless gardening, and despite the beauty of the paradise dream, there is a suspicion that life in Eden is boring. A holiday in paradise is one thing; a permanent life in paradise is another. There is indeed a serpent in the garden. Homo sapiens is a restless, ambitious, danger-loving animal and charged with aggressive and destructive impulses, essential to its survival during its almost 200,000 years life-and-death struggle for existence. Its sapientia, the curiosity and constant need to seek improvement, becomes the very serpent that urged Eve to taste the mythic apple.

For a fraction of its existence, perhaps 10,000 years, Homo sapiens has increasingly mastered its environment. The last century has so accelerated this process that the last few generations in the Western world have no necessary connection with their biological heritage and now live in unprecedented ease, safety and comfort. The present-day way of life in the Western world would seem like complete fulfilment even to the comfortable middle class of Dickens' time. For the generation born fifty years ago 'all mod cons' meant the luxury of an indoor bathroom. Now an 'en suite' is expected with the 'master' bedroom, preferably with a Jacuzzi. But, this does not seem to have brought the contentment previous generations might have expected. Even the most privileged individuals suffer psychological stress and even depression, often resorting to 'life coaches', gurus, counsellors, drugs, etc. to ease their angst and dissatisfaction. There is no need to exert themselves physically. This in itself can lead to sluggishness of body and spirit. It is also the case that the very sapientia that prompts man's hopefulness and quests for betterment has the negative effect that the creature cannot easily find contentment in its achievements, but almost immediately takes them for granted and looks ahead for more.

Modern technology has created a dream world in the Nevada desert. Las Vegas is an entirely artificial environment dedicated to satisfying man's thirst for pleasure and excitement. Colour, bright lights, movement, erotica, food, and the thrills of gambling— monetary tokens being at risk rather than bodily injury or life—challenge modern man who no longer has to wrest a living from the dangerous natural world. Las Vegas is the fastest growing city in U.S.A. and a magnet for tourists and holiday makers. It offers the heightened sensory experiences and adrenaline rushes man craves, albeit artificially.

Of course, it is also a matter of temperament, expectation, and social context. Western economies depend on stimulating consumption to maintain employment in order to disperse the community's resources and so generate more consumption. Consumerism is the result. Once the basic needs are satisfied, consumption depends on stimulating desires for the inessential. Thus, there is a prevailing atmosphere of discontent. However, this present malaise probably also relates to the lack of challenge in modern life. Perhaps the environment is too safe and unexciting for a creature with enormous curiosity and a low boredom threshold.

Restlessness

One of the cures for boredom is travel. Wanderlust has always lured the human animal past the next bend of the woodland path, round the next coastal headland, across oceans and now into space. Homo sapiens has wandered out of Africa to every continent, always looking for new experience or a better environment, following 'the quest'. The wagon trains moving west across unexplored North America in the nineteenth century may have been the last such movement. For this reason the settlement of the West has a powerful grip on the modern imagination. In recent centuries people have left the countryside for the town, migrated from city to city in search of streets 'paved with gold', and now travel from country to country. Until now there were always unexplored places on the planet to find danger and adventure, but for the first time in history the wilderness is disappearing. It is now also easy to travel across the globe for exotic holidays that were just fantasies a generation ago— first the seaside, then the Mediterranean, now the Pacific, where next? Space cannot satisfy this need to wander, as it is too inhospitable and the means of travel too limited. Future generations will be denied an outlet for their need to wander, unless exploration can be simulated in some as yet unimagined way.

Although man has always wandered, this wandering was conditioned by its physical limits. For more than 90,000 years, man simply walked. Then some 10,000 years ago came the horse and other beasts of burden. The coming of the steam engine and the railways just a 150 years ago allowed mass travel as never before. Thomas Hardy's short story, *The Fiddler of the Reels,* compares the six day walk from Dorset to London with a train journey of a day. Dorset dairies were then able to supply London as in *Tess of the D'Urbervilles*. Only then was time in rural England standardized with London in order to timetable journeys. People travelled, mixed and migrated. The invention of the internal combustion engine has had an even greater impact.

Any view of a motorway or congested modern conurbation, shows modern Homo sapiens perpetually on the move, a vast swirling mobile mass coming and going, frantic for the freedom to journey more and more, further and further. It is not just a matter of movement, but movement at speed. Modern man already moves at speeds far in excess of what nature intended, yet it seems any restriction generates huge impatience. A driver held up by a slower driver often becomes unreasonably angry, and any momentary hold-up rouses huge annoyance. Air travel in the last decade has become a mode of mass travel, allowing even more mixing and migrating. In 1900 no one could have envisaged a six lane highway in the rush hour in 2000; it is just as difficult to imagine transport in 2100. Already helicopters and private planes are becoming the transport of the wealthy, just as cars were in 1900. By 2100 roads could be almost deserted while the sky could be congested with 'skyways'; without agreed and enforced controls our great grandchildren may live under a hail of debris, constant disturbance, and clouds of flying 'cars' just as our lives are often blighted by road traffic. However, maybe by then technology may have replaced the need to meet in person and no part of the world will be distinctive enough to visit as a tourist.

It is difficult to account for this extraordinary restlessness which must be a biological imperative, a kind of geographic sapientia driving the animal on to find a better or at least a different place. Bands of walking Homo sapiens or even hordes on horseback explored the wilderness in previous millennia, but in less than a century human mobility has escalated beyond any imaginings of previous generations. This has happened so quickly and is still accelerating so that even if no longer fuelled by damaging fossil fuels, the mobility itself is environmentally and even psychologically destructive. So far this human behaviour is almost unnoticed and unquestioned, but it is likely that, like any indulgence, it will have to be understood, curbed and even rationed. Flying to the moon and beyond cannot solve the mobility crisis for six billion or more restless earth mammals.

A Danger-Loving Animal

Homo sapiens has a need for physical stimulus sometimes to the point of terror. This varies widely from individual to individual, and is particularly felt by the young—especially males. In Europe the running of the bulls through the streets of Pamplona, the horse races of the Siena Palio, the Spanish bull-fights, have for centuries generated excitement and allowed young males to test their courage, possibly mimicking primeval struggles with prey and predators, and the challenges for pack leadership. However, in most western societies there is no formal way for a young warrior-hunter to gain recognition. For some—often inadequate young men—'taking and driving' expresses their huge need for status and excitement. Perhaps teenage pregnancy performs the same function for young females.

Very young children enjoy the feeling of being held high and playfully dropped or swung through the air. The adult equivalent may be 'bungee' jumping, roller-coaster rides, hang-gliding, parachuting, trampolining etc. Could these activities be a relic of a once arboreal ape's pleasure in jumping across space high in the jungle canopy? Often the danger has to be real and there must be a possibility of injury or death; it is not enough to offer adventurous spirits activities that are safe and socially acceptable. Rock-climbing, mountaineering, pot-holing and extreme sports offer considerable challenge, but even these activities may be too well controlled. Quite young children choose to play 'chicken' on railway lines and adolescents become dare-devil drivers or 'bikers' taking appalling risks with their lives and the lives of others.

Burglars often find their crimes very exciting, as well as profitable, and there is plenty to steal in modern cities. Those groups which have no particular talent or inclination to discipline themselves find release in destructive activity, rather like dogs running loose in the countryside looking for something to chase or kill. Border collies' killer instincts have been redirected to herding. If these dogs are not given some substitute activity, in the words of a dog psychologist "They'll make it up for themselves, and you won't like it!" The same can be said of aimless gangs of teenagers. Lack of challenge in the environment is as damaging to some humans as cage-life is to zoo animals. Unfortunately, gang warfare and hooliganism are a self-invented alternative when young males are cramped into cities or adrift in over-stable suburbs with no outlet for their instincts to hunt and assert themselves. It should also be recognised that almost for the first time in human history youths are healthy, well-nourished, and free of the energy sapping labours needed for basic survival. Most young people do not even expect to walk to school, never mind fetch water or help with the harvest. On an overcrowded planet with most of the natural challenges eliminated what can be done with this appetite for thrills and danger?

Horror films, fictional emergencies, fireworks, rescue documentaries, daredevils exploits in the media, video games etc relieve boredom by proxy. Increasingly techniques are used to increase excitement—loud sound tracks, flashing lights, scenes cut into shorter episodes, for example. As for activity, Homo sapiens fortunately has great satisfaction in teamwork which can be positively directed to cooperative feats. At its best human teamwork, motivated by faith, built Stonehenge, the Pyramids, and Chartres Cathedral without the aid of machinery. It is the impulse behind sports teams, choirs or symphony orchestras, and a multitude of simpler, everyday projects. Sport formalizes a whole range of substitute sources of excitement, and has created a symbolic world of challenge, victory and defeat. It is no surprise that males are more interested in sport than females, and that sport has developed so strongly over the last century when the challenges from the natural world have largely receded.

Peace and turmoil

Homo sapiens has the ability to adapt conditions so that it can live almost anywhere on Earth, but biologically it belongs to sub-tropical Africa, the original Eden. It may relax on a palm-fringed beach at holiday time but it soon tires of inactivity. Homo sapiens with an instinct to wander, to hunt and take risks, with a mind programmed to confront enemies and predators, is not easily satisfied with too quiet a life. In folk tales, epics, dramas and novels, or their modern equivalent—video games, films, TV—-there have to be villains, threat, destruction, and often bloodshed. Satan is more interesting than the angel Gabriel; J.R. Ewing fascinated the audience as the anti-hero of the TV series *Dallas*. Even the scenes of film and video are increasingly 'cut' to generate more speed and excitement.

Psychologically man needs to experience change in contrast to familiarity, and danger as opposed to safety. Despite all the sufferings of war, there is less depression and mental illness because the problem of boredom is at least temporarily solved. The amazing achievements of man demonstrate its peculiar appetite for physical and mental stimulus. To challenge fierce predators, to hunt down dangerous prey, to fight off rivals, to cross oceans, to scale mountain ranges, and to fly to the Moon requires at the very least enormous animal nerve. There may be an ideal of peace, but the turbulent spirit of Homo sapiens, almost despite itself, seeks adventure, challenge and danger.

Fear of Famine:
Diet and Exercise

They dined on mince and slices of quince
Which they ate with a runcible spoon
And hand in hand on the edge of the sand
They danced by the light of the moon.
Edward Lear, 'The Owl and the Pussycat', 27-30

The Primal Diet
With the coming of daylight each morning, 'wild' man would
begin its search for food. There was no farmed meat, no grain,
no milk or dairy products, no highly-bred and carefully grown
vegetables, and nothing but water to drink. There was juice in
fruits, and moisture in leaves and flesh, but water was essential.
The food value extracted from uncultivated leaves, seeds,
berries, nuts, stems and roots was quite low in relation to the
digestive effort required. The human digestive tract is designed
to deal with this roughage but more digestible foods are more
appealing because the food value is more readily available, and
this saves calories. As the human groups moved from food
source to food source, they ate little and often. Occasionally a
successful hunt or find of carrion made for a feast and social
gathering. Other animals like polar bears and some whales can
survive months without food, but man needs a constant low-
level intake.

Like all wild animals Homo sapiens regularly faced hunger and
even starvation, and still does in many parts of the world.
Agriculture may have made food supplies more predictable, but
it made famines all the more disastrous when crops failed. There
are famines in the Bible, and famines in folk lore. Famine has
been a constant fear even in Europe; less than two hundred years
ago the Irish starved to death in their thousands. Charities like

Oxfam are aptly named, as they continue to struggle with famine. To survive such times, the human animal stores calories as subcutaneous fat, and a genetic predisposition to store fat was an important survival mechanism. Now for the first time in human history, hunger has been eliminated for the general population in some favoured areas of the world. This must be understood in the context of 100,000 years and more of human history. Three set meals a day and a constant supply of delicious food like that ranged in modern supermarket is a new experience for perhaps the last two or three generations. Such bounty is quite out of keeping with Homo sapiens' natural state.

Adaptability

One reason why Homo sapiens has survived and multiplied is its ability to eat a wide range of foods. The giant panda derives all its nourishment from bamboo shoots and the koala from eucalyptus leaves. These animals are unable to vary their diet; if there is no suitable food, there is no panda or koala. Most carnivores have very limited diets but remain healthy on a meat-only diet from which they are able to metabolize vitamin C and other nutrients. Homo sapiens' diet is limited by the animal's dentition and digestive system, but it is still able to vary its diet and so adapt to different habitats. It is the variety of its diet that has allowed the human animal to inhabit almost every corner of the Earth.

Food-Energy Balance

Over-eating in early man was a response to a fear of future famine—packing in the calories against inevitable hard times. The human female's hips and buttocks are designed like a camel's hump to hold a fat reserve of some 80,000 calories for her to draw on while pregnant and nursing her young. The intake of carbohydrate boosts insulin; this boost is followed by an insulin crash which provokes hunger so that the human animal is encouraged to return to the food source for more. Such sources would have been rare, and so the occasional binge had important survival value. While this is a useful mechanism in a 'wild' creature designed for famine, it has become entirely inappropriate in modern conditions. In nature wild man like other creatures balanced its food intake with its energy needs; chronic over-eating was rare, only observed in the occasional powerful and indulgent individual. Obesity would have been as unknown in man as it is in wild creatures, such as leopards, giraffes, whales or parrots.

Exercise

'Wild' man was not particularly athletic but was designed to survive in conditions where mobility was entirely through bodily movement; 10,000 steps a day is now suggested as a measure of necessary exercise. Within each tribal group there would be individuals who were, within limits, genetically adapted to store calories, while others shed calories and remained lean and active. Both body forms helped group survival. The fatter individuals survived famine; the leaner individuals provided food and protection. The food supply was irregular and uncertain and required much more digestive effort than modern food. Fat, carbohydrate, and salt were scarce. Food gathering in the tropics was not very energetic but it often required stamina. Gathering food took hours of gentle browsing, the animals eating along the way. It has been calculated that hunter-gatherers in a congenial environment can satisfy their dietary needs in about four hours a day. However, there were times when the environment was not congenial, and there were long treks from food source to food source. For all human history until very recently the hardships of ordinary living balanced the likely intake of calories. Just over a century ago the labour required to work the land, to transport and prepare food, together with washing heavy linens and wool cloth, churning butter, keeping fires lit, all required hard physical work. Ploughing a field with a team of horses meant walking many miles a day often through wet, heavy soil. There was a natural equivalence between the available calories and the exercise necessary for everyday life.

Calorie Conservation

The intake of food needs to balance what is expended, with perhaps a little held in reserve. If intake is one side of the equation, the conservation of calories is the other. Homo sapiens, like its ape cousins, naturally avoids exerting itself unnecessarily and uses all its ingenuity to find ways of 'labour-saving'. It will always take the shortest path, literally and figuratively. This had a purpose before man invented machines and discovered electricity. Now modern Homo sapiens can indulge its general reluctance to take exercise. It will ride rather than walk, and use a lift (or elevator) rather than climb the stairs. Bodily movement has been reduced to a minimum with mobility machines (cars, trains, planes etc.) and machines that perform almost every other physical task. There was once an inescapable need to walk, carry loads, do household tasks, and generally labour, but it is impossible to go back to this way of life. Substitute physical activities often do not seem purposeful, and are avoided. At the same time, the food supply is constant, abundant and easily digested and the ancient urge to store fat, and carbohydrate remains like an addiction. The result is an epidemic of obesity in the developed world.

Gathering

The impulse to collect perhaps derives from the ancient survival skill of food-gathering. Once a food source is discovered, there is a compulsion to pick and select the best specimens and sometimes carry them off like trophies. In some individuals collecting becomes an obsession, though the collected objects have no relevance to food gathering, but are artefacts, stamps, plants etc. There is then considerable satisfaction in arranging them, their relationship perhaps giving them additional meaning.

Food from the Wild

The human animal had to know its environment, mind-mapping sources of food and, more particularly, water supplies. Older members of the group, especially post-menopausal women, often held life-saving knowledge of remembered resources. A huge store of expertise in the use and preparation of food must have been passed on from generation to generation, like an oral recipe book. A group had to know which plants were poisonous, which plants had edible roots, and when foods were in season. Survival might depend on finding calorific staples, food that gave an excess of calories over the energy needed to find, process and digest it. There had to be knowledge of how to make different foodstuffs edible by mashing, soaking, smoking, drying etc. Above all, cooking hugely widened the range of foods, but for millennia there was no pottery and no metal for cooking pots. Food was cooked in fire-pits, on spits, or with hot stones. As well as knowledge there had to be a great sensitivity to the natural world, which became a kind of spiritual awareness of the life forces in trees and animals, and an awe for the sun, moon, and stars and their effect on the seasons. The flow of life carried with it the generations of man, and man knew itself as part of something it could neither resist nor understand.

Hunting

Hunting was comparatively unproductive while man evolved and meat was more likely to have been obtained as carrion. Meat was often tough, and torn from the carcase with much blood and offal, and eaten raw. Even the parts of the victim that would now be considered unpalatable were eaten—eyes, brains, lungs, genitals etc. However, fresh meat was probably not a regular or very large part of the diet, though man's change to a carnivorous diet stoked the growth of its great brain. The enlarging brain allowed man to hunt better and so acquire more meat, and a cycle of development followed. Homo sapiens may have evolved close to water, so that fish and crustaceans would have been an important part of the diet. This may be why fish and fish oils are now known to be especially important for human health while too much red meat or milk can be unhealthy.

Cats will naturally look with eagerness into hidden corners where small rodents are most likely to be found; dogs will be at their happiest chasing or digging out prey. Homo sapiens is also a predator with an instinct to hunt. Hunting still dominates the lives of hunter-gatherers, especially the lives of young males, in a way that is difficult to imagine for settled cultures. These predators relate to their prey in a complex and often deeply emotional way. They have to understand or even empathize with the animal; there is reverence, and gratitude as well as cruelty. The thrill of the chase and the need to express the killer instinct remains in some settled populations. These hunters are predators but the prey no longer promises relief from famine; it is just an object for sport, which to some observers seems unworthy. The Spanish bull-fight for all its cruelty gives some dignity to the dying animal. In former times the pleasure in killing gave rise to a delight in blood sports like hare-coursing, cock-fighting, bear, bull and badger-baiting. These sports are now generally considered too cruel and have become illegal in much of the Western world.

Stone Age hunting required short bursts of extreme energy, or sometimes long chases, but like most other big apes there was often time spent in socializing and just dozing. For more than a 100,000 years, Palaeolithic relaxation was balanced by the constant low level of activity needed to find food and shelter, by occasional spurts of extreme energy, longer pursuits, and walks into the endless wilderness.

Agriculture

Plentiful sources of gluten were not available until the beginning of agriculture and the cultivation of grain only some 10,000 years ago—a fraction of man's existence. The discovery of certain grasses that produced large grains meant the availability of a compact food source. The grain could be stored so that food supplies could be better controlled. The grains could be crushed into powder and mixed with water and baked. Similarly, before the domestication of cattle, goats or sheep, dairy products would have been unknown and are not part of the dietary heritage of man. Bread, milk, cheese, eggs and meat became available as never before, but disease, bad weather, or social dysfunction could still bring about a sudden collapse of the food supplies. With agriculture man became dependent on a new range of foods, rather than wild fruits, leaves, roots, and meat. The wandering life was over. From then on, many Homo sapiens became sedentary and developed new crops, and ways to process them.

Modern Food

Human taste particularly relishes sweetness, salt, and fat, and different textures of crispiness, crunchiness, juiciness and creaminess. Of course, this is partly cultural, but the worldwide success of burgers and fries and sugary drinks suggests a predisposition for food that is high in sweetness, salt and fat. The enjoyment of these tastes drove wild man to seek out high calorie foods, and foods with essential mineral traces which were comparatively difficult to find. The gatherers also looked foods that were easy to digest so that life-saving food value was immediately available.

To some extent foods are also colour-coded: green, red, orange, and yellow are attractive, suggesting ripeness and goodness while tones of blue, grey or black subconsciously indicate decay, badness or poison. Modern analysis corroborates these instincts; red berries and green leaves have been found to have valuable protective qualities. Vision plays an important part in man's selection and enjoyment of food. The modern food industry knows that colour is enormously important in attracting Homo sapiens to its food. Most processed food has colouring added to it because consumers associate bright colours with taste and goodness—an interpretation inherited from the primeval past.

Sugar

A sweet taste prompted Homo sapiens to gorge themselves when they found a source of sweetness so that they benefited from the rush of energy. Sweetness was only available in fruits, nectar, some stems and roots, and the occasional honeycomb of wild bees. As recently as the Renaissance and the voyages of discovery, sugar was principally medicinal and the individual intake would have been a few teaspoonfuls a year at most. The discovery of sugar cane and the refining process, and the colonization of suitable land for its cultivation led to the huge expansion of the sugar trade in the eighteenth century. The European taste for sugar was insatiable, and the planters made huge fortunes—literally off the back of African slaves. The fortunes of the sugar planters to a significant extent funded the British Industrial Revolution. For the last two hundred years the consumption of sugar has continued to escalate until the annual intake is measured in kilograms rather than spoonfuls, increasing the risk of diabetes and other health hazards.

Salt

Homo sapiens also craves salt because salt is lost in sweat and salt is also difficult to find in nature, away from the sea-shore.

Certain animals find rocks that contain salt, and return to these salt-licks for generations. So precious was salt that Roman soldiers were paid a salt allowance or 'salary'. Salt is also valuable as a food preservative. In modern times salt is freely available and ingested in unhealthy amounts causing high blood pressure and cardio-vascular damage.

Fat

Sources of fat were also rare. Few wild animals had the layers of fat found in modern farmed livestock. Nuts and berries like olives would have been seasonal. Northern fatty sea fish such as herring, or animals like seals would presumably not have been found in the primal evolutionary habitat. Bone marrow would have been the main source from which wild man could satisfy his craving for fat. The craving was intended to urge the animal to pack in the calories from this particularly rich source while it was available. In a warm climate without refrigeration, meat would have been eaten quickly, and the marrow sucked from the bones. In time the animal learned that lean meat could be left to dry in the sun and so preserved, but fat was not so easily stored.

Over the last 5,000 years and above all the last 50, the taste for sweetness, salt and fat can be satisfied out of all proportion to nature's intentions or the creature's dietary needs. The urge to store extra calories is still easily and repeatedly triggered even in conditions of secure overabundance, giving brief 'highs' that are experienced as 'comfort', leading to further unhealthy binges. The result is that junk food is consumed in massive quantities despite health education which seeks to control the damage. All in all, while modern Homo sapiens has made its life easy and comfortable, it now has to work psychologically to control some of its most powerful biological urges. These need to be recognised, and their power understood, so that sugar, fat and salt are thought of as treats for special occasions rather than staple foods.

Craving and Addiction

Humans are subject to addictions. This can vary from a compulsion to eat chocolate or a self-destructive craving for heroin. Man has an awareness that beyond the initial taste and comfort of a full stomach, food, or what is ingested, may have other effects. Some apparent instinctive awareness of the medicinal or healing effects of minerals and plants has been observed in some higher animals. However, most animals eat first and experience later without any awareness of a causal relationship. Any dog owner knows that a dog will eat whatever seems immediately palatable with no sense of the consequences. Humans, as animals, also can ingest thoughtlessly and often do. However, they also understand there is a causal connection between ingestion and after effects; medicine depends on this. Humans have learned that some substances, which are not particularly palatable or nourishing, heal; while others alter moods and some bring strange pleasures even though they may be poisons.

Why should an individual knowingly take a substance that will cause it harm? Sometimes the immediate pleasure of a delicious taste is just too seductive. There is possibly a search for excitement or the pleasure of risk-taking, which sometimes motivates cigarette smoking among the young. Some drugs stimulate dangerous over-excitement; others bring oblivion, peace and self-forgetfulness to those whose lives are unfulfilled or too stressful. Almost all cultures have an approved drug; alcohol has long been the choice of the Western world, though now other drugs are also available. Drug addiction alters body chemistry and this triggers a craving with the desperation of a hunger that overrides all reason and control. Alcohol has been called the 'demon' drink, as if the alcoholic is indeed possessed by an evil spirit—literally and metaphorically.

Eating Disorders

Anorexia, bulimia and other eating disorders can destroy the health of some individuals, particularly adolescent girls. Somehow starvation becomes addictive. It may be that without food, brain activity may change so that anxieties are damped down, and the individual feels more in control. There is still much to understand about the psychology of appetite. Extreme over-eating is now also being diagnosed as an eating disorder.

Food, Culture and Religious Observance

Food has enormous symbolic significance. All cultures have food preferences and expectations about how and what is eaten and drunk, but sometimes food is used more consciously for cultural bonding or religious expression. The ingestion of food affects the body, and most cultures consider certain foods unpleasant or even impure. Most Europeans will consider caterpillars or ants unpalatable. Some cultures are vegetarian; others will not eat pork or bacon. The pursuit of purity may be a religious duty, and sometimes fasting or denying some foods becomes a religious obligation. There may be strict dietary rules about what can be eaten, how the food is prepared and served, and who eats with whom. Sometimes the food animal has to be killed in a particular, ritualistic way. Fish, milk and meat sometimes cannot be mixed, and even the utensils used to prepare the different foods have to be kept separate.

Food as Wealth

In some cultures cattle are wealth. Food is the ultimate currency and money is actually called 'dough' or 'bread'. Food is used to motivate animals; money (symbolic food) is used to motivate Homo sapiens. Instead of stockpiling actual food, tokens or money are exchanged for food or other commodities and ultimately used to attain power and security. Human crime is largely concerned with one animal trying to take this symbolic food from another or others, just as pack animals will fight for their share of resources. Thieves, burglars, and fraudsters all try to take the wealth of others. The foolish and innocent are seduced by the hope of easy money and become easy prey to 'con men'. Though it may play out as a quarrel over land, oil reserves, or other sources of wealth, at root these disputes are an instinctive response to the threat to the archetypal food supply. If food supplies fail, gold, possessions, and all tokens of wealth and power are valueless. Charity too has many forms but often comes down to famine relief.

The Social Function of Food

Food is a central factor in human social interaction. Although there is basic animal selfishness, a special feature of the human relationship to food is the pressing need to share with other humans, and to feed other creatures. Other animals do not use food in this way. A group of animals like chimpanzees and even some pack animals may at times share food, but generally there is a hierarchical order and the process of a meal is self-interested and potentially quarrelsome. Only when threatened by starvation or other extreme pressures does man's basic animal nature surface and like other animals it feeds itself and its nearest relatives without regard to others.

To share food with others, especially those that are younger or weaker—kin, friends or animals—gives great satisfaction. Homo sapiens is enormously sociable and sharing food is an expression of this social impulse and, beyond that, of affection and even love. This may lead mothers to overfeed their children, possibly reacting to a primitive urge to protect their offspring from starvation as well as satisfying an emotional need to express affection. Sharing food helped the transmission of ideas from which culture eventually developed but sharing is above all a bonding mechanism. Sharing food is also the starting point for Homo sapiens' capacity for empathy.

The elderly, ill or weak were a source of a wisdom which was transferable through speech, and therefore they were sustained by the group when unable to find food for themselves. For Homo sapiens it is as if the action of offering food is the equivalent of offering 'life'. This is ritualized in religious ceremonies such as the Christian sacrament of communion (based on the Last Supper) and feeding rituals from other religions—even cannibalism, which is perhaps a kind of ultimate bonding. 'Feeding' is both a metaphor and a real act. Jesus of Nazareth is fabled to have fed the five thousand, and commanded his followers to 'feed his sheep'.

Human social life prioritizes food. Social meals bond families, working groups, friends, members of clubs, institutions, and communities. Sabbath, Christmas and Thanksgiving dinners and similar ceremonial meals in other cultures, bring together millions of individuals into a shared experience across the national or religious group. Most ceremonies have meals as part of their format, while state banquets and receptions ease official relationships.

The need to feed animals and birds is so pressing for some humans that it is difficult to prevent the public from spoiling the diets of pet and zoo animals, or from encouraging an unhealthy overpopulation of feral cats or pigeons. Humans want to feed almost any species that does not threaten predation or other harm, if there is food to spare. Loneliness and inner hunger must sometimes prompt this relationship with other species as an extension of the bonding achieved by exchanging and sharing food with their own kind. It is also often an expression of the capacity to care for the injured or weak. This must have aided the domestication of animals. It is something different from parental feeding in other species, and seems to be a need to relate to and enjoy other creatures. Homo sapiens probably developed its sense of justice and its ability to feel empathy for its fellows, both animal and human, from this strange and generous urge.

Perception, Communication and Fantasy

The barge she sat in, like a burnish'd throne,
Burn'd on the water; the poop was beaten gold,
Purple the sails, and so perfumed, that
The winds were lovesick with them, the oars were silver,
Which to the tune of flutes kept stroke...

...

...   the silken tackle
Swell with the touches of those flower-soft hands,
That yarely frame the office....

Shakespeare, *Anthony and Cleopatra.* II, ii, 199-218.

Communication has to start with sensory perception. The human individual is isolated within the self and the five (or more) senses are its windows on the world. Sensory deprivation is one of the cruellest torments as the human animal has an alert and curious brain. If an individual is deprived of sensory input, it is likely to hallucinate. Like all animals it has developed sensory organs which allow it to find its way safely about its particular environment.

Animals have organs that are appropriate for their different purposes—compound eyes, infrared vision, sonar receptors, lateral line sensors, organs of Jacobson, hearing at different wavelengths, scent receptors of incredible range and sensitivity etc. The thresholds of the different senses are also set differently for different species. Eagle-eye vision lives up to its reputation as the birds of prey can see a distance of several miles. Hawks have two foveas (the area of the retina that focuses images) so that one is used for short distance, the other for long distance like 'spectacles' for close and distant vision. Cats can see six times more clearly in the dark than man. Apes have enough colour vision to recognize leaves for food. Chameleons can swivel their eyes independently. Dogs can hear wavelengths too high, and grasshoppers can hear wavelengths too low, for human perception. Hammerhead sharks have receptors that detect the electric impulses given off by prey. Animals such as whales, dolphins and bats have a sonar system developed so far beyond human capacity it becomes equivalent to vision. Smell is much more important to most other animals. Dogs in particular are known to have extraordinary powers of smell, many hundred times more acute than those of man.

The five human senses, and possibly a sixth sense (or even more)—for instance, an individual seems to sense being watched, though the watcher is not in sight—are similarly adapted to the needs of a wild ape on the African savannah. All species have special needs and perceive their world accordingly; the observer is part of the perception process and knowledge of 'the thing itself' as electrical waves and charges of energy remains for ever unknowable. Like cause and effect, the perception of space and time are constructs of the human mind and its sensory organs. Film can speed or slow events; zoom lenses can magnify, and a plane travelling at 800 kph can seem to be motionless. Other dimensions not perceivable by man probably exist. Modern physics teaches that light bends near heavy objects in space under gravitational influence. In fact physics and metaphysics seem almost to merge in exploring the mystery of physical matter and both question the simple perception of the human senses. Einstein discovered the interrelationship of energy and matter, made up of unperceivable particles and waves. Human senses are tuned to interpret these as mass, and mass is moulded into the recognisable forms of the physical world. Other species perceive this same world very differently according to their biological needs. Beyond these species-specific perceptions is Einstein's mysterious reality, existing behind the veil like a life after death.

That world of 'wild' man would have been free of all mechanical noise and artificial light pollution so that there were only the sights and sounds of the natural world. Survival depended on interpreting signs which would lead to food or warn of predators. Sharp senses were important to survival. As the group moved through its environment its senses were attuned to the slightest variations. Man was simply part of the ecosystem. It could enjoy well-being when health and circumstances were favourable, and could relax in the safety of the family group. On the other hand, it was vulnerable to injury, disease, famine and predation. The merciless winnowing out of the ill-adapted operated for at least 150,000 years, 90% of Homo sapiens' history.

Vision

Vision is man's primary sense: 'one picture is worth a thousand words.' The animal's upright stance and bi-pedal locomotion made its light sensors or 'eyes' its primary awareness monitors, set on the flat forward-looking face. Unlike many other animals, Homo sapiens used vision rather than smell for its primal hunting and gathering. The mental process of detecting prey through vision was more complex than following an enticing smell. Animal tracks had to be consciously related to prey animals—a kind of cause and effect connection. This primacy of vision may therefore have contributed to man's cognitive development in a very important way. The human 'light sensors' allow for three dimensional, bifocal, colour vision within certain wavelengths (380-720 nanometres= visible light) based on three primary colours, and the perception of distance, angle, dark, contrast and speed. There is also the suprachiasmatic nucleus in

117

the brain that is sensitive to light and regulates the animal's body clock.

A notable feature of human vision is its restlessness. The eyes alter their fixation three times a second, scanning the surroundings without conscious effort. Even in sleep there are 'rapid eye movements' which are associated with dreaming, though muscle paralysis prevents the dream being activated. A third of the brain's resources are used in interpreting the impulses shunted along the optic nerves. With so much incoming data, attention has to be selective; the ability to direct awareness and focus is essential. If vision was simply random, the animal would often be distracted and unable to avoid danger. A car driver scans the road ahead for hazards and concentrates on particular features while peripheral vision takes care of the wider scene. Exactly the same mechanism served 'wild' man as it crossed the savannah.

The human animal can anticipate movement and position itself to catch something even before it starts to fly through the air or as it is falls almost too fast to be seen. This kind of coordination is extremely valuable in many sports; the goalkeeper in various sports, for example, seems to have an almost uncanny sense of how the ball will come at him. As wild creatures such skills were probably important for hunting or avoiding danger. There seem to be certain innate responses to what is seen. Most individuals experience some sense of vertigo when they look down from a high cliff or building. There is also an obvious fear of the dark when Homo sapiens' vision is limited.

Apart from the awareness of danger, human vision is most importantly adapted for relating to its fellow humans. Almost above everything, human vision is programmed for people-watching and group-living. The human group has a complex signalling system. Some species have coloured feathers, white fur on the rump or tail, or a fringe of white fur on the face like the colobus monkey. Dress and ornament take the place of fur or feather signals in human society and of course are infinitely variable. Gender is one of the most important aspects of this, and recognised above all visually. Females advertise their gender with their breasts; the male gender signals are facial hair, general body shape, and in some cultures something like a 'cod-piece' or 'lunch-box'.

Body language

Body language and gestures are very powerful and communicate social information to all higher animals, including man, at a subconscious level. Every nuance is instinctively interpreted so that tell-tale movements often reveal emotions. It is almost impossible to coach public figures to suppress these and avoid 'leakage', whereas actors learn to use them to convey their character's inner feelings. Companion animals, most notably dogs, are very sensitive to human body language, detecting mood, dominance, threat, affection and so on. Dog training mainly consists of learning the signals that tell the dog what its human owner or pack leader requires of it.

Most other animals have threat or submission postures and so do humans. 'In my face' suggests threat as a dominant individual invades another's personal space, and glares to intimidate. 'Looking down one's nose' suggests arrogance. A head held high expresses superiority. Averting eye contact, bowing, or otherwise lowering the body expresses submission. There is a whole repertoire of body language expressions instinctively understood across cultures. Otherwise, of course, there are gestures that are culturally dependent such as the British 'Agincourt' or 'V' sign, or the American raised middle finger. Some populations in India move their heads in a characteristic

119

'wobble' as they speak. This is obviously a cultural feature as is the Jewish nod or 'shockle'. Hand movements also vary from culture to culture, sometimes very controlled, sometimes very lively and expressive.

Facial Signalling

Most importantly, the human face is strikingly individual and particularly mobile and expressive with over 40 muscles, and 7,000 expressions. The animal meets face to face because of its upright posture, and relies on vision as its primary sense. The mouth and teeth are very expressive, especially when smiling, smiling being a gesture of tamed aggression. Broken, missing, bad or misplaced teeth can have enormous impact. A distorted, damaged or grimacing face has a very powerful effect, especially if it is suddenly revealed, as in a horror film. The faces of monsters like the Cyclops are the stuff of nightmares.

Facial expressions are read like a book across cultures and centuries. A smile, a frown, a stare, a wide open mouth all have innate meanings as Munch's painting *The Scream* illustrates. Greek drama used masks for comedy and tragedy, exaggerating the emotions for the audience sitting at a distance. The effect of masks is very potent both hiding identity, and eerily freezing the features. Carnival masks are used for amusement and subvert the facial expression communication system. This communication is so sensitive that a great film actor can use a blink of an eye or a slight contraction or relaxation of a facial muscle to convey powerful emotion. The first films were without sound, but could convey much of their meaning through facial expressions and gestures. On the other hand, writing, radio, sound recording, the telephone, and now mobile phones, internet and e-mail communicate without 'a face' or gestures. This lack of visual information can lead to misunderstandings or misjudgements, sometimes with disappointing or even dangerous consequences..

The face haunts the human imagination so that images of faces are compulsively imposed on quite abstract patterns, as Gestalt psychology demonstrates. The mind looks for the features of the human face in every ambiguous pattern—dots and lines are compulsively aligned to make a face. Decorative patterns, the fronts of cars and trains, houses, flowers, ducks, cats, rabbits—almost every surface with features can be perceived in this way, as is often illustrated in children's books. Faces therefore play a huge role in human relationships. The human mind has an enormous capacity to recognise the faces of its kind, and hold them in a huge memory bank.

Eye contact is always significant as it is said the eyes are 'the windows of the soul'. After death one of the first actions of attendants is to close the eyes if they are frozen open and staring. Almost unique amongst animals, Homo sapiens have large eyes with whites framing the pupils. This makes the eyes the focal point of the face. Goya's painting, *1808,* shows how the whites of the eyes express fear and panic. Staring is very intimidating, expressing anger and threat. Some other animals control their prey by staring at them, so that the prey become immobile, and 'play possum' in the hope of damping down the predator's killer instinct. Sheepdogs and other herding breeds need a 'good eye' to keep a herd under control. Perhaps the human stare of hypnosis is something similar. Averting the eyes and avoiding eye contact show submission or avoidance of relationship.

There are also learned responses to visual in-puts. Experiments have shown that the mind can compensate for upside-down spectacles after a period of time. The understanding of certain stylized drama traditions, opera, even western TV, may need an understanding of its cultural background to become meaningful. Paintings and even photographs have special individual meaning to the observer as they are experienced subjectively. Then there are all the symbols and signs of the costumes humans wear, all having significance with regard to gender and status. Much of this is cultural, and the body ornament of one culture can seem very strange or even ugly to another. A troop of guards on parade with red coats and bearskins would look as odd to native of a Borneo rainforest as their traditional dress looks to us.

The smile is an inversion of baring the teeth in aggression, and instead communicates pleasure and friendliness. (Dolphins appear to smile and this evokes a particularly warm response from humans.) Handshakes are a punch or slap transformed into a hand clasp as a way of showing non-aggression, and clapping expresses pleasure and excitement—a gesture shared with chimpanzees. Non-sexual kissing may similarly be a bite transformed into a light touch of the lips or cheek. Raising the arms is especially evocative. Punching the air with one arm expresses triumph or aggression, and is often seen after a goal is scored or a race won. Both arms raised, together with a swaying motion of the body accompanies great pleasure, ecstasy or self-surrender.

The primacy of vision is also apparent because the imagination is described as 'the inner eye' and dreams are mainly visual, observed as 'rapid eye movements' under the lids of a sleeper. For some 30,000 years Homo sapiens has used vision symbolically and represented the world it experienced in carved objects and then cave paintings.. Even abstract lines and curves communicate; direct lines suggest energy while curves suggest tranquillity. Then for the last 5,000 years, a mere fraction of the time Homo sapiens has existed, aural language began to be represented by simple, stylised pictures. These became visual symbols which then became more abstract until ways were found to record language and the ape became literate. This changed the world for ever.

Smell

Human acuity of vision has been achieved at the expense of the sense of smell. Bi-pedal locomotion means the nose is high above the layers of air close to the ground where smells are most apparent. In addition, the short muzzle, which aids man's facial expressiveness, has reduced its smell receptors. Instead of scent marking, man uses visual signs such as graffiti. It is said that smell is the most primitive of the senses, and evokes memory at the deepest level. In the primal state a family group probably shared the family smell. In modern western conditions the mother's ability to identify her infant by its smell is virtually all that remains of that family scent-bonding. There is evidence that sexual compatibility correlates with compatible smell; the smell of close relatives however is incompatible, and this is probably why other mammals do not mate with litter-mates, so avoiding inbreeding. Until the advent of the modern bathroom, personal smells must have been important and may even have been sexually arousing. On the African savannah the sweat and other secretions would have been trapped in tufts of body hair, and the personal odour would have been an important aspect of individual recognition and group bonding. Laurens van der Post describes the smell of a bushman:

> Even his smell was astringent with essences of untamed earth and wild animal being. It was a smell... archaic and provocative...

In some northern societies the family group until recently would remain in close proximity in a confined space through the winter. Clothing was not easily laundered and the space was often shared by domestic animals. However, as everyone smelt, smell was taken for granted, but the smells of other families or strangers may have been registered as unpleasant. Until recently smell was part of national or racial stereotypes, as different diets and practices of hygiene meant that different groups smelled differently. It may be that because families are now much more dispersed, the family smell no longer has a function. In fact, as there is more intermingling, most modern humans now try to suppress their personal smell, and natural body smells are generally registered as offensive.

Relatively little is currently understood of human pheromones. There may be an organ near the vomer in the nose which detects airborne pheromones. Pheromones certainly exist, but they do not apparently work at a conscious level. It is known that something like a human fear pheromone alerts other animals to human anxiety and distress, sometimes triggering a predator's aggression. There are reports that young women living in community groups synchronize their menstrual cycles, presumably as a result of some pheromonal influence. Perhaps in primitive societies this synchronization had a survival advantage. Caribou synchronize their births so that there are so many young at one time that predators are soon glutted and can only kill a small percentage. Homo sapiens may have had a similar group birth pattern. Other effects of human pheromones are more mysterious, but from time to time advertisements suggest that a particular fragrance makes an individual sexually irresistible.

Unpleasant smells have much greater impact than pleasant smells. Rotting flesh, vomit and faeces give off strong offensive odours and prompt evasion. This is protective as it makes the animal avoid infection. On the other hand, Homo sapiens experience pleasure from the scents and perfumes from flowers, herbs and other substances. Flowers are enormously symbolic, and from the time of the Neanderthals have been used to pay respect to the dead. They often mark the site of a tragedy, and flowers are widely used as tokens of love and affection. The scents of flowers, herbs, fruits, resins, oils and leaves attract man's interest, sometimes releasing feelings of happiness and even joy, and leading the animal to seek out substances that might be therapeutic. Frankincense and other scented substances can have a religious significance. On a simpler level aromatherapy uses the sense of smell to promote relaxation and healing.

Taste

Without smell, substances can often be difficult to identify by taste alone. Smell and taste are closely allied, and the enjoyment of food and wine is as much a matter of smell as taste. Homo sapiens is unusual in being an adventurous omnivore, part of the adaptability that has helped it survive. Other animals have limited taste; for instance, cats have no taste buds for sweetness. The human tongue detects four, perhaps five, tastes—sour, sweet, salt and bitter; there is also another possible savoury taste. Individual sensitivities vary a great deal, and many tastes are acquired. Children love sweet tastes, but it takes time for them to enjoy sour or bitter tastes. This is protective as it keeps them from ingesting unripe fruit or poisonous substances. Salt is attractive because salt is lost in the animal's sweat-based cooling system. Taste also has a tactile component because the feel of food is important, whether it is crunchy, creamy, sticky or crisp. Crispiness is also in part 'heard' through the bones of the skull. Cooking is the art of taste and smell, and to some extent, vision.

Touch

Touch is possibly the most basic sense of all—the first felt by the newborn infant and the last perceived by the dying slipping into oblivion. Touch receptors are spread very unevenly over the body so that the face—especially the lips, and tongue—finger tips, and toes are particularly rich in receptors, while the back is as insensitive as leather. Receptors in the skin detect temperature, pressure, vibration and pain. Combinations of the receptors produce other sensations such as texture. The face has to be protected for obvious reasons: all the sensory receptors—vision, taste, smell, hearing, and important touch areas—are located there and the brain sits behind it. The eyes are extremely tender, and lips account for half the receptors in the face and are sensitive for food, language and sex. Most of the body can respond sexually but the breasts, nipples and the genitals are the principal erogenous zones. The tongue is erogenous, but more importantly guards the digestive system and selects what is to be ingested. Fingers are highly sensitive because they are vital for feeding, manipulating tools, learning about the environment, and touching others; their dexterity has been a great evolutionary advantage. Mobility depends on the feet, and mobility means success and safety; a damaged foot in the primal situation may well have been a death sentence. Feet are, therefore, also very sensitive. In comparison, the back is merely a protective shell. There can even be pain from phantom limbs after amputation because the nerves above the amputation still convey pain impulses.

The human animal, like the other apes, enjoys being groomed. The hairdresser, the masseuse, the beauty therapist are perhaps modern versions of the chimpanzee who searches through the fur of a companion. Deep relaxation and a sense of well-being can result. Other pack animals enjoy being stroked and the action of stroking can itself lower human blood pressure and induce well-being. As in other primates, the pleasure of grooming and being groomed bonds individuals, and promotes trust. The development of spas and health clubs allows modern man deliberately to access the pleasures of touch without the bonding function. Stroking and caressing still has this function in sexual foreplay, but in most modern human societies bodily touch is carefully controlled because the group intimacy has largely been lost, and the sexual aspect of touch, therefore, has become more prominent. 'Massage parlours' are often not far removed from brothels because touch so easily links with sexual foreplay.

Balance and the kinaesthetic sense are related to touch. These senses help the animal orientate itself in space and are vital to its bi-pedal locomotion. A rocking motion has a soothing effect as the human animal enjoys the sense of freedom in space, like a pre-human primate. Swings, rocking chairs, cradles, hammocks and so on all give this feeling of well-being, perhaps reminiscent of the rocking motion of the womb in pregnancy. However, too much rocking and swinging can cause nausea, and a bumpy ride can lead to travel sickness. Disturbed individuals sometimes develop persistent rocking or head-banging as if to find some relief from their pain through such motion.

Hearing, Speech and Communication

At first man's hearing was simply a sense that would help the animal find prey, avoid danger, and communicate with its fellows. Like other animals it used screams, grunts, sighs, growls, laughter etc. These primal sound signals are still enormously powerful; the human scream arouses visceral responses of alarm and terror. The two ears allow the animal to locate the direction of a sound. The inner ear detects minute vibrations of air molecules—less than the width of an atom. Children have a hearing range of 16 to 30,000 cycles per second; this reduces to a range of 16 to 3,000 by the age of seventy. Many animals, especially birds, use sound patterns to communicate. Whales seem to 'sing' and convey information and emotion. Certain gibbons 'sing' quite complicated spontaneous songs. A monkey can warn its group that there is a leopard on the ground, or with a different cry that there is a bird of prey above. They can also recognise the cries of some other species. Some pack animals will join together and coordinate their 'voices' in a howl, probably consolidating the pack's identity. Many other creatures such as geese use contact cries to keep in touch as they travel. However, Homo sapiens communicate with sound at an altogether different level.

Homo sapiens has refined its animal noises into a huge range of symbolic sounds which gradually developed into language some 40,000 years ago. There had to be physiological adjustments to the chest cavity and throat to allow fine breath control and the functioning of the larynx to achieve this. With adjustments of the throat structure and mouth, human sound signals became more refined and precise; human thought became more abstract, and capable of using sound symbolically. Since then, whatever the impairment, other senses can be substituted to make communication by language possible: touch (Braille) for the blind, sight (signing and lip-reading) for the deaf, even touch for those without sight or hearing.

Speech has huge advantages; among these are the more subtle socialization of individuals within the group. The individual becomes hypersensitive to the whole social signalling system, but most particularly to the voice cues of its language. The unborn child knows its mother's voice in the womb, and as soon as it is born it begins to tune into its mother tongue and master its language in a predictable sequence. Speech is a powerful force in teaching the compromise of personal impulses with group norms. From family and spouse, the group widens to include acquaintances, then political, national and perhaps racial allegiances. The development of information technology is very recent in terms of human history; even the radio and telephone are merely a century old. The effect of this widespread flow of information must in time have a huge effect similar to the invention of printing on Western civilization five hundred years ago. Modern technology now allows Homo sapiens to inhabit a 'global village' where information and opinions are exchanged worldwide as never before. This is itself the 'message' of the new technology. There are benefits and dangers in this. It should, of course, promote the brotherhood of man. However, without skilled and knowledgeable mediation instant communication can foment misunderstanding or anger. For example, without some explanation a TV picture may set off a riot as an accident is misinterpreted as an assassination; a film of an angry leader stirring up a mob can seem unreasonable unless there is an understanding of the background.

Language in sound conveys far more than factual information. The tone and pitch of a voice suggests gender, age, and emotional state—the kind of information a dog can detect by smell. Science fiction robots are often given flat, expressionless voices to make them sound frightening and inhuman. A deep voice indicates a big, muscular, dominant male, a husky voice indicates sexual arousal, and a child's voice is immediately recognizable. Language has rhythm and pitch, and different languages have their own intonation patterns. With excitement, the rate of speech speeds up; with sadness or thoughtfulness it slows down. For the most part human aural communication is informal and imperfect, and much of the meaning is conveyed by facial expressions and gestures, so communication is more effective if there is face to face interaction between speaker and listener. Language is sequenced through time and the mind holds the individual components in memory until the message is completed from word to sentence to paragraph to perhaps a long speech or sermon. The longer message has to be structured, with summary and repetition inserted to help concentration on the argument

While language is represented visually in writing, it is still 'heard' in the aural imagination. Reading largely depends on phonics, and writing is monitored in terms of whether what is written 'sounds right' as if verbal communication is still primarily aural. English spelling is difficult because there are so many phonetic irregularities. Much of the artistry of writing, especially poetry, is a matter of word and sentence rhythm.

A great deal of verbal communication is more a matter of vocal grooming than the transmission of information, and a huge part of a successful social life. Talking is a favourite occupation and almost impossible to control in a group situation. A moment's silence is so exceptional that is often used as a special tribute. An hour's silence is almost unthinkable except in special circumstances like an examination or act of religious devotion. Trappist monks take a vow of silence and this is recognized as an enormous sacrifice. As the language flows, the minds of the participants shape the communication in the language centres of the brain. It is a mysterious process involving imagery, memory and emotions. A great deal of social information is transmitted through language. Words can be used to wound or caress. Many human beings have been driven to illness and death by unkind words, and gossip. The power of a curse features in many folk tales and legends but most religions have words that give healing, hope and blessing.

Sound has always been a communication mode. Sounds with rhythmic patterns and tonal variations expand meaning, often accompanied with movement, and ultimately become song and language. Dance, rhythmic sounds, singing, vocalizations like ululation have very primitive origins possibly in the human equivalent of a wolf pack howling. The power of rhythm in man may be part of the sensitivity to sound patterns which allowed speech to develop. It seems to be felt like the beating of the heart, and can even raise or lower the heart rate in response. Dancing and music play important parts in religious ritual. States of ecstasy, often accompanied by upraised arms and a swaying motion, can produce religious excitation and trance.

Words allow immediate aural communication but are generally ephemeral and leave little trace in the human memory. To make them memorable, poetic effects such as rhyme, rhythm, and alliteration are used. Sagas, scriptures, epics, poetry and other forms of aural language art have given expression to Homo sapiens' deepest thoughts for thousands of years. The natural pitch and tone of the human voice can be raised to become intonation and then song. Before the invention of microphones, the human voice had to project itself through its own resonating chambers—the sinuses of the skull. Melody first followed the 'song' of spoken language, as in plainsong or recitative, and then broke free to become an independent artistic expression.

Music
Singing can express the deepest human experiences combining emotion, words and music, and can at times lift the singer to an almost transcendental state sometimes called 'souling'. It seems appropriate that traditionally angels and the souls of the blessed sing in heaven. Beethoven added human voices to the last movement of his ninth and final symphony as if music and words together express the highest aspirations of the human spirit. There is sometimes a suspended moment of almost spiritual rapport between musician and audience after a performance before applause breaks the spell. Alternatively the performance ends with a crescendo to a climax, which merges with a roar of excitement from the audience.

With music to heighten emotion and make the words more memorable, songs have told stories and expressed emotion for centuries. As generation after generation learns the music of its culture, it seems likely that with minor variations some folk tunes may be extremely ancient: 'the hills are alive with the sound of music, with songs they have sung for a thousand years.' The musical heritage of a community is a powerful bonding mechanism. The songs are often repeated with slight variations from place to place and time to time. They were probably widely dispersed as human groups wandered from place to place. Traditions mix and evolve, and with increased mobility this process has accelerated. Folk songs from the Celtic and English-speaking world travelled with settlers across the Atlantic. African slaves brought their music to the New World where it survived despite all persecution. Other cultural communities have the same traditional song heritage as music is so persistent in the human memory. It is possible that modern folk singers are repeating music that was first heard in the Iron Age or even earlier—albeit much adapted and changed. In recent times these ancient songs have been collected and written down. Modern technology has now transformed the experience of music and song, and allows almost immediate global dissemination of newly composed material and makes successful performers worldwide celebrities overnight.

Classical western music is a complex cultural construct and needs to be learned and practised by performers and listeners to achieve the necessary understanding for its full appreciation. This has disinherited the hitherto uneducated majority of the population. High culture depended on hierarchy and was supported by the drudgery of an underclass. With modern labour-saving devices, and the possibilities of recording and disseminating music, Handel, Mozart and Beethoven are no longer the preserve of a cultural elite. Music illustrates the potential of the human mind to follow and interpret complicated interweaving aural patterns moving through time, and experience mood and emotions often at the deepest level. This has to be recognised as extraordinary behaviour, something unique in nature. Homo sapiens is an ape, but an ape that sings its soul.

Although it can be a solitary experience, music is primarily a communication medium. It can be a weird experience to sit in a large concert hall with hundreds of human minds 'plugged into' the same musical source and feeling the same synchronized emotions. A thousand humans sit expressionless and still while music links their minds in a spell of emotion and wordless meaning. At its height some individuals seem to be transported into a transcendental, self-forgetting state of mind—or spirit. Ceremonies, informal gatherings, gala occasions, huge gatherings of fans are all events that depend on music. Music sets the mood for rituals and ceremonies and conveys the group's emotions of patriotism, sorrow, excitement, religious fervour etc. together with special vestments and movements such as uniforms, marching, 'presenting arms', carrying flags and so on, but it is the music that defines the whole experience.

Popular music of the present day is of enormous importance in modern western culture, and its most successful performers have an almost royal wealth and status: Elvis Presley is in fact remembered as 'the king'. This music is usually song with a strong, repetitive beat, and electronically produced background effects. The audience usually participates, singing, calling out, waving arms, and screaming with enthusiasm. This popular music expresses the soul-life of its time. The lyrics of popular songs are preoccupied with physical and material pleasures and lack spirituality, but in this they are a true reflection of a secular era.

Fantasy

Spoken language for the last 40,000 years has allowed individual thoughts and fantasies to be shared. The collective mind can achieve more with a co-operative effort than a single mind alone. Language shapes and fixes a group's view of the world. Vocabularies reflect a group's environment and cultural background. Unfortunately, stereotypes can seize the group imagination, leading to irrational and dangerous theories of conspiracy, and group paranoia. However, an open-minded appreciation of 'difference' must increasingly counteract prejudice and mistaken ideologies in the modern world.

For over 30,000 years after the development of language, thoughts had to be exchanged face to face, or by a human messenger—the only way of transmitting ideas across time and space. Over the last 5,000 years the visual representation of language as writing has allowed the more exact preservation of knowledge. Language allows the transmission of facts, insight, memes, and ideals, dreams, hopes, and ideas of heaven and transcendence. Hallucinations and nightmares can also be shared. Strange stories such as urban legends arise simultaneously in different places as if from the group psyche.

Predation Fantasies

A fear of being caught and eaten by a predator is a staple of the human imagination. Such predation fantasies are full of existential fear and panic and must reflect the vulnerability of Homo sapiens in its primal habitat, ambushed by carnivores, chased by mammoths, stung by insects and bitten by serpents. Any weakness meant almost certain death. A small bite or scratch from a thorn might fester; a bad tooth might cause infection or make feeding difficult, a digestive disorder or a sprained ankle might leave the individual human animal vulnerable to watching predators. These predation fears are expressed in stories from ancient folk-lore to modern films—Grendel, the Cyclops, the Minotaur, dragons, serpents, 'the big bad wolf', sharks, dinosaurs, wicked witches, demons, Dracula, aliens from outer space, the Martians in *The War of the Worlds,* etc. The sea is full of monsters, ready to carry off an unwary aquatic ape. The film, *Jaws,* illustrated this terrible fear in a modern situation. Many a motorist has felt a frisson of ancient terror as a following car is seen like a threatening predator in the rear mirror, closing in and tail-gating. Steven Spielberg's terrifying film, *Duel,* uses just this predation fear. In the moral dimension the 'predator' is the murderer, rapist or thief of the TV or film story. Being killed is one side of the equation; killing is the other. Heroic humans outwit, maim and kill monsters, aliens, and other adversaries—-St George, Perseus, etc. The human imagination has generated such stories for millennia, and now modern animation techniques externalize these imaginings and fix them in the public mind.

The Power of the Imagination

The human capacity for empathy and projection allows endless possibilities for fantasy. Stories of historical figures, anthropomorphized animals, dolls, stuffed toys and even trains and cars, fantasies of the future, and so on, are endlessly generated for entertainment, information, and understanding. So many children's stories anthropomorphize animals, and while this, in many cases, is charming, it can lead to unrealistic and sentimental attitudes to animals in later life. Peter Rabbit is so appealing and 'human' that ever afterwards rabbits are thought of as little 'people' with all the perceptions of a human child. This is neither true nor psychologically healthy, and the difference between fact and fiction must be gently observed. While rabbits must be respected as sentient mammals, they are not capable of the psychological insights that cause so much human suffering. Peter Rabbit's limit is Mr Macgregor's garden, but the human imagination can also grapple with the complexities of a Hamlet, in the setting of a corrupt court.

Memory and experience can be re-interpreted, 'cut and pasted', and coupled with new and different emotions. The present affects the past; a couple will recall their first meeting with different emotions according to how their later relationship develops. Individual attitudes and memories are constantly adjusting to new and different experiences. The human imagination can source ideas from reality but also invent 'aliens', UFOs, ghosts and monsters beyond real experience. Elements from reality can be manipulated by the imagination to create new environments, relationships, sequences of action, and personae, or even break free from reality altogether. The creativity of the human imagination has not only expressed itself in art but also science, projecting hypothetical ideas and ways of testing them to arrive at new interpretations of the world.

Similar mechanisms are used in painting and other visual arts. Cave paintings, rock art, Greek sculpture, Renaissance paintings, modern cartoons, films, and videos externalize man's inner imaginings of hunting, predation, bonding, betrayal, rescue and heroic failure. The senses can combine in dance, drama, opera, film etc. using sight and hearing. In time there may be ways of mass-communicating smells. There is even a curious mixture of the senses when a song can 'taste' sweet or be 'seen' as green. This mixture of senses or synaesthesia is totally subjective, and varies greatly from person to person.

Towards the Spiritual

When 'wild' man roamed landscapes untouched by his intrusions, the wild life was unimaginably rich and varied. At night the moon and stars shone brilliantly deep in the dark sky; below, the land was lit by glow-worms or fireflies, and was full of deep shadows, strange shapes, and wild sounds close by and far in the distant. The howls of wolves and wild dogs, the calls of night-flying birds, the rasping and humming of insects, echoed in the dark wilderness. Homo sapiens often hunted by the light of the moon, and were hyper-aware of the night and its creatures. The moon excited some individuals to mania. It influenced the ebb and flow of tides, and marked the monthly cycles of earthly time. After the development of agriculture crops were often planted and harvested according to the phases of the moon. The Earth was the seed-bed of life, the nurturing Mother Earth—Demeter or Ceres. Planting seed mirrored the male inseminating a female, 'He ploughed her, and she cropped' – so Shakespeare describes the liaison between Julius Caesar and Cleopatra, and the conception of their son. The mysterious waxing and waning of the seasons seemed to be controlled by unseen, powerful agents like 'the Green Man', the spirits of the countryside, woods, rivers and seas. Everywhere was magic, beauty, mystery and danger.

As Homo sapiens wandered across the empty continents without map or compass, it encountered exotic new landscapes, animals, plants, some of which might not be fully understood. The settlers moving west across the American Prairies in the nineteenth century walked into an unknown land and were met by strange, alien people. The quest or voyage is a persistent fantasy where the hero—Gawain, Arthur and his knights, Odysseus, the hero of Westerns, and so on—face monsters, dangerous pathways, ambushes, mysterious happenings which challenge the traveller's strength and ingenuity. The mounted horseman is particularly charismatic—the chevalier, the knight, the cowboy. The quest can also be symbolic of the inner journey towards understanding and spiritual enlightenment.

Other animals with their super-sensitive senses, in their own terms, may experience wonder and an intuition of another dimension of being. They have an apparent awareness of an impending natural disaster, ghostly presences, and even a telepathic sensitivity. Primitive man as an animal had similar powers, such as a sixth sense, as noticed by Laurens van der Post among the Kalahari Bushmen. Over a considerable distance, the knowledge of a kill is 'felt' by the group left behind miles away. Such sensitivities may still exist below the threshold of modern life, but are denied by a secular, materialistic culture. There is still sometimes an awareness of the earth's magnetic field, an ability to dowse for water, to experience altered states of consciousness which allow psychic healing or cursing, telepathy, clairvoyance, pre-cognition, communication with the dead and other 'spirits'—quintessences, principalities and powers. As Hamlet remarks: 'There are more things in heaven and earth, Horatio, / Than are dreamt of in your philosophy.' Modern man lives in an environment of constant noise and light intrusion. Attempts to rediscover parapsychological powers have been largely discredited, or dismissed as dealing with 'something' dangerous or even devilish. However, the human propensity to 'believe' suggests there might indeed be some lost capacity for such a means of communication.

EROS—Sex and the Family: Breeding Behaviour

Here with a loaf of bread beneath the bough,
A flask of wine, a book of verse – and thou
Beside me singing in the wilderness –
And wilderness is paradise enow.

Edward Fitzgerald, *Rubiayat of Omar Khayyam,* 41-44.

Homo sapiens, as particularly aware creatures, are encouraged to mate by the promise of extreme physical pleasure. Sex is a powerful bonding mechanism and has little to do with reproduction for many couples; after all, sex leads to reproduction in only a fraction of instances. Homo sapiens' close relative, the bonobo, uses promiscuous sex for mutual pleasure, to defuse aggression—literally 'to make love not war'—and generally to promote good relations. Sex is, of course, biologically a mechanism for mixing genes. Sexual reproduction as opposed to 'selfing' (self-fertilization) promotes diversity and allows adaptations which aid species survival. Diversity promotes evolution as the cleverer, bigger and stronger animals are more likely to pass on their genes to the next generation.

The Human Family

Homo sapiens have extraordinarily strong emotional and sexual bonding mechanisms which control much of their lives. Not only are there bonds of familiarity and physical closeness but also the special human faculties of heightened memory and imagination. 'Family' is pre-eminent, above all the parental bond between mother and young child. The 'wild' mother and child, watched over by the father, was embedded in a clan of many interrelated individuals each bound to each by blood and familiarity. The adult males bonded as a hunting-protective group, while the females were interchanged with other clans to hybridize the blood lines; otherwise the females formed a cooperative breeding group, and the males wandered. This is probably more likely because it is reflected in the many stories where the hero is a brave young male who by chance passes by, performs some heroic act and then rides away. This importation of new blood was necessary because sex seems to be naturally taboo between those that share familial intimacy before the age of about six. Other animals will not usually have sex with their litter mates, and it is suggested that similar DNA expressed in a personal smell instinctively inhibits sex with close relatives. Humans recognise this consciously as incest.

Care of the Human Infant

Pleasure in caring for children is somewhat off-set by the work and stress involved. The Homo sapiens infant is particularly immature and helpless. Its gestation continues for another year after birth. It needs a huge in-put of affectionate attention. If this is lacking, it can seek negative attention rather than have no attention at all. No attention in the wild would have been tantamount to a death sentence. The infant's survival depends on parents and related adults feeling affection and protectiveness for it. When an infant smiles, chuckles, and reaches upwards towards its carers, it is almost impossible for them not to respond positively. The infant's large round eyes, chubby face with its small features are all naturally appealing and have been commercialized as 'cabbage-patch' dolls. The close relatives respond all the more readily if they recognize themselves, or those with whom they are bonded, in the new infant. The unnatural isolation of parents in modern society, sometimes far from supportive relatives, means that the children and their parents are often emotionally exposed and vulnerable. Women, in the west, increasingly have careers, often finding the solitary full-time care of young children unrewarding. This is all a long way from the social context in which hunter-gatherer groups reared their infants.

Mothers can recognize their infant's smell; fathers are less sensitive, and can become a danger, especially if not convinced the infant is theirs. There are terrible myths, like those of Cronos or Saturn, of fathers killing and even eating their children. As a protective device, it has sometimes been suggested that newborn Homo sapiens babies often resemble their fathers. A baby that secures the affection of its father is more likely to survive and physical resemblance reassures the father of his baby's paternity. Before DNA analysis, the male could never have complete certainty that an infant carried his genetic material. In nature, some male animals, such as lions and bears will kill offspring that are not their own if they set up a new partnership with their mother. The vulnerability of step-children is well-recognized in folk lore, and even in modern conditions step fathers are known to be a particular threat to their partners' young—molesting or even killing them. Cruel step mothers are also well-known figures of folk lore.

If for some reason the pair bond between the parents fails, the infant is less likely to survive. Other blood relatives will try to support the child, but may not have the resources or inclination. Throughout the centuries charitable organizations have tried to care for widows and orphans in recognition of their vulnerability. Even amongst modern Homo sapiens, a one-parent family is at greater risk, especially if the single parent is the mother. A long-term heterosexual pair bonding, or otherwise a powerful male figure bonded to several females, can avoid this vulnerability. With changing economic and social conditions the financial dependency of females and children is less marked, though the psychological burden of a lone parent can still be very heavy.

The Human Pair-Bond

The father is emotionally programmed to seek exclusive access to his breeding female. He tries to win and hold the female's loyalty; in turn, she tries to win his protectiveness for herself and her offspring. Exclusivity is however difficult to establish and has to be something more than the strong affections Homo sapiens feel for many of their family, friends and acquaintances; it has to be a bonding of a different order and is felt as 'love'. Bonding ceremonies publicly declare the socially sanctioned pair bond; adultery brings condemnation and sometimes heavy punishment.

Ovulation without Oestrus

Perhaps the most important factor in Homo sapiens' mating behaviour is the unusual fertility pattern of the female. Insemination in other apes seems to be a matter of pheromonal excitement aroused by the females' oestrus cycles. Other female mammals have a few weeks of fertility at widely spaced intervals; the female's behaviour changes and she arouses the males with irresistible hormonal signals so that she will almost inevitably become pregnant. At other times, the animals are released from sexual stimulation though they may still indulge in non-reproductive sex play.

Unusually, human females do not come into 'season'. Neither the female nor her male associates are conscious of her few fertile days that occur at monthly intervals, though it is now thought that when she is ovulating she unconsciously often behaves in an unusually seductive manner. This hidden ovulation gives the Homo sapiens female unusual control over her fertility. No one knows for certain when she is fertile and in ordinary circumstances she cannot be guarded all the time. She, therefore, has more options than most other female animals. Ovulation occurs secretly once a month making her fertile for just a few days. Ovulation is then followed by menstruation if no pregnancy is established. Most other female animals because of their breeding behaviour are unlikely to escape pregnancy, but if this happens they simply reabsorb the womb contents. In Homo sapiens the more frequent ovulation and constant state of sexual readiness requires a monthly shedding. During menstruation in many cultures the female is considered 'unclean', for obvious reasons, but also she is clearly infertile.

Another unusual feature of human mating behaviour is the moderate level of interest in sex all the time, not just in a mating season or when a female is fertile. Other animals are either frantic or switched off. They are consequently less identified by their gender, except when fertile. Instead of periodic phases of sexual interest, latent interest is there in Homo sapiens all the time and sexual attraction in humans is not indiscriminate—-a spreading of genetic material wherever and whenever nature prompts. The female oestrus is replaced by the attraction of personal features—the face, the crotch area, buttocks and breasts in women—the face, shoulders and crotch area in men. Other senses like smell, sound and touch also play a part—personal smell, perfume, tone of voice, firm or gentle touch. It has even been suggested that the couple may share compatible bodily smells which they intuitively recognize.

Love as a Psychological 'Oestrus'
Sexual attraction depends on previous family imprinting and personal compatibility. Intelligence is attractive as it promises status and greater access to resources; an ability to raise laughter is another kind of power play. When a couple check out their potential in these stakes and match with their partner, the feeling of suitability engenders a mutual excitement turning on a flow of

'happiness' hormones, felt as 'love', perhaps the most profound of all human emotions. The fulfilment of love can bring supreme happiness and physical joy. It is celebrated endlessly in poetry and song. Just as powerful unfortunately, is the experience of disappointment in love—frustration, betrayal, and loss—the themes of much literature and music. The romantic formula of courtly love is very much a construct of fourteenth century Western Europe; it is so satisfying that it lingers to the present day with testosterone-charged heroes tamed by beautiful, unattainable women. The combination of force and grace, chivalry and beauty, knighthood and elegance, suggests the best of male and female in exquisite balance.

The lovers are often said to be love sick or even temporarily mad. Love seems to strike inconsequentially like a fever or a drug. In Shakespeare's *A Midsummer Night's Dream* the juice of a special herb affects the eyes of the lovers and Titania so that they are emotionally transformed. The Queen of the Fairies falls in love with a coarse workman wearing an ass's head. The antidote is as easily applied. The onset of sexual excitement can be so sudden and overwhelming that it is like being struck or smitten, traditionally by Cupid's arrow. Ordinary behaviour is overridden by irrational obsession, very much like the mating behaviour of other species—in 'season', in 'must', in 'rut'. Any dog owner knows that a beloved, docile pet will become virtually unmanageable under the influence of its sex drive. In Homo sapiens this feeling of erotic love is the conscious experience of the equivalent of oestrus in other animals but instead of the females arousing the males pheromonally, the couple become more and more psychologically fixated upon each other until mating is inevitable. In nature the couple 'in love' would produce a pregnancy almost as inevitably as other animals 'in season'—erotic love is just as compelling and almost as impossible to resist. In this way, Homo sapiens are motivated to overcome their natural inhibitions to intimacy and open their private selves to each other.

Illicit Love

While the long- term pair bond is the Homo sapiens' ideal, there is a high level of dysfunction. Relationships are often threatened by infidelity. Moral systems try to police human relationships but biologically Homo sapiens is moderately sexually dimorphic, and this suggests it is programmed to be more or less promiscuous. The Homo sapiens male has large testicles compared with other great apes such as gorillas. Only the notoriously promiscuous chimpanzee has proportionally larger testicles. This also suggests that Homo sapiens males have an usually high sex drive, and need frequent copulations to maintain their equilibrium. The female is less easy to assess, but the widespread occurrence of illicit sex suggests she matches her male counterpart in her need for sex.

There are benefits for both sexes in other liaisons; between 5%—30% of all infants may be fathered outside an existing pair bond. The female balances the security of her pairing with a secret search for a more powerful male, sometimes an older individual whose longevity attests to strong genes. The male is prompted to spread his genes by seeking young, fertile females whom he can inseminate. Powerful urges for infidelity remain just as strong in modern conditions as they did in Homo sapiens' wild state, though they are very unlikely to be consciously recognized as the breeding strategies they are.

Unsanctioned human lovers challenge ordered society, and for many of them no threat of punishment or social disapproval can deter them from the present pleasure of their risky liaisons; the couples' immediate pleasure eclipses all thoughts of future consequences, however dire. Females usually risk more as there are more pressures on them to control their sexuality. Once the 'happiness hormones' begin to flow couples will risk home, career, fortune and even life itself while the heightened emotions last— for instance, Romeo and Juliet, Tristan and Isolde, Antony and Cleopatra, Dido and Aeneas, Paolo and Francesca da Rimini, Héloïse and Abélard, and Lancelot and Guinevere. Sometimes such liaisons change the course of history: Henry the Eighth's passion for Ann Boleyn changed the religious life of England; Charles Parnell's affair with Kitty O'Shea ruined his career and hopes for peace in Ireland. Edward VIII of England forfeited his crown for 'the woman he loved'. Sexual scandals still damage political leaders and celebrities, even in the more tolerant modern world— as President Bill Clinton discovered.

Non-Hormonal Sexual Attraction: Gender Markers

Male to female attraction in humans is particularly complex— psychological, as well as biological. Careful selection of a mate is by mysterious factors—some cerebral, other intuitive. Desmond Morris has analysed factors that promise health— symmetry of face and figure (trauma or disease can bring about distortions), shining thick hair, clear skin, bright eyes and strong white teeth and a well-shaped body, demonstrating oestrogen or testosterone markers. Over the centuries, artists and sculptors, and now also photographers and filmmakers, have projected the various cultural ideals, though real males and females rarely match these.

In females the breasts are the significant gender markers; their shape has little to do with lactation. Most other mammals, including higher primates, have very little breast tissue beyond the essential nipple for suckling the young. Female Homo sapiens have large swollen breasts. In the words of T.S. Eliot, 'uncorseted her ample bust/Gave promise of pneumatic bliss.'

As a bipedal ape, the breasts are very obviously on display near eye level and have therefore become the main female visual gender signal. In some cultures the breasts are carefully hidden; in others they are displayed without inhibition. The Minoans cut the bodice of the female gown to frame the exposed breasts. The tabloid press, artistic representations of females throughout history, modern plastic surgery, all reflect the obsessive human interest in the female breast.

However, the breast is also meant for lactation but a suckling infant compromises the breast's sexual appeal. A woman breastfeeding can offend prudish sensibilities, and in some societies the woman herself finds breast-feeding unpleasant or even disgusting. Many women avoid breast-feeding—in the past employing a wet-nurse, but nowadays bottle feeding. Many modern women are not prepared to sacrifice the sexual appeal of their breasts for an extended period, and breast-feeding is almost impossible in the workplace. However, in primal times there was no substitute for breast milk, and breast-feeding was a necessary part of most females' lives. As the mother of Jesus, the Virgin Mary is sometimes represented as lactating in recognition and even celebration of this essential female function.

A waist-hip ratio of 2:3 or 7:10 is also significant as the definite waistline signals that the female is not pregnant and is therefore potentially an available mother. The cushion of the female hips and buttocks instinctively suggests successful childbearing, but not because of a wide birth canal as is sometimes supposed, but because there is an extra calorie reserve for pregnancy and lactation. The 'Venuses' of prehistoric times celebrate female figures gross with rolls of fat, probably because they promised fertility at times when such surpluses were rare. Undernourished females are generally infertile. The buttocks are sexually exciting. For most other primates, rear-entry is the only sexual position and the human form seems to mimic this. From behind, the fattened human buttocks have distinctive deep horizontal folds at the junctions with the thighs; these folds meet the vertical fold that runs from just below the waist to the crotch, making that area a kind of 'target' which draws the eye to this particular erogenous zone. Rather similarly, many flowers guide insects to their female parts by special markings like the 'face' of a pansy or as D.H. Lawrence saw in a gentian:

> Reach me a gentian, give me a torch
> let me guide myself with the blue, forked torch of this flower
> down the darker, darker stairs, where blue is darkened on
> blueness...
>
> D. H. Lawrence, 'Bavarian Gentians', 11-13

Blonde hair (in Caucasian individuals), big eyes, fine skin, red lips, a small nose and jaw suggest youth and almost childlike femininity. Marilyn Monroe demonstrated this, and furthermore her drooping eyelids with their heavy lashes suggested sexual arousal. A lustrous, full head of hair suggests health and fertility. Its sexual connotations in some cultures require that this 'crowning glory' is modestly hidden under a veil. In nature the animal with its upright stance perhaps needed its patches of pubic hair to guide the eye to the genital area, as scent was less significant than in many other species. However, in Homo sapiens females the genitalia are deeply hidden. Western women, especially the Anglo-Saxons, are expected to remove most of their body hair. Women with hairy legs and armpits are considered unclean and ugly, though hygiene is no more implicated in women than it is in men. More probably the aversion to womanly body hair has more to do with the ideal of young, almost pre-pubescent beauty. This may also explain why models of female beauty in Western society are unnaturally slim, with girlish figures. After all, in traditional societies girls were often married almost before they entered their teens. Youthfulness promises less wear and tear and perhaps virginity—the precursor of exclusivity, and thus attractive to males likely to be anxious about their paternity.

Testosterone markers in males are a big jaw, heavy eye-ridges, broad shoulders, narrow hips and a bulging 'cod-piece', or 'lunch box'. The male should ideally project a promise of muscular strength and personal authority and so on, like Arnold Schwarzenegger. This attracts the female as the male promises support and protection, and she may appear innocent and weak in order to trigger his protectiveness. His deep voice suggests power and authority. Just as testosterone urges stags, bulls, and other animals to trials of strength, Homo sapiens males may in the past have similarly jousted for control of females. Sport, drama, legends and jealous rages show remnants of such behaviour. However, the unusual oestrus pattern of the Homo sapiens female does not rouse males as a competitive group like other species. Testosterone empowered 'wild' man to feats of heroism, and is still important in times of emergency, enabling the male to protect his mate, his offspring and his social group; in a high testosterone state the male is ready to face risk and danger. Females have long been considered unstable because of their hormones, and often denied leadership and status as a result. Testosterone-driven males however are also victims of their hormones, becoming unstable and dangerous; they inflict untold suffering on humanity and the natural world. Testosterone, especially when combined with human inventiveness, is one of nature's most dangerous substances, and can lead to violence, war, and genocide.

Sexual Conventions

In most societies there are codes of dress and conduct based on gender. Some societies expect their women to cover themselves completely from head to foot in public, whereas in others, women are free to wear almost whatever they want. However, the genitals are almost always covered even if it is just by a thong, loin cloth or bikini bottom. In Western society, women have until recently usually worn skirts, and men trousers. 'Wearing the trousers' has had a highly symbolic meaning. A male can sit open-legged while a female is expected to sit with her knees together as if protecting her genitals. A woman sitting open-legged is likely to be severely censured. In earlier times women riders were expected to ride modestly side saddle. When Elvis Presley began to gyrate and shake his hips in the 1950s, he aroused females to hysteria but fifty years on, and both male and female entertainers provocatively 'bump and grind' suggesting penile and clitoral excitement.

Over time and from place to place, societies have celebrated sexuality or suppressed it according to fashion, religious conviction, or the flow of events. Breasts, waist and buttocks have been emphasized in turn. Corsets, brassières, bustles, crinolines, padding alter the natural Homo sapiens female shape, and feet have also been bound to make them small; high heels make the feet dainty and also lengthen the legs. Hair may be covered for modesty, 'let down' in abandon or dressed for maximum impact. Male fashions have emphasized the waist, cod-piece or shoulders. Male facial hair allows great variations —clean-shaven, moustaches, and beards—while head hair can be long, short or even shaved. The shaved head or 'skin-head' signals masculinity, and may even suggest the baldness that is a testosterone marker in older men.

Most societies try to control sexual activity by moral and practical restraints. Although justified as health measures, some societies mutilate the genitals to reduce sexual pleasure, and make it less troublesome. Most humans masturbate, especially if not otherwise sexually active. Circumcision reduces a male's pleasure in masturbation so that he will be more productive of sperm in intercourse, while a circumcised or genitally mutilated female cannot fully enjoy sexual pleasure and therefore is more likely to remain continent.

Sexual Orientation

The bonded couple is the ideal but many individuals do not fit into this pattern. Almost certainly Homo sapiens' sexual identity is more of a continuum from homosexuality to bisexuality to heterosexuality, rather than the tidy dichotomy fixed by the gender codes of many languages. It has been estimated that about five to ten per cent of any human population is openly homosexual, but the actual number may be much higher. In many societies there is so much pressure to conform to the heterosexual norm that it seems inconceivable that individuals would choose to be homosexual. The reverse is often the case and many homosexuals try desperately to normalize and suffer to the point of suicide when they cannot. There is now evidence that chromosomal sexual direction can be off-set by powerful hormonal influences in the mother's womb at various sensitive times during gestation. Previous pregnancies might leave hormone residues which affect succeeding foetuses. These influences may also explain trans-sexuality. Some male foetuses may be subject to their mother's mitochondrial DNA so that they, like her, prefer male partners. There may even be a gene for sexual orientation. This suggests homosexuality is not a casually chosen behaviour in defiance of social expectations.

There is evidence of homosexual behaviour in other animals, as if same-sex contact is a normal part of nature. However, homosexual activity in animals and in 'wild' man is for mutual pleasure and bonding, or possibly a way of declaring dominance. This should not be confused with reproductive sex. The role of sex in fertilization has almost eclipsed sex as a bonding mechanism; sex has become almost entirely connected with family morality, so that infertile homosexual sex is regarded as unnatural, wasteful and therefore 'sinful'. The equation of sex with sin also derives from the location of the genitals near where defaecation and urination occur. If humans copulated like damsel flies—head to head—sex might not be condemned as disgusting and sinful so readily.

There is no way of knowing how such homosexual individuals were perceived in 'wild' human groups, but for them to have persisted in human society whatever the social sanctions suggests some adaptive value. Homosexuality may also have been a mechanism whereby sexually fulfilled adults were available as spare nurturers or protectors of the young, weak or disabled. Extra hunters or gatherers not trammelled with the breeding of the next generation could be very valuable to the group and were perhaps almost considered a third sex.

Sex in Homo sapiens is an explosive force. Both sexes are, if not sexually active, at least interested in sex into advanced age. Homo sapiens is an animal that is constantly looking for relationships, social and sexual. Sexual need in many humans, male and female, is very urgent and constant. On the positive side, the partners try to win each other's love: on the negative side, jealousy and suspicion prompt their efforts to maintain exclusivity. Unfortunately, sex as a bonding mechanism often malfunctions or is one-sided, causing great frustration and unhappiness. Sexual excitement often seduces partners into relationships that are otherwise unsuitable. Uneven sexual interest, personal incompatibility, unhealthy imprinting can cause terrible suffering—the inverse of the pleasure sex can deliver.

*   *   *   *   *

Non-Relational Sex and Perversion

Sex is pleasurable and although it is a bonding mechanism, if no partner is available the pleasure is sought for itself, sometimes purchasing sex or using fantasy images—in the modern context, on film, video, the internet, telephone etc. For Homo sapiens sex is very much a psychological experience. There is therefore a huge market for pornography, prostitution and sexual scandals in the media. Fantasy relief and self-stimulation are obviously safety valves for built up pressures. Uncivilized Homo sapiens would perhaps have been constrained by different social or other controls. Lower status animals may have copulated randomly—heterosexually and perhaps homosexually—whenever they could find an opportunity; or the higher status individuals may simply have terrorized the others, such as lower status individuals in packs of wolves, into acceptance of their celibate status. In this way the less successful individuals would be prevented from breeding. Poor nutrition, brief lives and lack of security may in any case have reduced libidinous activity.

Sexual feeling can attach itself to fetish objects such as shoes or shiny-wet materials—impersonal ways of releasing sexual frustration. If sexual feeling is not focused on a partner, it can divert into unproductive or even dangerous behaviours such as paedophilia, incest, sado-masochism, rape, necrophilia and bestiality. These expressions of human sexuality are far removed from sexuality's primary purposes of bonding and reproduction.

For a few psychopathic individuals bonding can only be negative and any partner becomes an object of hate and rejection.

Paedophilia

The line between physical pleasure from closeness to children and paedophilia is firmly drawn in cultures where the welfare of children is paramount. Children are physically attractive, and may occasionally arouse sexual feelings in an adult. If there is any danger that this sexual response to a child's body is likely to be acted upon, the adult is morally bound to recognise it and avoid any temptation at an early stage. The individual can 'talk' himself or herself out of any action, distance themselves from the child, or at least seek help. This takes enormous determination but as with any addiction, once the pleasure takes hold it is virtually incurable, and this addiction must be prohibited because it damages the innocent. Although young children are sexual in an immature way, their sexuality needs to be respected, especially in a society where there are negative connotations to unsanctioned sex. For an adult to risk damaging a child physically and psychologically for personal gratification is completely unacceptable. Unfortunately, the appetite for child pornography on the internet suggests paedophilia is far more widespread than might have been thought; its extent seems to have been hidden as society's dirty secret

Children are pretty with their soft skin, delicate hair, and engaging ways. Their innocent minds are non-judgemental, and therefore they are particularly attractive to adults who are likely to be unsuccessful in adult relationships. The extended family groups of 'wild' man could perhaps have been more watchful of their children, being always together and sharing communal living arrangements. There may simply have been more general indulgence of sexual needs. However, in many societies girls may be considered

154

marriageable in early adolescence, especially when life expectancy is short. Shakespeare's Juliet was just thirteen, and the Virgin Mary was probably of a like age when she was betrothed. Certain groups might even have accepted paedophilia; baby males as Cupid, cherubs and putti in art often seem to have sexual connotations, sometimes caressing a Venus or some other female figure. However, there seems to be a taboo against depicting baby females in such a way in western art perhaps because adult male nudes are heroic rather than erotic.

Incest

Incest contravenes the instinctive biological warning against harmful inbreeding. However, the unnatural privacy of the modern nuclear family and the concomitant loss of wider intimate contacts may make sexual frustration more likely to turn in on family members. Adults, especially the males, may molest pre or pubescent children, particularly girls, so that the incestuous act has elements of paedophilia. Females can also initiate incestuous relationship but the borderline between intimate caring and sexual attention is less obvious.

Sado-masochism

The intensity of sexual feeling can blur the borderline between pleasure and pain; extreme emotional and physical pleasure can itself be almost painful. Kisses can become the bites they imitate and love bites are the commonest pleasure-pain experience. In some circumstances, pain can release pain-relieving brain chemicals or endorphins. It is a short step to use pain to heighten sexual interest, and use its infliction as a sexual technique. Sado-masochism, bondage, flagellation and such behaviours are the result. Asphyxiation can bring intense excitement, possibly altering brain chemistry and the very danger may also raise excitement. Orgasm has been equated with momentary 'death', 'to die' being a synonym for sexual climax. Consenting adults experience mutual enjoyment, but a sadist may find pleasure inflicting pain on an unwilling partner, more as a matter of power rather than sexual pleasure. This can be very dangerous.

Rape

Rape is a form of attack shared with other higher primates, a testosterone-driven mating strategy. Female rapists are less common for obvious reasons. The resistance of the victim may heighten the rapist's aggression and his sense of achievement. Gang rapes and rapes in times of war are male rampages of a different order, the attack being encouraged and often public. The impulse is not so much sexual, as a territorial violation and symbolic humiliation of an enemy by degrading and possibly impregnating his women.

Necrophilia and Bestiality

Power confronting vulnerability can arouse a particularly primitive sexual excitement, and the murder of a woman is the ultimate conquest. Violent killers sometimes report experiencing an orgasmic pleasure in their murders. There is an undeniable link between cruelty and sex. A dead body is a victim whose silence is guaranteed. The inertness allows the necrophiliac to experience complete power. Farm animals and even pets may be used sexually. An animal is a secret partner and this very secrecy makes it impossible to gauge the extent of such contacts.

*   *   *   *   *   *

Courtship

The mating behaviour in other species is often much more obvious and usually set in a species-specific instinctive pattern. For instance, the male peacock displays his elaborate tail, or stags demonstrate their strength by locking antlers to impress the females. Homo sapiens, unlike other animals, can vary its mating display at will, and respond to transient social moods.

Although human mating behaviour is variable, there are certain definite signals and patterns. Dancing can resemble the mating displays of birds, the males and females adopting complementary roles, expressing sexual exuberance. Giving 'the eye' or the copulatory gaze is all that is needed to arouse interest. Relationships may start with just a glance, the female eyes often being emphasized by make-up. Flirting is developed to something of an art in some societies. Kisses are like controlled bites, just as a smile is a reversal of the aggressive signal of bared teeth. They also imitate suckling. Women have always used cosmetics to enhance their eyes, skin and lips, the latter having an unconscious connection with the other female lips—the labia. Red, gleaming, soft lips and wide 'deep' eyes are sexual signals, suggesting arousal and this, in turn, stimulates the male.

Mating

Other animal's pair publicly as nature urges, and copulation is quick, functional, and not particularly pleasurable. Female cats experience pain as the male ejaculates, and this triggers ovulation. Homo sapiens and some of the higher primates experience pleasure; for these special apes sex is fun. Human couples are likely to be focused on their pleasure rather than on biological compulsion and are therefore likely to prolong their sexual activity. This leaves the couple vulnerable to attack unless they seek privacy.

The human's naked skin, sensitive hands and full lips allow for special tactile contacts and sensations. Psychologically, there is a sense of heightened intimacy enhanced by unaccustomed nakedness and the withdrawal to a private place. Homo sapiens, unlike other animals, is able to be inventive in its sex play, adopting different positions and exploring new sensations. The Homo sapiens brain is a powerful sex 'toy'. Sex, particularly in a stable emotional relationship, opens up the psyche to ultimate surrender and reinforces the pair bond which may last well beyond the years of fertility, and is indeed often life-long. It takes maturity and tolerance to achieve such a relationship. The male sex drive often leads to promiscuity and damages the monogamous bond, although ultimately, males are happier and healthier in a stable relationship. Monogamous females are often burdened by the care of their partner and his children so that the relationship produces stress as well satisfaction.

The human female, unusually among animals, experiences orgasm, perhaps because male and female Homo sapiens have rather similar genitalia compared with many other animals. Homo sapiens' foetuses develop from the female default form to the male, so the genitalia of both genders are related. The clitoris is equivalent to the male penis, and its tissues extend deep into the pelvis and through the vulva to the entrance to the vagina. The 'G' spot may be a vestige of the male prostate. Orgasm can produce extreme physical stress almost like an epileptic seizure or heart attack. The female orgasm may be intended to suck the ejaculate through the cervix and hold it against the force of gravity, particularly important in an animal that stands upright. The psychological outpouring driven by pleasure hormones is even more significant. Oxytocin is a hormone that causes womb contractions, but is also a relationship enhancer. The reinforced heterosexual pair bond provides emotional stability for the couple and the children at the core of their lives. The couple enjoy familiarity, protection, emotional security and trust, long after their oestrus-like excitement has passed. The extended family shares this security and its interconnectedness, allowing ordered and well-defined social relationships. Promiscuity can damage the oxytocin effect, as it detaches sex from its relationship function. The teachings of the great religions recognise this, and generally forbid adultery, or even divorce.

Human mating can be compared to the mating rituals of other species. Doves pout and coo, then bill each other until the female is prepared to accept the male's mounting and entry. Homo sapiens kiss, which is a very unusual animal behaviour. Kissing varies from social kissing which has its own etiquette to erotic kissing with its progressive intimacy. The couple mutter endearments, caress and gradually arouse each other with foreplay until the female is receptive to the male's penetration. Humans, unlike other animals, have a whole repertoire of sexual positions, though the most common is the couple face to face, with the female under the male.

Successful mating followed by birth and the consolidation of the parent pair-bond is the intended biological purpose of sex, though sexual pleasure continues even into old age long after the female is no longer fertile. The loss of a spouse after a long partnership can be the most traumatic experience. This suggests that the pair bond has a purpose in itself providing older genetically connected carers such as grandparents. Grandparents in other species are hardly more than a general part of the kin group.

Mothering
Like most animals there are strong bonds between offspring and parents, especially the mother. This is essential. Compared with many other mammals the newborn human infant is so under developed that gestation continues for many months or even years after birth. While a foal or calf is able to walk very soon after birth, the human infant takes more than a year to reach this stage. The naked skin and bi-pedal locomotion mean that the

human infant is held closer to its mother than the infants of most other animals allowing very intimate bonding. This can be immediate or take time to develop. As with other animals interference can damage this bonding: a painful birth, separation of mother and infant, or post-partum depression may prevent the mother developing what she experiences as love. Neglect or even infanticide may be the result. Infanticide occurs in nature when a mother animal is disturbed, threatened, or has had poor nurturing herself. A famous experiment by Harlow in the 1960s used chimpanzees to examine the effects of poor nurturing. A naturally mothered female chimpanzee was compared with one nurtured on a towelling 'mother' and one on an inhospitable 'wire mother'. When the infants became mothers themselves, their nurturing clearly reflected their own experiences.

Human mothers are also affected by how they themselves were mothered. They may be unable to cope with the stress of child rearing, especially in deprived conditions. During famines, children are particularly vulnerable. In times of hardship infants have often been sacrificed so that the survival of stronger individuals is ensured in the ultimate interests of the species— the harsh workings of the 'survival of the fittest mechanism'. Laurens van der Post describes how a baby born in a time of drought threatened group survival and how the bushmen practised infanticide:

> At birth was the child was taken from her [the mother] before
> … 'it could cry in her heart' and was killed by the other women. The
> anguish and bitterness with which those who loved children performed this
> deed…proved how necessary it was.

In antiquity unwanted infants were left to their fate, and no doubt infants continue to be abandoned in unfavourable circumstances if abortion facilities are not available. Modern surgical abortion may be considered a kind of pre-birth abandonment.

Once developed, the mother love is all encompassing—intruding on the mother's life both physically and imaginatively, even into her dreams. She responds to her infant's special smell, needs to touch and hold it, and feels a self-forgetting protectiveness. In nature she would breast feed the baby until her next pregnancy, or even after that for several years. To wean the baby, its mother would mash the solid food by chewing it first herself, before feeding it to her baby; modern liquidized baby food lacks this intimate and personal touch. Until the last century or so, there was no substitute for human breast milk. If the mother could not lactate, her infant would almost certainly die unless a 'wet nurse' could be found. There may be exhaustion, hormonal imbalances, boredom and frustration, but the care of the growing infant through to puberty becomes biologically central to the mother's life for at least a decade. In nature, other related human females also share something of this bonding as is seen in other animals such as feral cats or wild lions.

Paternity

The biological bond is gradually replaced by habit and familiarity, establishing a likely life-long affectionate relationship. Fatherhood depends perhaps even more on this, as well as successful bonding with the mother, and contact with the infant. Above all the father needs to be assured the infant carries his genes. For the first time in history it is now possible positively to identify a father by means of DNA testing, but for tens of thousands of years the father had only circumstantial evidence of his paternity. The result has been endless deceit, suspicion, jealousy, violence and murder—the stuff of story-telling down the ages.

Siblings

Sibling relationships vary depending on habit, familiarity, genetic similarity, and family dynamics. Usually sibling relationships are close, affectionate and life-long but sibling rivalry can cause disastrous rifts. Cain and Abel is the biblical version of such family feuds, and Hamlet's murderous uncle recognizes his sin in saying 'It hath the primal eldest curse upon't / A brother's murder'. However, on the whole, Homo sapiens feel strongly bonded with their blood relations, recognizing 'blood is thicker than water', or that 'you're family'. This is the conscious expression of genetic similarity, as if the shared genes themselves could speak. Brethren, brother, brotherhood, fraternity, friar, fra, sister, sorority, mother (superior), father—all these family names are used for particularly close non-familial relationships like those in religious or political groups.

Kinship

The extended family of parents, children, grandparents, cousins, aunts, uncles, nephews and nieces usually gathers for ceremonies that mark birth, adulthood, pairing, and death. There are also ceremonial meals on holy days such as Christmas and Thanksgiving. These family bonds protect the young, the weak, the elderly, and the ill. The affection felt for family members, generates a spirit of cooperation and feeling of empathy which then often reaches out beyond the family to other social contacts. In modern times the family group is fragmenting, and these family duties are increasingly carried out by impersonal public services. Families still try to take care of their relatives, but as families move away and women take their place in the world of work, this is less and less practicable. However, there is virtually no way of replacing affection with paid care, unless empathy for the weak and disadvantaged is made a social priority or primary religious duty. Society will have to find some way of providing care as the population ages, and more of the disabled and injured survive. Their fate is otherwise unthinkable.

Socialization

Within the kinship group the child gradually evolves into a socialized member of the clan. The human child has an extended period of immaturity, followed by a sudden adolescent growth spurt. This unusual pattern of development is required for the growth of the large physical brain and the enormous volume of cultural or learned material that the human individual has to assimilate. It learns to share, and obey the moral rules of the group. These are usually founded on instinctive human morality, often expressed in some religious format. Homo sapiens hunter-gatherers were probably highly moral in their own terms. Group loyalty and interrelatedness made child-rearing a socially cooperative undertaking, so that deviance would be unusual. It is difficult to know how individuals whose socialization was defective or malfunctioning would have been treated. These were creatures that lived close to death and daily experienced the cruelties of nature that they were powerless to alleviate. The moral code that suited an isolated group of 100 or 150 interrelated individuals cannot be easily adapted to the huge unrelated populations of modern cities. Furthermore, the isolation of modern nuclear, or one parent families, exacerbated by the solitariness of computer and TV entertainment, make it more difficult to integrate the young into an increasingly uncoordinated and relativist modern society.

Into the World

As children become adults natural tensions prompt them to leave their parental home to seek a life for themselves, just as the grown offspring of other species are driven off to find their own mates and territory. Modern 'back-packers' may be acting out this impulse. Sex drives the young individual to seek its own pair-bond and so begin its own breeding cycle. What is experienced as filial and parental love by individual humans is the instinctive drive to ensure their genes survive. This is expressed as a desire to pass on a name and found dynasties, linking ancestors and descendants, particularly in families that have achieved wealth and power. In some societies ancestor worship is an overt awareness that the genes of the dead live on in their descendants.

Eros in the life of man

Homo sapiens are unique in their very variable mating pattern. Unlike other animals, sex is an undercurrent of its whole life and has as much a bonding as a breeding function. Frustrated sex causes terrible distress but the fulfilled oestrus experience has been celebrated endlessly in story and song from the time Homo sapiens began to speak.

PHILIA—'Brotherly'Love and Fellowship The Self and other Homo sapiens.

Thou shalt love thy neighbour as thyself.

Matthew 23,v. 39

'All you need is love'

The Beatles

Homo sapiens as a Social Animal

Homo sapiens are extraordinarily social animals, perhaps the most sociable animals that have ever evolved. Cooperation has made man successful and compensated for its physical vulnerability. Speech developed out of the ape's enormous need for relationship, and, in turn, speech enhanced that very sociability. Unlike other pack animals, it will instinctively try to rescue its fellows, and relieve suffering, even at a risk to itself. It has the usual animal bonding mechanisms for parenting and family cohesion, but beyond that there are intense feelings of fondness and even love directed at friends and others. Each individual has to leave the familiar haven of the family and find its place in many social groups based on religion, work, common interest— taking different roles in different situations and adapting to different gender groupings whether all male, all female, or mixed. Humans need to please others; to give well-received presents, to provide a treat, to give others happiness and pleasure. On a simple practical level Homo sapiens move around congested cities with astonishing ease, avoiding collisions on crowded pavements, and cooperating unconsciously with huge numbers of strangers. The love of friends and generous feelings towards others is 'philia' as opposed to 'eros'. Philadelphia was founded as 'the city of brotherly love', where its inhabitants were to live out this great ideal of loving human relationships.

Social Deprivation

The human animal hates social isolation. Castaways such as Ben Gunn in Stephenson's *Treasure Island* can go mad. Robinson Crusoe survived but was very pleased to discover Man Friday. Sometimes a community may exclude a member as an expression of disapproval as in Hawthorne's *Scarlet Letter*, or when a group member is 'sent to Coventry'. Solitary confinement is recognized as a terrible punishment tantamount to psychological torture. The Israeli Mordecai Vananu, who exposed Israel's nuclear weapons programme, was almost driven mad by years of solitary confinement. The punished individual may develop a more entrenched attitude or alternatively simply give up on life. Sociability is known to prolong life and many old and isolated individuals simply die quietly without it.

The Homo sapiens nervous system needs human society to develop; tales of feral children such as the Savage of Aveyron illustrate the damage done by isolation from human company during childhood. Speech is a product of community. A child deprived of human speech at a crucial stage of development may never make up that loss. Without speech, culture and even basic socialization are grossly impaired; the individual lives like the ape it is, rather than the Homo sapiens it could become. Some autistic individuals are unable to relate socially, as if some emotional faculty is missing or under developed. Such individuals may just behave inappropriately; others are so grossly impaired that they are unable to speak, and are emotionally unresponsive. Deafness is also a terrible affliction, and can impair the development of speech.

The Social Group

Primitive man must have had a very rich social life, usually living with those that it knew intimately from birth to death, and also a large extended family. Most modern humans, like their hunter-gatherer ancestors, have a social list of about a hundred friends and acquaintances but modern man has to be far more socially versatile. Social contacts are encountered in various contexts while individuals increasingly live in separate units with their closest family, or even on their own. It is now even possible to have a cyber social life. Instead of being a member of a tribal group, the individual associates with others by necessity, or choice. The open or public house features as the central meeting point in many communities, and British soap operas would be impossible to imagine without the 'pub'.

The Bonding Imperative

Homo sapiens experience a constant flow of relationship-seeking energy. This energy reaches out like tendrils of a climbing plant trying to catch on to any passing person or thing. It connects not only with other Homo sapiens but stuffed toys, cars, ships, pet animals, celebrities and religious figures. Dolls, 'teddies', cartoon figures, and fictional characters become the objects of imagined relationships. A personality can be projected on to a car or ship: 'he' can speed down a motorway; 'she' can ride the waves. The relationship of Homo sapiens with their companion animals is emotionally enormously fulfilling and important. If animals are kept for food, the keeper has to resist this bonding, and is usually advised not to give such animals a name. This may once have contributed to Homo sapiens' ability to domesticate other animals. Relationships are also commonly developed with intuited companions, spirits and presences, and even the dead whose existence continues after death. Other creatures stay with their own kind (or occasional substitutes), but man seems to be unique in its need to relate to many other animals, and the creatures of its imagination.

While relationships bring great emotional satisfaction, the corollary is enormous sadness when a loved one is lost. Other animals may mourn for a few days but Homo sapiens can mourn for a lifetime. Sometimes a dog seems to mourn its master, but it is probably simply at a loss without its 'pack leader'. Only elephants and perhaps a few other higher animals bear anything like Homo sapiens' burden of sadness.

Group Membership

Homo sapiens feel integrated into a group so that 'me' and 'not me' become 'us' and not us'. This can be felt strongly when there is a disaster: different accounts are taken of 'our' casualties as opposed to those of others. Loyalty to the group was supremely important as hominids hunted and protected themselves in their primeval habitat. That instinct survives and is easily aroused. Human loyalty can be the motive force behind team sports, group projects and acts of great nobility. However, it can also be misdirected into gang rivalry and general antagonism. Tragically, it can lead to massive and unnecessary sacrifice. It was this sense of loyalty that sent 50,000 British soldiers to death and injury on the first day of the Battle of the Somme in an effort to cross just a few hundred metres of no-man's land.

Other animals rely on scent, plumage, skin or fur patterns and body language to identify themselves with their group but Homo sapiens is able to alter its appearance at will. It therefore uses symbols—insignias, logos, badges, colours, flags, tartans, uniforms, dress codes, fashion items etc. to denote group identity, almost like a brand image. It can tattoo its skin, pierce its body, and wear ornaments or use secret signs such as a special handshake or passwords.

Groups usually have rituals of membership and rites of passage—initiation, graduation, pairing and passing on. These are communal celebrations, which consolidate group identity.

Hospitality is a sign of generosity and parties are general celebrations of social contact. Anthems, flags and parades may unite a political party, or a whole national group. Individuals within the groups almost merge to become something more than themselves, bonding together and synchronizing their emotions. In man, music, songs, banners, even drugs excite and extend group feelings. It is very comfortable to feel 'us' as opposed to 'not us'. There may be general involvement in a jubilee, sporting event, wedding, anniversary, or funeral of an important person. This is particularly likely in a monarchy. There is often a military parade, not so much as a demonstration of power but rather as a spectacle. In human society pageantry and ritual can play on the emotions, heightened by the group psychic energy and lead to a feeling of unity, which is usually experienced as very pleasurable.

Social Intelligence

Like other herd or pack animals, wild man had a need to coordinate its actions and thinking with the needs of the group, even at times to its own individual disadvantage, and some emotional control must always have a been an important social skill. Human relationships are so significant, a successful human life depends, in large part, on having the emotional intelligence to choose the most appropriate response to a particular situation:

> Two roads diverged in a wood, and I
> I took the one less travelled by,
> And that made all the difference.
>
> Robert Frost, *'The Road not Taken'*

Better-socialized individuals had better chances of breeding successfully as they were likely to attract more mates. Their emotional intelligence also helped them to be successful in other interactions. When the survival of the fittest worked

169

unmercifully, the intellectually and emotionally intelligent were more likely to survive, so that selection worked in their favour. However, because socialization is so influential, even genetically exceptional individuals can easily be damaged by circumstances and fail to fulfil their potential, while genetically ordinary individuals may exceed expectations if given special advantages.

Social success brings great pleasure to all involved. An individual who is socially attractive has enormous advantages. In modern situations sales staff use charm techniques to achieve sales and in hostage situations, hostages need to relate positively to their captors. When charm fails, the well-socialized individual has to learn the social ciphers that defuse aggression. Verbal apologies, gestures of submission, gifts, bunches of flowers, etiquette, humour and manners, all reduce tensions and disagreements. Well-regulated societies develop a repertoire of techniques to keep relationships sweet. It reduces tensions in debates if remarks are channelled through a chairperson or 'speaker'. Speech interactions between individuals are very subtle; catching and holding attention, sharing the conversation, keeping interest, breaking off the interaction, are all culturally sensitive. Cell phones give offence because there is as yet no etiquette for their use. A speaker on the phone catches the attention of those nearby as if about to talk, but then ignores them and talks on the phone instead. On some trains there are phone-free carriages so that other passengers can avoid this annoyance. This is a long way from the African savannah, but sensitivity to others, and negotiating social impasses are skills as important now, as they were then.

Socialization

The development of a well-socialized individual requires the consistent care of the family and wider community with agreed standards. Homo sapiens societies vary greatly in how they balance 'brutal' and 'humane' nature. Some societies may applaud cruelty and violence and encourage the strong to predate the weak without mercy; other societies live peacefully and share resources. The group develops its behavioural and moral norms and the child as a little animal has to be programmed in accord with these. Of course different children have different levels of receptivity and human social conditioning is a complex and very variable process.

Training minds and emotions means literally routing neural pathways so that impulses are to some extent conditioned. If a situation exerts extreme emotional pressure, good conditioning may allow just a moment when reason, self-control, foresight or some process of detachment prevents the animal reaction overwhelming what most Homo sapiens would consider the higher response. An attractive female may draw an otherwise conforming male into behaviour so rash that he loses family, career, and social position. Though his reason tells of the risk, the promise of present pleasure is irresistible. Similarly, a moment of primitive anger can wreck a whole life. The avoidance of such self-destructive behaviour depends on suppressing the primal reaction by habits of rational control. Even recognising and understanding animal reactions can to some extent defuse their power. By using the imagination and verbal habits, perhaps even prayer, the animal impulses can be 'turned off'. For instance, fear may be conquered by thinking of 'my favourite things' – in the words of the popular song. With practice, this sort of verbal deflection can become a kind of psycholinguistic switch that turns off 'the beast'. Anger management is just this sort of process. Homo sapiens can practise free will in this moment of pause. It is hard won but on such moments civilization ultimately depends.

Group Dynamics—Conformity

Homo sapiens have a tremendous impulse to conform and be part of a group. A group often resonates with the biological family unit so that its members feel themselves to be a 'band of brothers'. Individuals within the groups almost merge to become something more than themselves, bonding together and synchronizing their emotions. This can work to the benefit or the detriment of wider society. Fellow spirits will bond together to form pressure groups, protest movements, political parties, unions, or religious movements. Social progress has usually depended on the commitment of such groups; the individuals support each other as they challenge accepted social practices and sometimes arouse bitter reactions. On the other hand, a group may be a terrorist cell.

The drive to conform has its dangers as has been demonstrated by a famous psychological experiment. One innocent individual was placed in a small group that had been instructed to answer questions wrongly. The answers were obviously wrong, but after one or two group sessions, the innocent individual became very stressed and often agreed with the group. The need to be liked and accepted was stronger than the need to be right. The security of being part of a group can sometimes be stronger than the validity of a group's ideology. There is terrible danger in this but in a primal group out on the African savannah, there had to be unquestioning coordination for the group to survive.

The power of group conformity in an antisocial group can be extremely dangerous to the majority. It can bond outlaw groups such as pirates, gangs, the mafia, terrorist cells, some cults, rebel armies and even whole societies. The Nazis knew how to choreograph enormous rallies to huge effect. It is very comfortable to feel 'us'—'KKK', hooligans, war parties, neo-nazis, etc.— as opposed to 'not us. The criminal group claims as a right its self-gratification at the expense of others. Loyalty to the brotherhood usually requires some detachment from the influence of wider society. The group becomes the primary influence in each individual's life, to the exclusion of other relationships. Group loyalty can become apocalyptic to the point where a cult may commit mass suicide, or individuals willingly sacrifice themselves to their cause as suicide bombers. Just two individuals may fulfil the clichés 'partners in crime' or 'folie à deux'. Just one companion is enough—Butch Cassidy and the Sundance Kid, the Kray twins, Bonnie and Clyde, Ian Brady and Myra Hindley, to name a few.

Group Dynamics—Independence

As opposed to conformity there is also a powerful need to assert individuality. The balance between conformity and individualism shifts from society to society and historical circumstances. In the Reformation and Counter Reformation terrible tortures and executions were used to persecute those that would not conform. Most tyrannies similarly demand unquestioning loyalty. It is therefore, usually much more comfortable to conform. However, there are always a few individuals who have the spirit to rebel and over the centuries some have gradually developed new concepts of personal, political and religious freedom. Those that rebel may simply be antisocial nuisances. Others may be the heroes that move society forward usually against its will or the will of its leaders and often at terrible costs to themselves. Social progress requires a tolerance that can consider new concepts and is therefore likely to be associated with more open and democratic systems which are prepared to risk the challenge and upheaval of new ideas.

In tolerant societies an individual usually has the freedom to be aberrant within legal limits—'freedom under the law'. Individuals that become outstanding in art, science, sport, etc. at some point often have an 'ignition' or 'eureka' experience or find some other source of enthusiasm which can direct the rest of their lives. These are the geniuses, the creative thinkers, the eccentrics. They are devoted to their particular interest or cause whatever the discouragement. They often challenge and disturb the majority with new ways of seeing the world and society. As the world's population becomes more intermixed and the global village makes for instant communication, communal values may become less unified, and conformity relaxed. The result will be some social confusion. This may lead to more tolerance and understanding or fundamentalist retrenchment and rivalry. Uncritical and media-naïve populations are easily persuaded to cling to old certainties. Too much change all at once can be deeply distressing. The future requires enormous goodwill and open-mindedness. The world's peoples must cope with their natural dismay as they have to leave behind many traditional ideas. Behaviours that may cause misunderstanding and friction in a global context will have to be moderated in the interests of a peaceful future for everyone.

Group Dynamics—Antisocial Behaviour

Burglars, rapists, murderers and other criminals are often individuals who have not learned to master their animal instincts. This is possibly genetic, familial or cultural. If, for whatever reason, the individual does not develop internal security and a sense of well-being, the psyche seems to close in as if preserving its emotional resources for itself. This is perhaps a primitive mechanism to increase the individual's chance of survival, but such failure to relate is socially very damaging. The emotional damage causes detachment, so that even satisfactory relationships are without much warmth or consistency; the damaged individual may become a 'loner', or even pathological and a danger to him or herself and the wider society. This condition has been termed 'anomie' or lawlessness, an empathy disorder presenting as an alienation from the feelings and needs of others.

There have always been a few individuals who have to be eliminated from the group, either by exile, execution or incarceration because they are irredeemable or psychotic beyond cure. They may have some sort of mental disorder caused by injury, abuse, drugs or genetic defect; some criminals actually have a smaller pre-frontal cortex so that they are impulsive and easily irritated. Whether damaged or not, often just a small number of repeat offenders can be responsible for a surprisingly high percentage of crimes. One antisocial individual can damage a whole community out of all proportion to his or her personal importance.

An individual who thinks society has treated him or her badly, may feel no obligation to that society. Someone rejected by a social group, may take dangerous revenge—sometimes a criminal response, a psychopathic impulse to hurt and even kill. Some dysfunctional individuals are like a poison in society, weakening and corrupting the group with bullying, drug addiction, animal cruelty, disturbed social contacts, anger, withdrawal and other pathological symptoms. If antisocial attitudes become habituated the pattern may be difficult or almost impossible to change, the neural pathways being too strongly reinforced.

Anti-social attitudes need to be diagnosed early so that there is some chance of reprogramming the group or individual. Punishment and its anticipated deterrent effect is society's main way of attempting to make antisocial behaviour, at the very least, unproductive by associating pain, discomfort or social exclusion with the antisocial act. However, punishment is itself a kind of conditioning that can alienate as much as reform. Its

175

implied social rejection tends to justify negative attitudes: 'Society does nothing for me, so why should I do anything for society?' The effect of imprisonment can simply be to bond alienated and dysfunctional individuals. Punishment can give some legitimate satisfaction to those wronged. In many societies past and present, there is a danger that the victims' understandable wish for punishment may connect with savage animalistic instincts to justify and even enjoy excessive cruelties. An individual who has been wronged may feel entitled to bloodthirsty revenge, or vigilantes may equally feel sanctioned to carry out brutal beatings.

Strong social mores, redirection of negative energies, certainty of detection and the elimination of desperation would be more effective than deterrence but they require exceptional societal understanding. A fairer distribution of wealth and benefits, education, family support, expert counselling, psychiatric treatment, and diagnostic testing as early as possible, would almost certainly be more likely to bring about reform than the social rejection implied by punishment.

Remorse and Confession

It might be that the spiritual exercises of the great religions can bring about a change, making an alienated individual feel forgiveness, love and hope. It is very difficult for most people to be self-critical; it takes great emotional maturity to accept the burden of fallibility and show contrition. Individuals that have a weak ego or a low sense of social integration anyway, will find this even more difficult. However, penitence is the first stage of reform. Many religious observances incorporate some form of confession in the context of a loving and forgiving deity. This inculcates a habit of self examination, acceptance of error, and resolution to reform and encourages a mind-set that challenges arrogance and self-righteousness. For a dysfunctional individual such a spiritual exercise may help soften the antagonism between the self and society.

The Psychological Function of the Antisocial

Criminals, deceivers, thugs and fools, despite the pain they cause, are of enormous psychological importance to society. They define the boundaries for the moral majority. News and stories about crime and betrayal, folly and deception fixate the imagination. 'Breaking news' brings an excitement to a news bulletin, but why is news so often negative? Why is bad news somehow more exciting than good news, (provided there is no personal involvement)? An awareness of danger, from natural disaster, crime, and the actions of others, perhaps acts as a warning and so helps survival.

Understanding Others

Each Homo sapiens has a sense of self as opposed to others, but societies vary from extreme individualism to an almost complete identification of the self with the group. Whatever the social pattern, the individual has to judge the reaction of others, and attempt to work relationships to its advantage, or at least avoid disadvantage. This happens at many different levels of depth and complexity. Homo sapiens has the imaginative power to understand the minds and emotions of others, and is able to anticipate and perhaps manipulate their reactions. This may involve assessing multiple responses of several other individuals or groups simultaneously. For instance, breaking news may delight some, dismay others, spur some to action, others to reaction and have further repercussions that may take great wisdom to anticipate. Shakespeare's *Othello* makes superb theatre. The audience observes the developing tragedy, and projects into the minds of all the protagonists, experiencing the events from multiple perspectives. In life itself an individual often has to calculate how a remark or action will be perceived

177

by others from various points of view. This has become so complicated that 'public relations' has become an important career. The mental adroitness required for such interactions is far beyond that of other animals.

Analysing relationships and interrelationships is the driving force of fiction, gossip, news, 'reality' and 'voyeur' TV, situation comedies and the media generally. Over the last few centuries there has been a revolution in communication: story-telling, writing, printing, mass media and now IT, websites and chat rooms but the subject is human interactions, especially for women. 'Soap operas', feature films, plays, even advertisements, all examine relationships. The tabloid press supplies scandals and gossip about celebrities and the royal family; any sensational story or photo-scoop boosts sales and is eagerly sought. This reflects the readers' obsessive interest. When reality fails, fictions have endlessly sufficed—for example, in western culture stories of Odysseus, Aeneas, Arthur, Beowulf, epics, dramas, novels, Western films and present day TV situation comedies and 'soap operas'. To be invisible and observe others and so detect their secret selves is enormously interesting. Literature, especially drama, often satisfies this social curiosity. The audience is unconsciously learning social strategies and practising whom to trust, as trust is central to human relationships. The characters of soap operas can become substitute friends and intimates, especially important as modern society fragments and social contacts in the real world may be diminished, with resulting loneliness.

Trust

No doubt there was gossip as soon as there was speech. Sharing secrets is the stuff of gossip, itself a kind of 'verbal' grooming and a bonding mechanism. With speech, secrets became the material for a confidence and sharing secrets a way of expressing and testing trust. There is an almost involuntary gesture of covering the mouth with the hand as if the very act of revealing the secret is itself secret. Knowing whom to trust was probably a survival skill in primitive societies, and still remains vital. A huge amount of human imagination and energy is expended on judging the reliability or otherwise of relatives, partners, friends, colleagues and acquaintances, other clans and in modern times—nations and other religious communities. The interest in 'reality' TV programmes may be that participants are put under so much pressure that the real personality is revealed below the public persona.

Trust is the cement that bonds relationships at all levels from intimate personal relationships to great financial and political and military movements. The betrayal of trust is so damaging to any relationship that betrayal is almost always followed by rejection of the traitor; a group that is interdependent must be able to trust in emergency. Reputation is an important testament to character. Othello's lieutenant, Cassius, cries 'Reputation, reputation, I have lost my reputation'. The loss of reputation can still have terrible consequences. On a modern practical level, employers usually require testimonials and references in order to minimize deception. A criminal record is a kind of negative reference as society guards itself against those that might be untrustworthy.

There is always a temptation to share the secret with another recipient, and widen the circle of trust by betrayal. In sharing news face to face on the street corner; the individual with the news momentarily becomes the centre of attention. There is also a pleasurable sense of intimacy and trust. This is probably why confidences are notoriously difficult to keep. The secret of Midas' long, donkey ears was such a burden to his barber that he felt his heart would burst, so he dug a hole and whispered the secret into it. In another version it was Midas' wife that could not contain herself:

> The unfortunate Midas grew a superb pair
> Of ass's ears…
>
> …
>
> Apart from his wife, no one knew
>
> …
>
> And she vowed that not for the world,
> Would she be so disloyal
> As to betray her husband.
> In any case she would then share his humiliation.
> Nevertheless she thought she would die
> Keeping the secret to herself.
> She felt her heart begin to swell
> Till she thought it would explode.
> Afraid to confide in anyone
> She ran down to the marsh
> And reached the reeds. Her heart was aflame.
> And like a bittern booming in the rushes
> She whispered into the water, at ground level,
> 'O water, please do not betray me!
> I confide in you alone.
> My husband has a pair of ass's ears!
> What a relief to share the secret.
> I just could not keep it to myself.'

Chaucer, 'The Wife of Bath's Tale', *The Canterbury Tales*
modern version by M. Rennie

Unfortunately, the reeds then rustled and broadcast the secret to the whole world. The myth shows how a secret almost inevitably bubbles to the surface and escapes into the world. The repercussions of leaked military or political secrets can be hugely significant. Informers are usually subjected to very savage punishments; spies and spy catchers figure as heroes and traitors in fact and fiction.

Group Achievements

Under rational control Homo sapiens' sociability makes it an enormously cooperative creature. Other group animals may build communal shelters or hunt in packs, but no other animal has achieved anything like the cooperative enterprises of man. In the modern world this has become 'work', often in huge industrial operations. If work is creative and valued, work brings satisfaction; if it is forced by authority or financial pressure, it is often burdensome. Whether in a modern factory or out on the primeval savannah, individuals banding together in mutual support vastly enhance their combined single efforts to succeed in extraordinary feats of ingenuity and strength. A group inspired by a grand project can work together to achieve astonishing feats such as Stonehenge, the great cathedrals, the Pyramids, or the discovery of the New World. Symphony orchestras, sports teams, ceremonial occasions are all huge cooperative efforts. It is not only the obvious achievement that is accomplished but a tremendous sense of bonding. Even very modest enterprises bond groups and give them purpose. The village needs its annual fête not so much to raise money as to experience itself as a village community. Without projects, the group and its individuals can suffer aimlessness and depression. The social aspect of work is so important that unemployment and retirement can be experienced as lonely and demoralizing. War, despite the suffering, gives such a purpose that mental illness is diminished and for many, war becomes their defining life experience. War stories and films reflect this. Camaraderie in war is probably the Homo sapiens' equivalent to the bonding of other social animals hunting and protecting themselves.

Group Bonding and Paranoia

Social cohesion is strongest at the time of outside threat and group cohesion is emotionally very satisfying. It simplifies life and gives the participating individuals an enormous sense of purpose and focus. George Orwell's *1984* shows how a population is bonded by hate for an enemy, and how a prolonged war is used to head off civil dissent. The leader can assert control more easily by triggering group paranoia. Those that feel they are likely to be attacked feel fear and panic— primitive emotions intended to protect animals from predation. They sharpen alertness, and stimulate huge efforts to enhance survival. Until the development of modern commerce, only religion— with the building of Stonehenge, the great cathedrals, and the great temples of other faiths—drove Homo sapiens to anything comparable to the cooperative efforts of warfare. Mere threats have motivated enormous defensive efforts such as the construction of huge castles, enormous walls in China, northern England, Berlin, and Israel, and fortified earthworks, other structures, and massive technological programmes such as 'Star Wars'.

Leadership

In undertaking a group project, there has to be some sort of leadership. Every herd, flock or pack develops a hierarchy; there will be an alpha male or female wolf, a gorilla silverback, sea-lion beach-master, an elephant matriarch, a 'cock o' the walk'. It is a survival mechanism so that a group takes decisive, co-ordinated action in an emergency.

The group is always evolving, and the failing or wounded leader is likely to be immediately challenged. Among group animals there is no democracy. It is a cut-throat system but effective in securing group survival. Leadership among Homo sapiens is similarly of huge importance. The hunter-gatherers would have known their leaders personally and to that extent would have been able to limit their power. Since Neolithic times and the need to organize large populations, there has been more entrenched social stratification, often held in place by cruel oppression. It seems such problems begin to arise once the primal group size is exceeded. The organization of a large population requires strict rules. Leaders often become paranoid because throughout human history crowd loyalty is notoriously fickle with a leader being feted one week and executed the next. Shakespeare's *Julius Caesar* illustrates how easily Mark Anthony is able to manipulate crowd emotions from sympathy to hostility towards the assassins and towards a demand for revenge. Crowds welcomed Jesus of Nazareth into Jerusalem and within days were shouting for his crucifixion. Crowds are often unrealistic in their expectations, and their inevitable disappointment goads them to disorder and violence.

It seems almost inevitable in modern human society that 'the leader of the pack' is a male although there have always been charismatic females who have become leaders, such as strong-minded, intelligent women like Queen Elizabeth the First of England. The hunter-gatherers may well have given power to their matriarchs. Females are generally less driven to participate directly in the power struggle but matriarchal power can still subdue the brute force of males. Women are more likely to rule by negotiation rather than force, using the Homo sapiens' natural spirit of cooperation rather than confrontation. Because males have usually held power, macho attitudes are more familiar so that at the moment gentler and more sympathetic approaches are often felt to be weaker alternatives.

A good leader can hold the society together and achieve valuable and extensive projects but for the most part leadership in large modern populations is very difficult, so that politicians usually seem mediocre or worse. Under a good leader there is satisfaction and purpose, but it is hard work to maintain morale. The good leader constantly monitors and adjusts the group dynamics, keeping them fluid and responsive to situation and personalities. A weak leader may deliver chaos, and often does. If a parental generation fails to lead its children and teenagers, the result can be anarchy in the home and streets. For most of human history the older generation passed on the essential skills that were necessary for survival. This guaranteed respect. This natural authority is no longer appreciated in many modern societies where old skills and knowledge have been entirely superseded. When a pack of dogs becomes leaderless, the animals will fight viciously until a new leader emerges and restores order. Similarly Homo sapiens' society can quickly fall to mob rule under a failed leader. It takes a strong and often ruthless leader to quell social disorder, and the population prefers oppression rather than continuing anarchy, at least in the short term.

Absolute Power: The Tyrant

It is an enormous risk to allow a single leader to take power without any constitutional safeguards. 'Big Brother' in Orwell's *1984* demonstrates the terrible power of a dictator like Stalin once his authority is beyond challenge. As Edmund Burke is reputed to have said 'All that is necessary for evil to triumph is that good men do nothing'. It is easier to let events take their course than contest them at an early stage. History shows that lack of watchfulness can be catastrophic. A seemingly superhuman leader such as Hitler can all too easily seduce a population with promises that answer their hopes. Stalin, Mao and others have felt justified in seizing power, driven by ideologies, promising utopia and the settling of old injustices. Robert Mugabe led Zimbabwe to independence, but in holding power he has failed to fulfil the expectations of his people. This has made him ruthless and cruel, and ruined the country.

The leader who is a wounded spirit easily becomes intoxicated by flattery and the power to command and intimidate. They begin to believe their own myth of invincibility, however their underlying insecurity often gives rise to paranoia, and an inability to accept any criticism. They soon arrange matters so that they are not controlled by public opinion. Their position allows them to indulge themselves, and justify their privilege while they exploit the rest of the population. This kind of corruption appeals to other wounded spirits who accept inequalities and privileges and often offer blind loyalty and flattery to the leader. Most dictators have their police who without qualms impose the corrupt rule with threats, terror and cruelty, the KGB, Gestapo, SS, Stasi etc., often working a terrifying secret network of informers. Their motivation might be fear, or hope of self-advancement, probably a mixture of both. This inevitably leads to the acting out of ideologies that encourage racism, nationalism, sexism, serfdom and slavery. Such leaders as Stalin and Mao used their power to impose their political agendas, whatever the cost in human terms. Hitler and Saddam Hussein are terrifying examples of misfits achieving political power, and acting out their brutal ideologies. In such societies justice and compassion are simply ignored or despised as weak and degenerate.

The Mystique of Leadership
Once pack animals such as wolves or wild horses accept a particular individual as their leader, they presumably feel some sort of emotion such as loyalty, fear and even admiration. The training of dogs depends on the human pack leader asserting authority by body language, and tone of voice. The well-trained dog exhibits total loyalty to its master to the point of adoration.

Homo sapiens similarly have a need to feel loyalty to a leader and acceptance of being dominated and knowing 'their place'. Military training depends on this. The non-commissioned officers exert strict discipline to instil group solidarity and then the commissioned officers, like alpha males, take command.

Political and religious leaders often enjoy a hopeful, honeymoon period, a suspension of critical faculties, as the group first accepts a new leader. If a leader wins his followers' respect, they find security and satisfaction in accepting their subservient position. The leader is easily seen as superman with almost magical qualities; the followers are all the happier if this loyalty becomes inflamed to a kind of adoration. Monarchy with all its pageantry is designed to encourage just this. In the complexity of Homo sapiens' social life this can be very dangerous. Primogeniture in many societies was accepted as the principle for inheriting hierarchical power, and this has, at times, developed into a divine right. Homo sapiens have a dangerous tendency to idolize an impressive leader.

Leadership Cults: Man or God

Beyond celebrity there can be personality cults; dictators such as Hitler, Mao, and Stalin encouraged these, seeming to believe their own fantasies. Beyond this, both leader and followers can collude in raising the leader to divine status. Some fans believe Elvis Presley 'lives' and is in some way transcendent. Pharaohs, kings with divine rights, emperors like Caligula, or in modern times Hirohito of Japan, or Haile Selassie of Ethiopia, have historically claimed or been given godlike status. For centuries the Roman Catholic Church ruled much of Europe, and it was a long struggle, because of its religious significance, to reduce its political power to the tiny Vatican state. States that use religion to support their secular rulers tend to be ruthless, fundamentalist societies.

Resisting the Mystique of Power

Modern open societies often deliberately separate religious influences from political power to prevent the danger of a leader claiming divine appointment. Turkey and France are determinedly secular states. The United States takes great care to separate the powers of church and state. Such societies have developed political systems that prevent abuses of power, but still answer the strong human need to idealize a leader. In the United States the President is at once one of the people—Mr President—but once elected is hailed as 'the Chief'. As head of state he has a glamour which gives him an almost royal status. However, his power is limited by the constitution which allows only two terms in office. This averts the danger of the President consolidating his 'quasi' royal status, and escaping democratic control. As it is, second term Presidents sometimes become hubristic, overreach themselves and become embroiled in scandals. The corrupting effect of power is well documented.

Gradually over the centuries Britain has developed a constitutional monarchy. The monarch projects the 'magic' but has virtually no power. As head of state the monarch leads the pageantry the populace craves, and embodies the sense of nationhood but this is de-coupled from politics. The power resides with the elected representatives of the people, and the Prime Minister can be criticized with no loss of patriotism. Far from the monarch being a mere tourist attraction, and the main actor in rather irrelevant events of pomp and circumstances, he or she is a priceless safety valve protecting Britain from overbearing political power. A British Prime Minister might stay in government far longer than an American President, but cannot assume any higher status, because the monarch blocks the way. The continuity of the British monarchy gives it a special mystique which would be lost for ever if Britain became a republic. When Queen Victoria died, Henry James observed 'She was a sustaining symbol, and wild waters are upon us now.' Juan Carlos, the King of Spain, in the early years of his reign thwarted a military coup. Instead of allying himself with the generals and dictatorship, Juan Carlos chose to use his kingship to support Spanish democracy. Other states certainly function well enough without a monarchy, but most populations need or at least enjoy celebrity and pageantry. Constitutional monarchy, adapted to modern society, accommodates this at a particularly exciting level with dignity and security.

The Good Leader

There have at times been good leaders, who are themselves enlightened and have the maturity to accept criticism and welcome debate. This is likely to generate real loyalty from balanced, generous minded individuals. There is freedom of speech. Creativity is welcomed and the population flourishes. There is general agreement about the aims of the society, and the codes of behaviour. A fair-minded police or some such force, accountable to the people, manages public conduct. A disinterested system of law dispenses justice where there is disagreement and a conflict of interests. There is tolerance of the harmless deviant. This, in turn, releases creative energy. There is 'freedom under the law' for all, so that prejudices are challenged and defused, and the weak and vulnerable are protected. This avoids exploitation and grievance. The Statue of Liberty is the icon of such an ideal, a gift from France to USA in 1876 to mark the centenary of American Independence which had inspired the French Revolution.

Power to the People

The good leader is however rare, and the best way of achieving fair government is for the people to elect their leaders, and so hold them accountable. Some societies over the centuries therefore have taken the risk of developing social strategies which have shared power with the population. This has encouraged communities to operate in accord with the deeply felt sentiments of natural justice. Democracy is socially fragile and easily damaged. It may be faked by leaders who refuse to give up power; they create one-party states, buy votes, intimidate voters or otherwise corrupt the system. For their part the populace may try to falsify votes, intimidate other voters, or boycott the election. Democracy requires enormous social maturity both on the part of the leaders and the populace, and may need a particular social context and tradition.

Group decisions have been shown to gather the intelligence of the mass and far from expressing the lowest common denominator, demonstrate a superior insight and wisdom. 'We, the people'…celebrates the wisdom of the common man. Democracy depends on this. In functioning democracies leaders are voted from office without significant social upheaval. Defeat is accepted without the need for revenge or violence. Under most dictatorships group wisdom is suppressed and creativity stagnates. A failed dictator may be executed or exiled, often leading to more social instability which is likely to make for more oppression.

Performance and Leadership

Most political or royal leaders have to make public appearances and address their followers. It is easy to see how performance becomes an aspect of leadership and why most modern celebrities are performers of some sort. The leader-performer is often very powerful and popular. Performance and public display requires special personal qualities, seldom inherited in dynastic lines. The audience is merciless to poor performers, but idolizes the successful, rewarding them with enormous wealth and affection. The poor performer, apart from lacking necessary skill, often fails to rise above self, feels exposed and vulnerable and projects nervousness and anxiety and so fails to communicate. The good performer is forgetful of self and becomes a conduit for common emotions. He or she becomes a special kind of leader, something quite unknown in the rest of nature.

Celebrity

The near worship of celebrities is in some ways a modern version of the longing to follow a magic leader. This susceptibility is often exploited and deliberately managed by the modern media and astute public relations. Outstanding personalities in various fields—music, film, TV, or sport—attract huge followings. It is ironic that in times of growing equality, adoration of celebrities is so prevalent. It is as if the celebrity fulfils the need for a magic leader for modern times and the animal need for a pack leader resurfaces in a new manifestation.

Sharing Experience: Art and Music

There is a tremendous compulsion for most human individuals to share their inner experience because of their huge sociability. An individual will verbalize the self, to others, to pets, even to the wall or mirror. Cave paintings, decorations and modelled figures survive to show this peculiar animal activity from perhaps 30,000 years ago or more, comparatively soon after the beginning of language. The performer's power or 'X factor' lies in the ability to make this public for the whole group and to become the surrogate for less talented individuals. Songs, in particular, can be known and loved by millions to become expressions of mass emotion.

Individual abilities vary widely, and in time language arts would have become practised more by certain members of the group who would become the storytellers, the bards, and soothsayers. From this sprang poetry and drama, saga, prayer and prophecy. The rhythm of words works with the sentiments and resonances to heighten the emotions and at best touch deep into the psyche. Language almost passes into music.

The power of song uses language and music to express very personal experiences which the listeners can relate to their own lives. Popular music, folksong and art songs pour out highly personal confessions—'Yesterday all my troubles seemed so far away', 'Oh Danny Boy…', My Love is Like a Red, Red, Rose', etc. The singing ape announces how it feels sexual awakening, hope, sexual ecstasy, loss, and loneliness, despair, and renewed hope. Religious music is often a group expression of thanksgiving, awe, prayer, and a retelling of the religious myths. Emotions are synchronized, elaborated and strengthened.

There is a strong impulse for individuals to join their voices together in a chorus, rather as wolves howl in a pack. When melodies were sung by different voices at different pitches, polyphony developed—melodies running parallel at different levels. With more independent movement of the levels, more complex musical effects were created. Harmonies occurred, and then these were deliberately sought. Eventually melody, harmony, rhythm, tone and volume were employed to convey strong emotions sometimes quite independently of words, and music of all different traditions developed. Tubes, blocks, strings, reeds, membranes, boxes, were hit, blown, plucked, bowed until after thousands of years the modern symphony orchestra developed. The skills and technical excellence concentrated in a great modern symphony orchestra make it one of the supreme achievements of human ingenuity, even before the musicians begin to play.

If the performance is skilled and sincere it is an enormously powerful experience for both performer and listeners. The performer shamelessly confesses ' I feel…' whatever the pain or exhilaration—often associated with a sexual relationship—over and over again, in thousands of different formats. The human pair-bond is endlessly reflected in human art. The listeners empathize or feel the performer is speaking for them. The performer is 'me' in the sense that they are individuals but as a performing persona they are also a more generalized 'me' who incorporates the individuals in the audience. At other times the performer may take on the persona of an altogether different character such as a 'wandering minstrel' or 'jolly sailor' or a narrator that knows the story of 'Eleanor Rigby', which connects with the feelings of performer and audience. This sharing of emotional experience never palls; favourite songs and favourite performances can be repeated over and over again with the same intense enjoyment.

The result can be synchronized emotions in dance, marching, choral singing, or with more sophistication simply sitting and listening. The group can synchronize their vocalizations with each other and with body movements, generating extra excitement. The rhythm of language combined with the stamping of feet or waving of arms soon becomes singing and dancing. The most neutral rhythm is close to the resting heartbeat, one or two pulses a second, faster or slower are perceived as 'fast' or 'slow'. Rhythm is the most primitive aspect of music and has a visceral response, especially in response to an insistent repetitive rhythm. Marching to a beat is far easier than just marching. Ritual dances can almost intoxicate the participants, and religious ceremonies often incorporate elements of drumming and dancing. The excitement of popular music is largely generated by loud, driving, repetitive beats.

Modern technology allows music and drama to be enjoyed in solitary circumstances, but they are essentially group experiences of the cinema, theatre, church or concert hall. The effect is a synchronization of group emotions, a raising of feelings above the individual. The oral tradition reaching back into the folk-loric past would have been group entertainment and the source of very significant bonding and cultural transmission.

Performance: Humour

Homo sapiens has another particular social phenomenon—humour. Those that can make others smile and laugh also have enormous celebrity. Other group animals will tease, and chimpanzees have something of a smile and laughter but Homo sapiens enjoys a joke as no other creature. Humour is a group experience, a shared release of tension or anxiety. There is a safe, coded acknowledgment of the forbidden—sex, class, bodily functions, or a deflation of pomposity, and other absurdities such as inflexible behaviour. In interpersonal relationships humour can defuse antagonism and even hostility.

The black side of humour is mockery and violence to others, and bullying usually involves this sort of cruelty. In performances of 'slapstick' humour, one group enjoys the apparent discomfiture of others, the 'not me' or 'not us', and in turn celebrates 'our' escape or survival. However, the audience knows this is a performance and not a real happening, and the humour is usually playful rather than vicious. Some forms of humour have been defined as a 'momentary anaesthesia of the heart'. The cartoon *Tom and Jerry*, is full of cruelty, but it is clearly unrealistic and neither character is permanently damaged. The humour lies in the ingenuity of the situations, and the exaggerated effects of the violence, which makes violence amusing in a socially acceptable way.

An important element of humour is incongruity and surprise. Darwin decided humour often depended on the clash of two incongruous ideas. Good timing builds up the expectation of a particular outcome, and then shocks with the unexpected. Laughter is socially cohesive. The emotional release of laughter can help a social group perceive a new truth. Is it possible that the great religious leaders enjoyed a joke? It is not usual to associate humour with Jesus, Mohammed, Moses or the other leaders, but at its best humour is a god-given gift and representatives of the divine are likely to have been socially attractive, and humour to have been part of their appeal. Humour, power, and charm, go together. GSOH—a 'good sense of humour' is a common requirement probably because it suggests a very desirable emotional maturity.

Hierarchy

Below the leader there is inevitably a hierarchy. Hierarchy is a mechanism, which gives the stronger and cleverer animals more chance to survive, for the good of the group rather than the individual. The place in the hierarchy therefore decides an individual's survival prospects—its chance of accessing food and achieving matings. Males assert themselves by winning and holding a female or a harem of females. Females try to attract males that will enhance their hierarchical position. The wife of the President of the USA is actually known as the First Lady. Once the hierarchy is established, an individual's place in it is very emotive. Even in modern society with all its security, there is a primitive impulse to assert and hold a place. This probably explains the enormous feelings of aggression experienced if a driver cuts in front on the road or when someone pushes ahead in a queue. The very relationship between pedestrians, cyclists and motor vehicles is also hierarchical, the vehicle usually demanding road space, at the expense of other users. Equality may be the ideal but as Orwell so memorably writes in *Animal*

Farm: 'All men are equal but some are more equal than others'. It seems the human need for hierarchy keeps reasserting itself.

Modern marketing takes advantage of the hierarchical sense. Symbols of rank become part of the dress code in humans— stars, medals, crowns, hats, uniforms etc. Fashion, accessories, and the tiniest details are all class, caste or other markers. Even designer labels become themselves labels of status. Advertising often defines products with status. Makes of car, trophy wives, and fashions in almost every commodity all declare status or would-be status. 'Keeping up with the Joneses' expresses the innate tendency to compete with markers that denote status.

The chance of winning and asserting a higher status is the motive for most competitive activities,—'fame is the spur...'. War gives this satisfaction but at huge risk and expense. Sport provides a cheaper and more humane alternative. The enormous emotional and financial investment in sport must suggest a symbolic significance far beyond its reality. Sport takes up whole channels of the media and many individuals—especially males—live almost surrogate lives through sport. Successful warriors in the past carried off booty; today successful sportsmen carry off huge rewards. This suggests that sport is not so much surrogate hunting or war, but an outlet for the need to assert hierarchy and dominance. League tables and rank orders record hierarchical positions; medals and trophies are symbols of success. A winning team can raise the morale of a whole country. The team or fighting group carry the identity of their community; their supporters chant such slogans as 'We are the greatest' or 'Homeland for ever'. The fans share the success of their team and feel the same triumph. As if it has the importance of politics or war, modern sport is celebrated in victory parades, huge fame and honour for the heroes, souvenirs, archives and museums.

At a time when equality has been apparently an ideal, there are media competitions that command huge audiences. The blunt, sometimes cruel comments of adjudicators are greatly enjoyed. It is as if these contests recognise the need for hierarchy, to the relief of the audiences.

There are also intellectual and other cerebral contests. Quizzes are entertaining competitions both for knowledge and intellectual agility. Although there is no physical challenge, competition is still intense. Educational achievement, grades, scholarships, competition for jobs and success in the workplace are all assertions of hierarchy. However, in education there has to be a balance between competition to spur on the most ambitious, and opportunities for less privileged and less assertive individuals who may nevertheless be very able. Offering opportunity is one thing, but there must also be the means to take advantage of that opportunity. Resources are usually limited and it is all too easy for the more ambitious and able to take more than their share. This has often been justified in the interests of the wider society, but is likely to leave a frustrated, ill-informed majority, which in modern societies cannot be simply ignored or intimidated into submission. Sport importantly challenges racial and other stereotypes and is an important democratic force as individuals are judged simply on their sporting ability, regardless of social background, nationality, or race.

Whole societies can dominate other societies, and be indifferent to their suffering as slavery, colonization, and oppression has proved over the centuries. In present times the rich west is largely indifferent to the poverty of the rest of the world. Any attempt to redistribute these resources is resisted and rationalized as a fair return on investment or a justifiable protection of the home community. It takes enormous generosity of spirit in a large percentage of the population to challenge such justifications.

The Symbolic Meaning of Wealth

Ambition, or striving for a high place in the hierarchy, is in animal terms the primitive drive for greater access to resources, either directly or by alliance with powerful individuals or groups. In animal groups power usually depends on brute strength. In modern Homo sapiens' society power has become symbolic, represented by money and its equivalents—gold, silver and jewels. The animals with greater stores of these symbols command access to the real resources such as food, shelter, sexual partners; they can also intimidate those lower in the hierarchy with displays of their wealth. This is the Homo sapiens equivalent to animal displays of dominance, and is probably why no amount of wealth is ever enough. The need to win at sport, to acquire possessions, to mix with a particular social group, all derive from the need to assert a hierarchical position and enormous satisfaction is felt by an individual or group becoming top. Each year there are lists in the media of the wealthiest or the most influential individuals. Honours are awarded in recognition of status. However, lesser Homo sapiens often do not simply acquiesce like other animals but can react against triumphalism. The losers may simply turn spiteful or in more important situations may react with a sense of injustice and fight back to redress the balance. There are always challengers for power in animal groups, but the sense of justice seems unique to man.

Dynasty and Genetic Survival

The tendency in human society is for dominant individuals to attempt to hold their position and pass it on to succeeding generations as inheritance and dynasty. Human elites are able to protect their genetic line from the harsh effects of 'survival of the fittest' and therefore develop protective strategies. Status, snobbery, elitism and claiming special privileges prevent the pitiless workings of nature. This desire is likely to be the conscious working of the genetic instinct to pass on and survive in future generations. Males, especially the first-born, are usually dynastically favoured perhaps because male genes can be more easily dispersed. 'Breeding' and 'pedigree' are often the terms used to describe a family line, rather like the genetic histories of cattle or other animals. *Burke's Peerage* and *Burke's Landed Gentry* record the pedigrees of Britain's social elite. Ironically human breeding, rather than producing a superior gene line, is as likely to produce the English 'chinless wonder' or pass on a hereditary condition like haemophilia. These attempts to be exclusive can, on the one hand, raise resentment and on the other, give a false sense of security or superiority. Some groups widen the dynastic impulse and seek to keep a national or racial bloodlines pure—breeding partners being selected for their racial, religious or other characteristics. The ancient Greek Ptolomies even married their siblings, and marriage between first cousins is common in some societies. Throughout history such theories of purity have led to horrendous discrimination and even genocide.

Emily Brontë's *Wuthering Heights* tells how the hybrid vigour of a charismatic misfit, Heathcliff, achieves complete and pitiless domestic power, destroying the effete local gentry and almost ruining another well-established family. Modern democratic societies prove that concepts of superior breeding have little or no validity. Furthermore, they conflict with Homo sapiens' intuitions of cooperation and mutuality.

The Moral Sense
As far as can be deduced only Homo sapiens and perhaps the higher primates have any moral sense. Dogs seem to feel guilt,

and this suggests an awareness of wrongdoing but is probably an association of a particular action with retribution rather than an indwelling moral sense. Homo sapiens evolved a sensitivity to others of its species because of its intense sociability. While animals communicate with cries and calls, speech has allowed human relationships to be deepened by common interests and shared hopes. The human individual is able to reflect on its own feelings, and most significantly develop an awareness that the 'other' also has feelings, and that 'I' can affect 'you'. From this develops the emotional intelligence so necessary for successful social relationships and beyond this comes a sense of reciprocal altruism. The animal has the imagination to understand that by a generous response, both parties benefit. This then developed into a sense of fairness. Uniquely Homo sapiens has a sense of natural justice and an impulse to share resources. This implies that all individuals have equal value, in direct contradiction to the values of hierarchy.

Hierarchy or Equality

The American Declaration of Independence announces, 'All men are created equal' and since the eighteenth century western societies have struggled to develop political systems which control the power of the powerful. Unbridled capitalism or the excessive powers of an aristocracy or other elite, allowed the few to exploit the many. Communist theories went to the other extreme with common ownership as the ideal for the brotherhood of man. However, communism lost its vision in the process, and became punitive in its efforts to enforce its ideals. Collectivization led to huge resistance and the stagnation of initiative. In Poland during the 1980s the workers of Gdansk formed their solidarity movement. The international status of the Polish Pope and the global situation eventually helped undermine the heavy-handed Communist government and began the disintegration of the whole Soviet system. Since then other popular movements against dictatorships, corrupt democracies, and racially oppressive regimes have also been successful, probably because the world is increasingly monitored by the global media. The campaign to 'Make poverty history' may be the beginning of a fairer world order. There is enough food to feed the world; it is the mechanisms of trade and distribution that are lacking and these need the cooperation of the power elites. Equality will be hard won and its maintenance will need constant vigilance.

Culture and Equality

In human society there is more than physical survival at stake. Cultural traditions take generations to establish, and high culture takes careful education and ready access to resources. In the past an accumulation of wealth and power was usually needed to sponsor great thinkers, artists and traditions of music and drama. Modern societies patronize the arts through individual, corporate or institutional sponsorship, and once established writers, artists and musicians can become free-lance, professionals.

Genius, Achievement, and Equality

Until modern political and technological conditions set the mass of Homo sapiens free from daily drudgery; the cultural success of the few depended on the oppression of the many. To some extent technology is needed for equality. The majority are otherwise usually excluded, though the need for culture is so insistent that alternative folk traditions usually develop.

In every population there must be the seeds of genius, but only special circumstances allow the genius to flower—ancient Athens, eleventh century Baghdad, mediaeval China, Renaissance Florence, Elizabethan England, eighteenth century Vienna, etc. The ideological backgrounds of these societies evidently had special qualities that encouraged creativity and the emergence of multiple geniuses. The whole society must have focused on some aspect of artistic and intellectual life as supremely important, beyond trade or wealth, though the wealth was needed for sponsorship. These comparatively small populations gave rise to an astonishing cluster of supreme geniuses. This must mean that such latent abilities remain undeveloped in other populations.

> Perhaps in this neglected spot is laid
> Some heart once pregnant with celestial fire;
> Hands, that the rod of empire might have sway'd,
> Or waked to ecstasy the living lyre.
>
> But knowledge to their eyes her ample page
> Rich with the spoils of time did ne'er unroll;
> Chill Penury repress'd their noble rage,
> And froze the genial current of the soul.
> …
> Some mute inglorious Milton, here may rest,…

Thomas Gray, *Elegy Written in a Country Churchyard*, 45-52, 59.

The Virtue of Humility

The great religions go beyond equality and endorse humility. Christianity and Judaism envision a self-sacrificing leader, a leader who lives to serve his people even to becoming a 'suffering servant'. Those that serve enjoy 'perfect freedom'; the meek, and poor are valued. 'Blessed are the meek' suggests disapproval of the powerful and arrogant. Jesus of Nazareth, as teacher and leader, washes the feet of his disciples. Some Anglican Bishops perform this ceremony at the ordination of their priests. In Christianity's *Magnificat* Mary celebrates the fact that the Lord 'hath put down the mighty from their seat and exalted the humble and weak', an overstatement perhaps, but an attempt to at least question the balance between power and weakness, and restrain the powerful in their relation with those over whom they have power.

For practical purposes in an imperfect world there has to be a compromise, meekness allied with physical strength. For instance Chaucer's perfect knight is 'as meek as is a maid' although he is a military hero. Chivalry and the concept of the 'gentleman' suggest strength controlled by mannerly behaviour; 'manners maketh man' is not so much about etiquette as consideration and kindness in relating to others, the behaviour that sets the gentleman apart. By the code of courtesy, the strong are enjoined to help and protect the weak and so endorse the ideal of equality.

The vision of equality may be a guide to the ultimate destiny of Homo sapiens and all its ape forerunners; it may indeed be a return to the primal state of man when the group lived closely together without possessions, and survived by co-operation. There has to be to be justice for there to be peace, and justice implies fairness and equality. The French Revolution attempted to achieve 'Liberté, fraternité, and egalité', all three concepts interlinked. Over and over again, modern humanity sets out with such ideals, and briefly they seem achievable. Then ideal is somehow hi-jacked by disorderly or ambitious personalities and corruption sets in. The vision however, remains.

Beyond Justice, Empathy, Philia or Brotherly Love.

Speech probably developed because of the animal's sociability, and speech, in turn, has deepened and extended its social behaviour. At all levels and in all cultures, Homo sapiens is programmed to look for the affection and approval of its fellows. Each animal finds its place in its various groups as a leader or a follower, and generally works out a moral attitude to its fellows as it matures. It often demonstrates the supreme human capacity for empathy, and empathy responds to empathy, developing into an understanding of weakness and vulnerability. Even beyond empathy there may be 'agape'—a complete selflessness and generosity of spirit. It has been a long social evolution to reach this stage. While predatory animal impulses still underlie much human behaviour and are given expression by a deviant minority, there is also a strong philanthropic drive towards the noble ideal of brotherly love.

AGGRESSION

Hamlet watches Fortinbras' army prepare for war.

> Witness this army of such mass and charge
> Led by a delicate and tender prince,
> Whose spirit with divine ambition puff'd
> Makes mouths at the invisible event,
> Exposing what is mortal and unsure
> To all that fortune, death and danger dare,
> Even for an egg-shell. Rightly to be great
> Is not to stir without great argument,
> But greatly to find quarrel in a straw
> When honour's at the stake...
>
> ...
>
> I see
> The imminent death of twenty thousand men,
> That for a fantasy and trick of fame,
> Go to their graves like beds, fight for a plot
> Whereon the numbers cannot try the cause,
> Which is not tomb enough and continent
> To hide the slain.

Shakespeare, *Hamlet* IV iv 46-65.

Aggression and Survival

As a highly social animal, Homo sapiens is very positively programmed to protect and advance its group, if necessary at the expense of others. In this, Homo sapiens behaves like any other herd or pack animal. Homo sapiens groupings were originally the family clan or hunting band in a life and death struggle for survival. Kill or be killed was a reality so that there could be no sympathetic feeling for predators, victims or enemies—rather the reverse. As animals, the group is prompted to attack as 'the

204

best form of defence' rather than hesitate and risk betrayal or predation.

This tendency to fight was vital to Homo sapiens as a wild creature. The teeming world of nature knows no pity and Homo sapiens is on one level simply a hominid ape and part of this world. Like other animals it had to use violence to hold or take territory, assert a hierarchy or protect the family group. It also had to kill for food, and at times killing enemies became a kind of hunting. For most of its existence it has killed and been killed in close animal contact, feeling the flesh and blood of its victims, and being wounded, torn and battered itself without mercy. Homo sapiens is still part of this animal system and its quarrels still often express themselves literally with 'brute' force. Not only is the violence threshold set low by nature, but there is also a natural emotional impetus to violence. In Homo sapiens alcohol and other drugs known to particular populations, add to the mayhem.

Animal Violence

Animals on the whole do not indulge in gratuitous violence. Predators kill for food, and prey animals have their natural defences. Quarrels within the same species are a simple matter of 'might is right', and a loser just wants to escape and survive. There is in most of nature an inhibition against killing the same species, and an animal facing attack from others of its kind will make signs of submission or flee to avoid unnecessary injury or slaughter. Only rarely do groups of the same species fight each other to the point of destruction. However, recent research has shown that chimpanzees demonstrate just this behaviour. Their brutality anticipates Homo sapiens' savagery with uncanny similarity. Unfortunately, Homo sapiens have the ability to link this innate primate brutality with abstract principles such as revenge, justice, pride and honour. These principles have no currency in animal relationships so that most animal conflicts flare up and are quickly forgotten.

The Excitement of Aggression

Anger, fear, panic and suspicion are unpleasant survival mechanisms helping the individual or group avoid predation, infection, or loss of resources. However, aggression is also exciting. It is difficult to say what emotion is experienced as a dog guards its territory, an alpha wolf asserts his leadership, a stag fights for his harem, or a pride of lions hunts a gazelle, but the animals certainly have a strong impetus to maim, kill or at least chase away their adversaries. Such primitive animal emotions are vital to basic survival, and must be easily and strongly triggered. Aggression delivers high excitement in animals and man. Combat has been described as the 'ultimate rush'. Brain chemistry changes so that low serotonin and high testosterone impedes higher brain function. The 'red mist' descends. The amygdala rules so that the frontal lobes are incapacitated. Adrenaline makes the blood run 'cold' and the animal is rewarded with a shot of pleasure hormones. These encourage aggression, and act almost like psychological anaesthetics—damping down for that moment wider anxieties and troubles. The impetus for aggression, war, or genocide is so strong that one Homo sapiens group will fight another group, as Shakespeare says, 'even for an egg-shell'

Hunting

Nature uses this excitement to motivate its creatures to hunt. Hunting was once the animal's way of supplying fresh meat for the family group. Hunting for man and beast gives an instinctive satisfaction so that it continues into modern times beyond any need for meat. Predators enjoy the chase, the capture, the kill, and ultimately the comfort of a full stomach. Anyone taking dogs for a walk observes their delight as they run about randomly searching for excitement, which is basically something to chase and kill. This wolf-like behaviour has been deliberately exploited in hunting with packs of hounds and although the prey species are no longer meat for humans, the hunters and their dogs become intoxicated by the same excitement that has fired carnivores through millennia. In whatever way hunting is rationalized, at base it is motivated by the enjoyment derived from the instincts of the predator.

War Bonding

Pack animals are programmed to bond into groups to fight off intruders and corner prey; the instinct in man is still as strong and as dangerous as ever. Most human combatants attest to the unprecedented camaraderie of war. War bonding is an extension of intense bonding beyond the family group. Unfortunately, human group loyalty can be murderously perverted. Military hierarchy can lead to discipline without responsibility so that the natural inhibition against the killing of the same species is neutralized. The Nazi Waffen Schutzstaffel or 'SS' illustrated the extreme of dehumanised discipline. The 'SS' were said to put on their cruelty with their uniforms. Such loyalty prompts appallingly wasteful group sacrifices such as the charge of the Light Brigade or orders for thousands of young men to go 'over the top' to almost certain death or injury in the battles of the First World War.

The Bias towards Violence

While Homo sapiens has great potential for goodwill and generosity, goodwill and generosity have to be almost consciously set in motion, as if they are secondary to basic survival. Remaining calm requires control and is not immediately satisfying; conciliation can seem like weakness, whereas aggression is immediately exciting. Nature, therefore, makes it extremely difficult for Homo sapiens to solve disagreements without violence but unfortunately violence does not necessarily favour the just. Force can be morally wrong; the wicked can be victorious. War and violence can settle quarrels decisively but this does not necessarily promote the betterment of mankind. It is therefore a terrible risk to allow raw violence to arbitrate quarrels. The great challenge is how to control aggression otherwise than matching force with force.

The Huge Waste of War

Arms races have sapped the economic strength of communities at the expense of their general well-being and so many conflicts with hindsight seem almost completely pointless. The First World War with its terrible toll of casualties, sometimes tens of thousands in one day, was out of all proportion to the quarrel it was intended to resolve. Economic rivalry and differing styles of government—austere authoritarianism as opposed to more liberal openness—caused untold grief and destruction. Furthermore, the Second World War might have been avoided if that first quarrel had been more wisely settled.

With the world's population a fraction of its present size and life anyway short and fragile, Homo sapiens groups quarrelled. Though subject to famines, epidemics and natural disasters, and enduring the pain, hunger and insecurity now suffered by only the poorest of the third world, one group would still readily persecute another, sometimes to extinction. The Hundred Years' War continued even while the Black Death ravaged the population of fourteenth century Europe. In modern times some of the poorest societies in the world prosecute futile wars despite disease, famine, and terrible degradation of the environment. Homo sapiens groups seem always to have virtually destroyed each other by war, their populations unleashing terrible cruelties on each other whatever cost. The cost is enormous, even before the killing and destruction begins. The expenditure of effort, ingenuity, and resources on murderous weaponry has often been a priority—above any other social need.

It is as if the lesson that war is destructive and cruel cannot be learned. The excitement of imminent action easily eclipses any awareness of the suffering and destruction that will inevitably result. A First World War combatant wrote of the 'damnable frivolity of war', and his horror as he watched 'a mischievous ape tearing up the image of god'.

The Small Investment in Peace

There is a huge disparity between spending on warfare as opposed to spending on aid and disaster relief, though in the long term such generosity might be far more effective in solving future disagreements. Nations spend huge sums on armaments; aid budgets are trivial in comparison, and disaster relief is often left to charities. It is not just a matter of hardware, but also institutions. There is hardly any attempt to study ways of achieving peace as opposed to prosecuting war. Secular peace studies in comparison with war studies are virtually non-existent, yet with the invention of weapons of mass destruction, peace studies and ways of promoting peace are supremely important to the future of the species and the Earth itself. Although religion has all too easily been perverted to justify aggression, at present it is mainly the great religious traditions, as opposed to secular peace studies, that try to combat the animal tendency towards aggression, by endorsing goodwill and peaceable, tolerant behaviour. However, this hardly makes any impression against centuries of propaganda for war, embedded in myths of heroism, conquest and victory.

'Blessed are the Peacemakers'

With modern technology, Homo sapiens' mental capacities combined with its lethal animal impulses are more of a threat than a benefit, all too easily leading to the possibility of mutual assured destruction—'MAD'. Each side seeks to deter attack from the other, by threatening the annihilation of both defender and aggressor—and all other innocent living things within hundreds of miles and it seems worthwhile to the protagonists while they are locked into their hostile mindsets. It was calculated that even if the USA had won the nuclear conflict, it was likely 130 million Americans would have perished. As it happened, the strategy did keep the balance of power during the Cold War, but it could so easily have tipped over into catastrophe. The impossibility of all-out warfare now means the present is a watershed in human relations. No disagreement can be allowed to unleash the equivalent of a man-made 'natural' disaster on the planet.

Apart from nuclear war, there is also the suffering of more traditional conflicts. Perhaps in time, the rules of war will allow combatants to be temporarily disabled by some sort of soporific or some agent that induces vomiting or diarrhoea, so that the moment of crisis is suspended before the destruction and killing begins. This will reduce the glamour of war. Perhaps at this point wise statesmen can test the validity of the quarrel, and help the combatants empathize with their enemies rather than demonize them. This, of course, requires enormous emotional intelligence, and such statesmanship needs to be valued in the media above military success, so that avoidance of war is valued beyond victory.

There should be no more propaganda for war, but rather any resort to violence should be equated with brawling in the streets—something crude and degrading. On the contrary, peacemakers need to be seen as the heroes, rather than the warriors. Strategies for peace-making need to be studied and developed with a whole sub-culture of legends and stories celebrating peaceable, tolerant, and far-sighted behaviour. Human readiness to go to war is encouraged by the well-rehearsed stories of aggression, heroic as they often are; the imaginative context of war must therefore be changed. Each individual, in the words of St Francis, should seek to be 'an instrument of ...peace'.

'Man's Inhumanity to Man'

Homo sapiens' affection for its family and friends is balanced by a of dislike or stronger antipathy towards anyone or anything outside the group that might present a threat. A new dog in a household or hen in a hen run is likely to be ferociously attacked. At base, man has the same instincts, though its response is usually moderated by some curiosity or other inhibition.

Conformity

The group naturally demands conformity of its members. The members may sometimes try to preserve racial, cultural or religious purity by mating with others of their kind. Families band together into clans or tribal groups. Protection of their conformity sometimes involves pre-emptive aggression against those that are different. The group feel their genes, or the cultural equivalent, are precious and must not be diluted by any mixing.

This kind of thinking promotes antagonism towards those that are not of their kind, with predictable reactions, sometimes as extreme as Nazi anti-Semitism. While there was a wilderness into which to disperse these different groups, the aggression could to some extent be dissipated. In recent centuries in an increasingly crowded and mobile world, national, racial or other groups inevitably encounter each other and often have to live together. Antagonism between races, political parties, geographical groups, classes, etc usually arises because both groups believe the other group should conform to their views. Such inflexible attitudes can seem to justify bullying, racism, terrorism and even genocide.

Religion has been used to promote the worst aggression and cruelty. This often occurs when a tribal, national or racial group identifies itself with a particular form of religion, usually distorted to fit their cause. Any sense that God endorses a group's convictions can justify appalling aggression especially when military power is allied with spiritual belief of a fundamentalist nature. When religious leaders focus on the most unreasonable, prejudiced, and superstitious readings of their scriptures they drive populations to terrible excesses in obedience to what has been interpreted as the word of their god. The resultant religious disagreements are particularly brutal—crusades and jihads, Christians against Moslems, Moslems against Jews, Hindus against Moslems even Protestant Christians against Catholic Christians, and Shia Moslems against Sunnis and so on. More mature societies take care to separate the political power of the state from religious power and so guard against the dangerous conjunction that has visited so much suffering on mankind.

However, secular ideologies like Nazism and Communism, have similarly perpetrated terrible cruelties and have been just as ferocious in their persecutions of those that will not conform. It seems that the motivating force is not so much religion or ideology, but an instinct or biological drive that encourages groups to assert their identity by attacking others. It is not religion or ideology that is to blame but something in the very nature of man—that need to feel part of a group engaged in some great supra-human endeavour. The understanding of this aspect of the human psyche must have top priority in our crowded and diverse modern world.

Strangers

Strangers are a threat; they are suspect because they are unknown and might be dangerous deceivers. They might introduce undesirable ideas or habits, or even bring physical contamination. Minorities such as Jews or Gypsies are always vulnerable and have often been marginalized or persecuted. If the minority feels threatened, it often finds security in clinging to its own cultural traditions; this, unfortunately, is the more likely to antagonize the host population. The minority that does not conform can easily be felt to threaten the cohesion of the majority. Cultural misunderstanding can be a dangerous matter. In order to accommodate these outsiders, the majority has to compromise on some aspects of its own identity, and this requires unusual generosity of spirit. The minority also has to be sensitive to this and compromise in turn. Multicultural societies have to find a very delicate balance, but such a balance is vital in modern circumstances.

Prejudice

Prejudice can have the most catastrophic results. At a low level it might simply lead to discrimination; at another level it might lead to lynching or genocide. Genocide is the ultimate atrocity, which occurs all too frequently, even in the modern world. To this day when one group triumphs over another, the killing of the men and raping of women occurs with sickening predictability. The vanquished women seem to be used partly for gratification, but also for spreading genes and so symbolically claiming the territory. The Holocaust is so horrifying because well-educated, even cultured personnel, used their management skills to industrialize killing as if it was just another process. Infants, children, pregnant women, nursing mothers, the old, and young

213

adults all became objects of hate beyond any threat they could possibly present. Colonizers of nineteenth century Australia shot native Tasmanians as 'game', and native Americans were ruthlessly dispossessed, or worse. Even after death the defeated sometimes had body parts taken as trophies—scalps, shrunken heads, skeletons, some having religious significance. There was no inhibition about exhibiting the remains of the enemy, and only recently has this been perceived as offensive.

Moreover there are covert forms of prejudice: the insensitivity of the first world to third world debt, the lack of response to the massacres in Rwanda and Indonesia compared to those in Kosovo, even the imbalance of African Americans subject to the death penalty as compared to the majority population. In the novel, *To Kill a Mockingbird,* this prejudice is exposed with telling impact. Caucasians are not alone in demonstrating the human propensity for racism though modern genetics have finally proved that no one race is superior to another. Just as poisonous are the conflicts between religious, national, tribal, clan and even family groups.

'Ancient Grudges'
Many other animals will attack and fight ferociously to protect territory or other resources, but 'ancient grudges' lasting generations are unique to man. Homo sapiens can record and remember. They have imagination and a faculty for abstract thought, and can also take note and share their experiences. They can pass on group memories and are capable of forethought. They are intensely social so that language tends to sustain and amplify any group disharmony or antagonisms. The antagonism can become obsessive and self-propagating. Suspicion and enmity may become part of a cultural tradition. From birth children are taught social attitudes to other groups so that to question these prejudices can seem like an attack on the group's

very identity. Shakespeare's *Romeo and Juliet* makes memorable tragedy out of just this situation. It seems that man's ability to abstract and think symbolically can link into animal patterns of behaviour with devastating effect. In the modern world, prejudice and antipathy are luxuries of feeling that cannot be afforded as diverse groups intermingle and confront each other. What once had survival value now can raise the terrible demons of hatred and cruelty.

Man's alert and inventive mind personalizes and projects these defensive feelings on to another group or individual, especially in times of social stress. These are then elaborated and indulged, often generating intense dislike and prejudice. If this happens, it robs the enemies of their individuality, and so turns off any sympathetic or humane emotions. It is as if a group psychosis takes over. The aggressors detach themselves from the humanity of the victim and generalize the enemy as sub-human, dangerous, and contaminating, so that they need to be exterminated. The child-killers of Auschwitz were normal family men but in the context of that terrible camp saw the captive babies and children as genetic pollution and killed them as vermin. When conflict starts, actions often confirm the polarities. Each side demonizes the other. This justifies antagonism, anger, and appalling cruelty. The fear and anger spread and groups are pitted against each other, perhaps for generations until one is effectively in control or both suffer so much that, conflict-weary, they make peace—a peace far more costly than it would have been if it had been achieved before the violence started.

> ....Capulet! Montague!
> See what a scourge is laid upon your hate,
> That heaven finds means to kill your joys with love:
> And I, for winking at your discords too,
> Have lost a brace of kinsmen too: all are punished.
> Shakespeare, *Romeo and Juliet,* V, iii, 291-95.

215

Bullying: the Scapegoat

Quite apart from groups fighting groups, an unfortunate individual may carry the antagonism of a whole group and become a scapegoat. The scapegoats are likely to be those that are perceived as outsiders or 'not us'—immigrants, those of a different colour or religious faith, of different status or sexuality, etc. This also occurs among animals when one individual is driven from the pack like the lone wolf. The persecution of the scapegoat usually takes the form of a kind of bullying. The insecure or damaged personality may gain security by asserting a hierarchical position. They might discover that 'not mes'— rather than being a source of company and social pleasure—can be used for self-validation and the assertion of power. It is necessary for the 'not mes' to be in 'my' power, and for 'me' to have no fear of unpleasant immediate consequences. 'Me' is safe while 'not me' can be hurt. Bullying generally and domestic violence are the result. The armed services and many all male schools for much of their history were hotbeds of bullying. Flashman is the arch-bully in Thomas Hughes, *Tom Brown's Schooldays* and C.S. Forester's stories of Horatio Hornblower depict episodes of bullying in the British navy. Pack animals assert a hierarchy by symbolic or even serious fights, so bullying may be a human form of this.

The attack often arises at the time of the initiation of new members just as pack animals usually drive away or even kill an outsider. It is probably the human equivalent of the animal reaction. In human society on first meeting there is an immediate judgement. There may be a 'halo effect'—a tendency to think the best without real evidence. Similarly there may be an instant dislike which may be equally unjustified. 'Hazing' or 'beasting' (an all too appropriate term) might originally have had survival value in that it revealed the newcomer's strengths or weaknesses for the good of the group. It might also indicate the newcomer's place in the 'pecking-order'. However, the cruelties of bullying often generate an appetite for brutality which is itself damaging to group morale.

Psychological Bullying

Female bullying is usually more psychological though males also use such tactics. This kind of bullying can cause terrible harm. Poison pen letters, slander, libel, gossip prove that 'words' do indeed 'hurt you'. Cruel words still have a very real effect and can make an individual feel cursed and even bring about illness. Malevolence is hard to bear, and even in a secular age cruel words can still have the force of a curse. It is the sense of violation and the intruder's malevolence that make burglary so traumatic. A group might fear individuals with apparent special powers such as witchcraft. Thomas Hardy's story, *The Withered Arm*, tells of an unwitting curse, which led to tragedy in nineteenth century rural Dorset. The effect of a curse was often catastrophic both for the 'cursed' and those that are thought to 'curse'. Witches were traditionally female and at times horribly persecuted by their paranoid community. As women, they were thought of as inferior to men, fallible as daughters of Eve, and possible sexual partners of the Devil. Spells, horoscopes and curses even in modern, scientific times can still have their effect, and some societies may still persecute individuals—even children—suspected of being possessed by evil powers.

Aggression against the Vulnerable

As well as the scapegoat, the vulnerable can attract instinctive hostility. In nature a weak or ill animal may attract predators so the herd will often drive it away. Homo sapiens' animal nature can prompt the strong to take advantage of the weak, especially where there is no family relationship or bond of familiarity. Unprotected infants, children, women, the ill, the disabled, the

217

old, and many animals cannot defend themselves, and may easily be abused. 'Kicking someone when they are down' describes the terrible temptation to take advantage of those unable to protect themselves. Even today there has to be constant vigilance to prevent child, elder, animal and other abuse. Shakespeare's *King Lear* illustrates how in old age a once powerful king is reduced to madness by abuse and neglect. Lear's arrogance has made him vulnerable and he suffers the consequences.

Aggression and Modern City Living

A hundred thousand years ago aggression was purposeful. 'Wild' Homo sapiens would have had a real need to hunt, and protect themselves. They would have been constantly challenged to find food, shelter and security, and their vital energies were chronically reduced by parasites, injury and illness. Modern humans now enjoy secure food supplies, sure shelter, freedom from predation and exuberant health. Their energies run at the full, but with no essential purpose. There are plenty of possessions to steal or vandalize, and cars to take and drive, but the modern housing estate or suburb otherwise offers no challenge to basic human drives.

In the anonymity of modern cities a 'war party' of young Homo sapiens is released from familial restraints and goes looking for excitement which all too easily takes over an individual and worse still, the group mind. This mirrors the Homo sapiens hunting or war-party group that ranged the African savannah a 100,000 years ago and literally shows feral Homo sapiens behaving like the animals that at base they are. Football hooligans deliberately look for a fight with rival fans. 'Demonic' young males fire each other to hectic excitement like a pack of hunting dogs, but in modern urban environments there is nothing to hunt. The killer instinct is therefore likely to express itself in substitute behaviour—smashing, destroying and spoiling property.

Aggression, Sport and the Imagination

In modern life, violence and aggression is increasingly experienced vicariously. The expanding populations of nineteenth century England began to codify and set up supervisory associations for football, Rugby, cricket, tennis, etc. The development of these modern sports coincided with the movement of populations to the cities during the process of industrialization. Although work in the factories and mines was exhausting, there was some free time when large populations had to find entertainment in their cramped urban environments. Sports are surrogate battles and hunting exploits, but beyond the rough play is the prize of hierarchical position. This spills over into antagonism between fans who take their status from their team; a bad-tempered match can trigger real violence. However, sport is fundamentally a valuable way of re-directing aggression.

Fantasy Aggression

Even if violence and aggression are not acted out, the human imagination constantly fantasizes about killing, from cave drawings, myths and legends, dramas, to today's films, computer games and other modern media, these imaginings are compulsively rehearsed and illustrated. Every society is indoctrinated with legends of violence. Ulysses puts out the Cyclops' one eye with a burning stake; St George slays the dragon; David kills Goliath; Theseus despatches the Minotaur. Perhaps even more vivid are fears of predation: the human imagination is full of threatening creatures—giants, Cyclops, Minotaurs, serpents, dragons, sharks, bears, wolves etc. The human at risk is often a child, a young woman, or puny humans facing a huge alien predator. In the natural world predators do indeed select weaker individuals as prey, and possibly the human imagination still retains this awareness. So-called children's fairy stories have had to be sanitized for modern tastes but even so are stories of threat, predation and bloodshed. Usually in the myths the humans escape because of their ingenuity coupled with experience and the nerve to overcome shock, panic and fear. The film cartoons of *Tom and Jerry* act out predator and prey episodes with humour and endless inventiveness. The Arthurian tradition at least tempers valour with self-control and mannerly charm. The myths of the Wild West are probably so enthralling because, perhaps for the last time after more than a 100,000 years and almost within memory, they act out the primal state of man, entering new territory, encountering alien people, and somehow surviving against predation and attack.

The Fascination with Death and Bloodshed

Probably because of this heritage there is a troubling excitement in death and injury common to even the most sensitive modern humans. Often despite themselves, they are fascinated by bloodstains on a road. A car crash quickly draws a crowd of on-lookers, and motor sports and other dangerous activities, to some extent, exploit this interest. This betrays not just curiosity but something more, a compulsive interest in injury and death. An instinctive curiosity in blood and killing may motivate the animal to spill blood in hunting, butchering the kill and similarly dealing with enemies. Perhaps such detachment is necessary in a meat-eating creature, and one that had to kill at close quarters. The curiosity may also be related to a need to understand the borders between life and death, health and injury, comfort and pain. There is a recognition that the observer has survived while another suffers and dies. This awareness of injury and death may subconsciously alert the animal to dangers, and so warn and protect. Killing and the boundary between life and death is always emotive; sacrifice, execution, murder or self destruction provides the most dramatic climaxes and crises in the human psyche.

An analysis of TV programming reveals how much death, violence; the mysterious and macabre fascinate the human mind. The Chamber of Horrors at *Madame Tussaud's* exploits this thirst for blood. News bulletins are full of disasters. Video 'nasties', computer games and gruesome websites feature shows of blood and sudden death. Medical emergencies, rescues, police dramas, courtroom scenes almost always portray some kind of attack, violence or murder. The most successful films are action movies with special effects of destruction and danger. Many video games are particularly gruesome and exploit the fascination with blood and injury.

Bloodshed in the Past

There is much debate about the de-sensitizing effect of TV programmes, internet websites and video games. Scenes of blood and violence may be cathartic—answering a pressing need in a socially acceptable way— or they may actually stimulate the aggression. Different individuals react differently. In the past it was not fictions of cruelty, but cruelty itself that provided entertainment. The Roman Colosseum staged unimaginable scenes of animal and human carnage. The Romans pacified their citizens with 'bread and circuses', often very bloody entertainments. Most dog breeds were developed for hunting, fighting or the baiting of bears, badgers, bulls etc. The crucified dead hung in hundreds along the Appian Way. The heads of horribly executed enemies were displayed on pikes above public places in London. A local community would watch as an old woman, one of their neighbours, was burned alive in front of them. Political rivals were hanged, drawn and quartered. Hanging fairs persisted until well into the nineteenth century and were witnessed with horror by the young Hardy and Dickens, but most of the population found the spectacle highly entertaining. No Post Traumatic Stress Disorders in those days!

The Context of History

Present sensitivities have developed so recently that it is an enormous effort to put them into some sort of historical context. Until the twentieth century even in the western world, children would have regularly witnessed animal slaughter and human death. The general population indulged in hunting and trapping, quite apart from being present when accidents, illness, birth and death were treated domestically. Imagine the horror of a family member dying over many months of facial cancer with no medical attention in a crowded labourer's cottage, or a dead miner being laid out in the front parlour. D.H. Lawrence describes this intimate process in his short story *Odour of Chrysanthemums*. Country people had routinely to slaughter chickens, kill the family pig they had fattened as a pet, and even drown the elderly sheepdog no longer able to earn its keep. Animal fertility could not be controlled surgically so litters of kittens and puppies just had to be drowned.

Country children would have participated in snaring, trapping, killing, and the butchering of birds and animals. Whaling, the bludgeoning of seals, the harvesting of nesting seabirds, the snaring of rabbits and hares were simply a part of everyday life. Injured, sick and deformed members of society with their obvious suffering would have been highly visible. Lepers and otherwise disfigured, mutilated and handicapped individuals often displayed their deformities as they begged. Medical practices were bloody, crude and extremely painful. The population must have been constantly confronted with the news of domestic violence, fighting in the local community, accidents in the workplace and the effects of warfare; everywhere a reminder of cruelty and its awful effects. A report on conditions in mid-nineteenth century factories records the nonchalance with which a factory owner explained why he had a hatchet beside the machines where small children worked for long hours a day. The hatchet was used to sever the hand or arm of a child if it was caught up in the whirling parts of the machinery so that the machine was not damaged. The ill-treatment of children chimney sweeps, apprentices and servants seemed of no consequence. Slavery was sometimes justified because slaves were given better food, clothing, and medical care than many European peasants. Slavery, cruel as it was, was age-old and took place in the context of general social barbarity. The press gang, flogging, and summary executions were routine in the British navy. While the modern media exposes the population to gruesome images, in the past children watched public hangings or the killing of the family pig in all its gory reality:

> The killing was a noisy, bloody business, in the course of which the animal was hoisted to a rough bench that it might bleed thoroughly and so preserve the quality of the meat. The job was often bungled, the pig sometimes getting away and having to be chased: but country people of that day had little sympathy for the sufferings of animals, and men, women, and children would gather round to see the sight.

> The whole scene, with its mud and blood, flaring lights and dark shadows was as savage as anything seen in an African jungle.
>
> Flora Thompson, *Lark Rise to Candleford*

> The time arrived for killing the pig which Jude and his wife had fattened in their sty during the autumn months....
> "Upon my soul I would sooner have gone without the pig than have had this to do!" said Jude." A creature I have fed with my own hands."

> "Don't be such a tender-hearted fool! There's the sticking-knife—the one with the point. Now whatever you do, don't stick un too deep."
>
> "I'll stick him effectually, so as to make short work of it. That's the chief thing."
>
> "You must not!" she cried. "The meat must be well bled, and to do that he must die slow. We shall lose a shilling a score if the meat is red and bloody! Just touch the vein, that's all. I was brought up to it, and I know. Every good butcher keeps un bleeding long. He ought to be eight or ten minutes dying at least."
>
> Thomas Hardy, *Jude the Obscure* .

These behaviours to most modern Western humans seem unnecessarily cruel, though this may be a luxury of a world where the food supply is detached from its source. Modern sensibility may be a very new development, a result of the industrialization of food production. Instead of killing in a hunt and butchering the carcase, slaughtering is now hidden and the meat appears neatly packaged in the supermarket. There is no relationship between the live animal, its pain, fear, blood and offal and the consumer. (However, it may be that the factory farming of pigs, calves and chickens inflicts a chronic suffering on sentient creatures, which is worse than being quickly torn to pieces by a predator after at least some life of freedom and natural behaviour.)

The Fragility of Civilisation

Because of the animal bias towards aggression, the modern taboo against killing is all too easily broken:

> Jack was on top of the sow, stabbing downward with his knife. Roger found a lodgment for his point and began to push till he was leaning with his full weight. The spear moved forward inch by inch and the terrified squealing became a high-pitched scream. Then

Jack found the throat and the hot blood spouted over his hands. The
sow collapsed under them and they were heavy fulfilled upon her...
William Golding, *Lord of the Flies*.

An episode in New York's Central Park in the summer of 2000
illustrates how easily apparently civilized Homo sapiens can
revert to the primitive. Groups of young men became a
marauding, irrational mob sexually assaulting the women in the
Park. More usually the 'prey' of a group are rival gangs such as
other football fans, or 'out' groups or individuals that are
different in race, culture, sexuality, or disability. Joseph
Conrad's *Heart of Darkness* is a study of how easily a civilized
European descends into gross barbarity.

The Triggers for Aggression
Homo sapiens' aggression has much in common with other
animals. There are four main areas that give rise to conflict.
Threats to territory and food supply are obvious triggers. Man
then reacts with surprising aggression to any threats to its
hierarchical position. In addition, competition for sexual partners
and threats to the family group and its cohesion arouse
aggression. Jokingly, American troops in England during the
second World War were said to be oversexed (competition for
sexual partners), overpaid (threat to hierarchical position) and
over here (threat to territory)'. However, there is one trigger to
violence in Homo sapiens that is hardly found otherwise in
nature, and that is an innate sense of justice. When an individual
or group feel they have been treated unjustly, they react, rebel
and revolt. This sense of justice causes violence but has also
motivated human society to develop new and fairer systems of
social organisation.

1. Territory

Adults are above everything driven to pass on their genes to healthy children. This imperative impels the group to keep rivals off the area that supports it. The food and water supply is essential and these depend on land or territory. Animals are primarily motivated by food as is well understood by animal trainers. In modern terms, money has become like token food, and motivates Homo sapiens to some of its most aggressive actions. Money, property and land are intimately connected. Early on, populations of Homo sapiens would have been widely dispersed in a landscape of virgin forest and unexplored grasslands. The groups that enjoyed security of shelter and food supply would probably have felt attachment to their home and stayed fairly localized. However, as the population expanded or food supplies failed, the groups had to migrate.

This wanderlust may be a search for 'lebensraum'; it might be a kind of endless migration like that of other herd animals; it might be an instinctive impulse that stirs young adults to set up their own breeding territories, or in modern terms to wander off as back-packers. Undoubtedly, the urge is felt as a curiosity to explore. Modern travel and tourism may perhaps be acting out the ancient impulse to see new sights and find new territory, even to the exploration of outer space. Eventually Homo sapiens moved into every habitable area of the earth until there were no new territories. Populations, including perhaps the Neanderthals, therefore, had to turn and challenge each other, with the more powerful and resourceful surviving at the expense of the weaker. Even now in times of stress, competition for territory can all too easily lead to violence. Homo sapiens has endlessly migrated but the 'new world' is now full up. Asylum seekers and economic migrants present altogether new challenges. Antagonism is instinctively felt towards large influxes of immigrants, or unauthorized gypsy encampments. Even without such stress, perfectly civilized neighbours can still become murderous over a hedge. Irrational quarrels between neighbours, the extreme reactions in earlier centuries of landowners to poachers, and gangland's 'turf wars' may be instinctive reactions to what are unconsciously perceived as ancient threats to territory and its underlying significance to the food supply.

Now, the populations of the world are fluid and expanding as never before. The rich world visits tourist attractions and the more mobile individuals of the poor world try to access the wealth of the rich by migration. The rich world has amassed much of its wealth by colonization, or preferential trading arrangements, as well as its ingenuity and enterprise. These societies have developed comfortable systems of welfare for their own citizens. Globalization has now made the citizens of the world aware of this wealth and welfare. Tensions are unavoidable.

However deplorable it is to modern sensibilities, and however successful rational thought combats these cruel impulses, deep within the human psyche is a fear and dislike of alien people and different cultures—though there is also a curiosity and friendly interest if numbers are not intimidating and living conditions are propitious. Racism is natural and must be recognized, understood and de-conditioned, rather than simply denied with the hope it will go away. This dangerous innate aversion probably had survival value in protecting territory, consolidating group identity, and sharpening the group's defensive strategies.

Caucasians have in recent centuries invaded the lands of other races. The Caucasian population often feels antagonism to immigrants; how can that antagonism be compared to the emotions felt by the populations of the lands they once invaded? The invaders were fortunate in coming from the temperate zones of the world, rich in natural resources, and often were imbued with the Protestant work ethic and individualism. Their spirit of enterprise and technological superiority prompted the colonization of the territories of other populations. Caucasians have prospered materially. The results have often been tragic for the aboriginal peoples they have in many cases almost unthinkingly exploited, enslaved or destroyed. Colonized populations and the poor in a community are usually subject to discrimination with its self-fulfilling consequences of escape into drug addiction, alcoholism, apathy or else anomie, rebellion, and sometimes terrorism. A threat to territory combined with man's sense of justice will almost inevitably lead to violence.

While there is an impulse to wander, Homo sapiens also have a very rooted sense of a 'home'. Neighbours will argue over small details of their territory; car parking can cause huge tension. Doors and thresholds are important as territorial markers and there are formalities of entry, knocking or, in some way, giving notice of intention to enter and waiting for permission. Boundaries have expanded enormously with increased population mobility—village, town, county, region, nation, continent. In modern conditions there is much confusion about the entries and exits across these boundaries. The group sense of belonging to a place conflicts with the ability and desire to wander. Now that nearly all the surface of the Earth is owned, it is almost impossible to follow the lifestyle of the hunter-gatherers, as the Bushmen of the Kalahari and the Australian aborigines are learning to their cost.

For an individual, the invasion of personal space can be very threatening unless there is a pre-existing intimacy. However, the perception of appropriate personal space is not fixed but varies from culture to culture. A crowded commuter train or lift often evokes a feeling of unease at the too close proximity of strangers. Accidental pushing or bodily contact can arouse irritation or even aggression. Because of their animal significance such slight matters can arouse disproportionate negative reactions. This is a defence mechanism, to protect an individual from surprise attack. This sense of vulnerability is reflected in room layouts. Offices, restaurants, any public space, the preferred seats are those by a window, with their backs to a wall, or in a corner preferably facing the door. Most workers dislike open-plan offices and working spaces, and almost inevitably divide up the space into personal zones with screens or whatever furniture is available.

Very simple barriers such as a ribbon or parking cones are respected as territorial markers. Even leaving a garment on the back of a chair is a place marker which most individuals will respect. Even if there is a spare seat at a table or in a train, it is a matter of negotiation for someone to take it, usually with the question 'Is anyone sitting here?', rather than simply sitting in the seat without asking. For the most part it would be considered rude to turn the newcomer away, but if there are plenty of spare seats, the intrusion may be resented.

There is also a wider sense of personal territory. In modern conditions this sense can be experienced very strongly when motoring. The driver is safe inside the car, which adds to the sense of power, particularly as far as pedestrians or cyclists are concerned. The driver is alone. Other drivers are not perceived in human terms as their facial cues are reduced or non-existent. If another car cuts into a line of traffic, the emotional reaction is often irrational, and calling it 'road rage' suggests its power. This may in part be a reaction to danger. However, the anger can be so intense that there must be some other factor involved. The car that cuts in has in a sense taken territory, but also implied a hierarchical threat. The age-old competitive urge fires up as if the drivers were vying for prey, or is it simply the need to be the fastest, strongest, cleverest? Evolution has not designed man for modern road conditions.

2. Hierarchy

Any threat to the place in the hierarchy is very explosive. The sense of hierarchy is expressed in racism, sexism, ageism and many other prejudices. The root of the discrimination is usually at least in part a sense of being of a superior race, sex or age, and so entitled to a higher place in the hierarchy. The psychiatrist, Alfred Adler, recognized that Homo sapiens seems wired for dominance; the 'will to power' has long been understood as almost the primary motivational force in human relationships. This is evident when perfectly mannerly individuals can become violent and abusive if their place in a queue or a stream of traffic is usurped. Someone in a queue has accepted his or her place amongst others in an orderly sequence. If someone pushes the others aside, this causes great hostility because the perceived hierarchy has been subverted. If one driver allows another to move ahead, some acknowledgement of this concession is expected, otherwise the whole interaction can turn sour. It is as if the second driver has taken the concession for granted and so assumed a higher place in the intuited hierarchy. It may also be that a gesture of reciprocal altruism has not been acknowledged, and the norms of justice have been infringed.

In the primitive past the group benefited from a hierarchy, and a need for the group to conform to agreed patterns of behaviour. It would be more likely to survive if its strongest members were given the best chance to breed. This would mean competition for the best sexual partners and then protection for the offspring. However, in the small band of wandering Homo sapiens, personal contacts and bonding would have been strong so that kindly feelings might often have overridden practicalities. As

Homo sapiens stopped wandering across terrain in small groups, and began to live in populations of thousands, more complex social rules had to develop. Social contacts would have been less easy to sustain across the whole population, and rival factions and class systems developed often with cruel consequences. The human animal feels most comfortable in a group size that resembles the size of the original hunter gatherer group. However, these groups move amongst each other within the larger population, and at the interfaces this can generate conflict. Forced into unnatural proximity with other groups, quarrels arise, but it is surprising how tolerant humans can be, moving around crowded cities.

Only individuals of accepted high status can treat lower status individuals with indifference without giving particular offence; but even so, a gracious acknowledgement of the lower status individuals engenders affection and loyalty—'noblesse oblige'. The Royal walk-about illustrates just this kind of rapport. The public is enchanted by the apparent friendliness, but can resent too much familiarity. It is a matter of fine balance. Monarchs, aristocrats and celebrities can enforce their place at the top of the hierarchy, and before the development of democratic ideals, they often did. Titles, body language, uniforms, possessions, and many other subtle indicators all demonstrate an individual's place. Manners are a highly developed system of defusing the potential conflicts associated with hierarchy, and in former times knowing one's place was a virtue. Showing respect is perhaps the more modern equivalent.

Somehow there has to be some way of defusing the aggression associated with the need to claim a place in the hierarchy, especially where populations are crowded together in modern cities. Fortunately, there is sport and sport is a symbolic hunt or perhaps more importantly a symbolic trial of strength with the power to define a place in the hierarchy. Most sports have leagues or other systems that rank teams or individuals. The names of teams often take the name of a town together usually with some aggressive, often animal, association—sharks, bears, wolves, bulls. After a score, the successful player will often run to exult before his supporters with gestures of triumph—the clenched fist thrust upwards, or arms lifted and waved with fists clenched, while the supporters roar approval in their hierarchical triumph— 'We are the greatest'. Sportsmen in modern society 'live to fight another day'. Sportsmanship also inculcates the values of fair play, generosity in victory and philosophical acceptance of defeat; such attitudes in wider social encounters would indeed prevent much suffering. 'It's not cricket' was once a motto for fairness and restraint. The losers usually learn to be good losers, and accept their hierarchical slippage philosophically. Graciousness in success and defeat is a very necessary virtue; arrogance and bombast are themselves powerful triggers to hate and violence. Referees keep order and while there are sometimes challenges to their authority, it is generally recognised that the game is more important than personal grievance.

3. Sex, Family and the Survival of the Genetic Line.

Dysfunctional sex is also a potent trigger to violence. Jealousy, honour, suspicion can madden otherwise controlled and law-abiding individuals. These feelings may also be a survival of the hierarchical need to ascertain who were the most powerful males. The biological imperative to pass genes on to offspring born of a chosen partner or partners is often reinforced by passionate bonding emotion, the psychological aspect of Homo sapiens' sex. Other animals might fight for access to sexual partners, usually males against males but this is not the same as human jealousy. Once the females of other species are safely inseminated, the males often lose interest. The sex pheromones are turned off, and while the animals or birds may bond to bring up their offspring or even for life, there is no longer any continuing sexual interest, until the next breeding season. The unusual mating pattern of humans means that the sexes are always sexually attractive to each other, rather than just at times of oestrus. This increases emotional pressures beyond the animal function. While the Homo sapiens pair bond is a source of great pleasure and emotional satisfaction, it can also be a source of pain, anger and violence.

Unlike other animals humans have an awareness that sex engenders offspring, and most males have a powerful need to be reassured of their fatherhood. Until recently there was no way of having this certainty. In some societies sex is repressed either by strict controls on breeding females, or social rules that separate the sexes socially. Female virginity is prized; promiscuity is seen as an infringement of the cultural norms and punished by ostracism or sometimes, even death. The concept of honour has a resonance of courage, respect, and in terms of sexual relationships—a certainty of a partner's exclusivity.

Honour Codes

Honour is a matter particularly for males. A male's honour depends on his female's chastity, and her infidelity has often been grounds for violence against her and her other partner. The male is motivated to defend his right to his female's womb, so that so-called crimes of passion are often not considered assault or murder, but accepted as an understandable defence of his honour. What this means is a tacit understanding that he has a right to ensure it is his genes that are passed on to the next generation. Other members of the family may become involved and the issue of family honour may arise. This may involve honour killings. Even a female that is raped may become rejected by her society although she is innocent. Her womb may

233

be tainted by unwanted genetic material, so she is 'impure'. Her rape may be seen as the ultimate insult to her partner. The whole emotional context of rape even in modern times is one of shame and guilt, and not so long ago a woman who had been raped was often thought to have caused the crime by dressing in a particular way, or walking in a particular area, almost 'asking for it'. She was therefore given little sympathy. It is as if she is to be rejected as soiled rather than the victim of a crime. Some societies guard against this by making the females completely cover themselves so that they become virtually asexual. This no doubt lessens tensions, but at the expense of women's personal freedom, although many women agree with the dress and seem to feel protected by covering themselves.

Sex and Violence

Sex is such a strong drive that very repressed individuals can become dangerously deviant, and sometimes murderously violent. There may be a fantasy relationship with a celebrity which leads to stalking behaviour that can become irrational and dangerous—perhaps not so much sexual as hierarchical. Quite apart from these and many other pathologic aspects of sexual behaviour. Sex can be one of the most powerful triggers to violent behaviour in the general population.

Individual or Group Survival

Homo sapiens' family bonds are very strong; in most circumstances mothers will fight to the death to protect their offspring, and fathers will fight to protect their mates and their progeny. Other animals will also fight to protect their young, but some will desert, kill or even eat them if frightened. Some hard-pressed human tribal groups will rather similarly expose children or abandon the elderly as if reverting to a more animal behaviour pattern. 'Wild' man had to protect the group at the expense of the weaker individuals. The old walked off or waited behind when they intuited they were becoming a dangerous burden to their group. Laurens Vanderpost observed just this among the Bushmen of the Kalahari:

> 'But these old people, how will they get on?' I asked....
> 'They'll go as far as they can,' Ben answered. But a day will come when they can't go on. Then, weeping bitterly, all will gather round them. They'll give them all the food and water they can spare. They'll build a thick shelter of thorn to protect them against wild animals. Still weeping, the rest of the band...will move on. Sooner or later, probably before their water and food is finished, a leopard, but more commonly a hyena will break through and eat them. It's always been like that... They've had to do it to others...Life was only possible for all of us, because in our past, there had been those who put the claims of life itself before all else.

In part the abuse of children and elder abuse may be a relic of this primitive behaviour.

A perceived threat to a family or the larger group also came from those individuals that were disabled, diseased or deformed. The group could not afford a risk of infection or an over-burdensome commitment to ailing, injured or otherwise non-productive individuals. In herd animals a weak individual is often driven off as its presence may attract predators, and jeopardize general safety. Fear of contamination, of genetic pollution, of disease, of disability can still arouse dislike and fear as AIDS has recently demonstrated. As wild creatures there was no comfortable surplus to support the congenitally weak or disabled. The weak, injured or disabled had to be abandoned without sentiment to ensure general survival. The millennia of scarcity have left their imprint of dislike and fear of the weak and deformed, even into modern times of plenty and ease. Until very recent times, the handicapped were hidden away in institutions, and it has taken determined campaigns to overcome discrimination against them. Fortunately, with greater prosperity and understanding such discrimination is now felt to be completely unacceptable.

4. Justice: Animal and Human Sharing

Pack animals will compete mercilessly for their share of the group's resources within some sort of hierarchical structure; the strongest and cleverest take what they want at the expense of the rest — the survival of the fittest in action. Homo sapiens though, have another source of conflict which is rooted in its new order of being. Most unusually man also has a very strong contrary impulse— to share resources. The perception of justice requires mental functions above the capability of almost all other animals —the power to envisage and compare, as well as an ability to empathize. The ideal of justice can prompt quarrels, and can underlie conflicts over territory or other resources. Justice is complicated as one claim can be in contention with another, hence the whole apparatus of the law. International law is still developing, and still lacks the authority to impose its judgments on uncooperative states. Justice is in any case an ideal that is easily betrayed because it has developed beyond basic animal nature. The animal impulse to take more and protect the self is easily triggered. In a settled human group the individuals will try to relate to each other with an innate sense of fairness or justice. However, episodes of panic buying illustrate how quickly civilized behaviour can break down under competitive pressures. If society becomes dysfunctional, some individuals may make a grab for resources and begin looting and stealing. This then begins to drive others to similar behaviour and the social fabric quickly disintegrates.

Human Justice

The sense of justice is unique so that only the highest primates demonstrate anything similar in the rest of nature. Recent research on capuchin monkeys shows that the monkeys will sulk or become uncooperative if they feel they have been discriminated against. This seems to suggest that a sense of natural justice developed as primate species evolved. Pack animals in recognizing their social rules such as their place in the hierarchy, demonstrate that there is already in these animals a sense of what is appropriate—almost a primitive sense of justice.

The Homo sapiens' sense of fairness or natural justice is felt from early childhood. Children in the nursery are watchful that they receive their fair share of everything dispensed by their carers. Homo sapiens' sense of natural justice within families, unfortunately sometimes results in poisonous sibling and other rivalries. Throughout life there is dissension if other individuals or groups do not seem to behave fairly. Generally anger and violence are felt against those that claim more than their fair share of resources while exclusion leads to unrest whether in families, nations or racial groups. Those that feel wronged may take their own revenge, starting vendettas and quarrels. Revenge is a product of justice, but it can unleash a chain reaction which can last for generations. Basic justice is a brutal 'eye for an eye, a tooth for a tooth'. The more far-seeing and generous-minded societies have gradually sought to control such vindictiveness, and over recent centuries, systems of secular law have tamed such savagery, though honour killings, reprisals and gang warfare are still threats to public order.

Law and Trade

Within primitive Homo sapiens groups there must have been a developing sense of fairness, and how one individual should relate to another, according to perceived status. A small group of hunter-gatherers probably acted this out almost intuitively. An arbiter of justice supported by group endorsement would have ensured the system would be observed and any deviance would bring sanctions. In this, the hierarchical sense served the cause of justice. This was perhaps the beginning of law, protecting an individual against its fellows and codifying social rights and duties. Legal systems have gradually developed and the rule of law has become the supreme mark of civilisation.

Very importantly, bartering and trade would be impossible without a sense of justice. The value of one commodity has to be compared with another, the value agreed on, and an exchange contracted. This would be impossible without some sense of equivalent value, and an acknowledgement that the exchange should be fair and just.

Inequality

However, after Homo sapiens began to live in large settled populations some 10,000 years ago higher status individuals became detached from the general mass. The hierarchical impulse stratified society. The rich and powerful felt they could indulge themselves while the ordinary people often suffered terrible privations. Religious authority was often distorted to justify these inequalities. The Christian Church often sided with economic and political powers even if they contradicted the message of the Gospel arguing, like other hierarchies, that privileges for some were in the interests of the group as a whole. Privileged classes usually interbred and kept an oppressive hold over their societies, sometimes for millennia. The hardships of the masses were often ignored or even justified. In *A Christmas Carol* Dickens makes Scrooge articulate a widely held sentiment, derived from Malthus' *Essay on the Principles of Population* (1803) that the poor should be left to suffer and die, so that nature could take its course and 'reduce the surplus population'. Ironically, the privileged made sure that such pressures did not operate on their own families or social groups.

Justice and Conflict

Enforcing and maintaining justice can lead to conflict because different individuals or groups may have different perceptions of their rights. For instance, two populations claim the Holy Land, but on different and incompatible grounds; the historical and territorial rights of the Palestinians conflict with the religious rights claimed by some Israelis. Somehow the cruelties of the continuing quarrel need to be balanced by a vision of the prosperity and peace both communities could enjoy if they could moderate their mutually exclusive claims. The cost of absolutism is so much grief and violence.

A society evenly divided in conflict may resort to civil war. Where the balance of power is unequal, and where the smaller or less powerful group has no political voice, their sense of injustice may prompt 'direct action' to make their claims on the majority. Somehow such desperation must be understood and defused, and this requires a generous open-mindedness. The leadership on both sides is hugely responsible. Unfortunately, the power play of leaders usually makes conciliation unlikely. The attitude of the majority hardens into indignation and worse. Meanwhile the minority looks to their leader, often charismatic and with religious authority, who justifies their grievance and endorses their plans. Hatred may be deliberately indulged. This is always the root of political violence. The minority that can resist hatred may just become a nuisance with acts of passive resistance and non-cooperation; those who indulge hatred may try to force change with acts of random terror. Such dissidents view the whole majority population as the enemy and no one is innocent. This is obviously irrational, but hate is beyond reason.

239

If the planned attack fails to achieve its purpose, at least there is the satisfaction of revenge.

Terrorism

Second generation immigrants can suffer from identity confusion as they have lost their age-old sense of belonging, but do not feel fully part of the host culture. Their parents were simply grateful to have better opportunities for themselves and their children. The next generation take the opportunities for granted, but feel alienated from the host society and identify with the lost culture of their ancestors and the injustices they are perceived to suffer. They find solidarity with others with similar identity crises, then may turn against the host culture, as happened in London in July 2005. Four young British Moslems from the north of England became suicide bombers and killed over fifty innocent civilians on the London transport system. They were so driven by hatred that they taped sharp nails on to bottles of explosive to prepare a kind of cluster bomb that would horribly tear flesh. The cause of such malice has to be understood and measures taken to prevent its development.

Control of Anger

Anger management, and sometimes ancient or religious wisdom, helps violent individuals cope with their aggression. It has been thought that anger needed to be expressed or it would become more explosive and damaging. However, the expression of anger, far from being cathartic, can actually increase the capacity for violence. There is, of course, a difference between complete denial and repression of emotion which is damaging. It seems that chimpanzees attack less ferociously if they 'swear', as if their vocal expression is a kind of safety valve. Humans can use their language to talk up or talk down their anger, and need to take responsibility for the choice they make.

Justice and Mercy

Too unforgiving a sense of justice, can lead to self-righteousness and aggression towards others. The story of Jonah and the gourd, or Christ's parables of the workers in the vineyard, or the Prodigal Son challenge a petty-minded or over rigid attitude to justice. The dispensers of justice, God, the Master and the father, choose to act with generosity when challenged by Jonah, the party of vineyard workers and the other son. Forgiveness, mercy and generosity allow for rehabilitation and when used with discretion prevent extremes of hate and alienation in reaction to too oppressive an imposition of justice: 'Forgive us our trespasses as we forgive them that trespass against us' neatly articulates this balance.

Justice and Social Evolution

A surprising number of Homo sapiens accept martyrdom for their beliefs, including suicide bombers. These may be articulated as 'King and Country', 'freedom', 'faith' but often at the root is the sense of justice, unfortunately sometimes misconceived. Many human communities feel justice is so important that they will resist attempts to deny it to themselves or others, banding together to assert it as an inalienable right. Their resistance may turn to violence, or in wider situations rebellion, revolution and even war. Other campaigns may use sanctions and passive resistance to achieve justice. Over the centuries despite many false steps, a true and humane justice has gradually asserted itself. Inequality is now questioned more and more; universal human rights are acknowledged and the Brotherhood of Man is widely accepted. In achieving justice there may be aggression and violence, but justice is nevertheless an important motive force for social evolution. The human sense of justice is the creative irritant that keeps pushing the evolution of society forward.

Towards Peace and Justice

It is easy to be discouraged. Violent crime seems to keep increasing. There have been recent episodes of racism and genocide, for instance in Rwanda, Darfur, and Congo. Even in Europe under pressure, the old animal behaviours emerge all too easily as in Kosovo. Too often in human history a gentle community has been overrun by brute-like aggression, often prompted by the victims' weakness or passivity. Only a stronger super-group has the power to intervene like a referee, and stop conflict. Homo sapiens as a species is struggling to enforce some kind of system to contain the belligerent.

The Holocaust demonstrated the full human potential for cruelty, recorded by modern media to demonstrate for ever what ultimately happens when humanity cultivates its most bestial instincts. Attempts are now made for the international community to prosecute perpetrators of crimes against humanity. The Nuremberg trials set an important precedent. Simon Wiesenthal pursued Nazi war criminals not so much to bring such individuals as Adolf Eichmann to justice, but to warn those tempted to commit future atrocities that they will eventually be held to account. Fifty years on in South Africa, the process of reconciliation after the end of Apartheid avoided the anticipated blood bath and a pioneered mature and humane way to escape from a cruel past. The Truth and Reconciliation Commission demanded truthful confessions from the accused in exchange for an amnesty. In this way, Archbishop Tutu demonstrated a process by which the past was not forgotten but did not imprison the present or future. This must be immensely hopeful, and reflects with enormous credit on African humanity.

It is as if humanity is beginning to emerge from the long, dark tunnel of its animal nature, and pre-history. Gradually in recent centuries in the more fortunate parts of the world the age-old cruelties have been reduced. In the Second World War the 'blitz' deliberately targeted civilians; now there is an outcry if civilians are killed or injured as 'collateral damage'. Practices like bear, badger, and bull baiting, cock and dog fighting have been banned. Slaughtering animals has been regulated, and cruelty to animals is subject to legislation. Those states that retain the death penalty use methods that do not cause unnecessary suffering or cause mutilation. Executions are no longer public spectacles, and increasingly states are abandoning the death penalty. Myths and legends (*Punch and Judy*), folk songs ('Wee Cooper of Fife') and sayings such as: 'A woman, a dog and a walnut tree/ The more they are beat the better they be' show how domestic violence was long considered normal and ignored by the authorities. Now, domestic violence is treated as serious assault, and duly prosecuted when it is reported and proven.

The Choice

The Preamble to the UNESCO Constitution states : 'Since wars begin in the minds of men, it is in the minds of men that the defences of peace must be constructed.' Homo sapiens can use their reason and imagination to look ahead to where prejudice and hatred are likely to lead. It is very much easier to stereotype, generalize and stigmatize their adversaries. To resist this is hard psychological 'work', and needs both practice and commitment, and perhaps a compassionate religious belief or at least a set of humane philosophical principles. There is an emerging agreement that there are universal human rights, that their acceptance is better than barbarism, and that beyond animal survival there can be a greater, cooperative spirit of well-being. In future it may be more important to have teams of psychologists, anthropologists and sociologists in addition to politicians involved in negotiations at points of conflict. If force still has to be used, it must be under the control of the international community, drawing on the wisdom of the various cultures and systems of justice.

Over 2,000 years ago Isaiah had a vision Homo sapiens' future':

> 'They shall beat their swords into ploughshares, and their spears
> into pruning hooks: nation shall not lift up sword against nation,
> neither shall they learn war any more.'
>
> *Isaiah,* 2, v4.

The Self: Assertion, Surrender and the Life of the Spirit

These our actors,
As I foretold you, were all spirits and
Are melted into air, into thin air;
And, like the baseless fabric of this vision,
The cloud-capp'd towers, the gorgeous palaces,
The solemn temples, the great globe itself,
Yea, all which it inherit, shall dissolve
And, like this insubstantial pageant faded,
Leave not a rack behind. We are such stuff
As dreams are made on, and our little life
Is rounded with a sleep, –

Shakespeare, *The Tempest*, IV, i.148-158

The Self

Other pack animals and possibly some closely-knit human tribal communities have little sense of themselves as individuals separate from their fellows. This is difficult to understand after centuries of individualistic Western culture where the persona spends a good deal of time and energy in asserting itself.

The self is the product of genetic and mimetic (learned and imitated ideas) history in a given environment. Each individual is unique and irreplaceable. Like other creatures the human animal will instinctively protect itself, struggling to live the safest and most comfortable life it can. It will clean, groom and nourish itself; it will seek safety and comfort. Beyond this man is capable of fully self-reflexive thought; it is an ape with a sense of self. A very significant aspect of this human awareness is its ability to tell the story of 'the self'. Memory and experience are connected through time in the individual mind to make a narrative of paramount importance.

245

Language obviously is an important tool for this; other animals without language and the sequencing ability on which language depends, do not have this sense of themselves, their history and their ancestral background. They may well have a memory of a happening associated with a particular place, a memory of water or a food source, a place where they suffered attack but that is not the same as the kind of connected personal history.

This story of the self tends to be edited according to the individual's needs. Other individuals who share the same memories can corroborate or challenge the account, and keep it in touch with some sort of reality. Even with the modern aids of recording, film, and video it is difficult to hold on to the shifting memories and experiences that are felt as the subjective self. For the first time in human history the old and the dead can be restored to youth and life in photographs and film. The individual can now be perceived on a continuum from birth to old age and even death, rather than a vivid living presence surrounded by shadowy memories and vague future possibilities. All animals are driven to pass on their genes, but uniquely in man this has become conscious. The self is understood as participating in a dynasty which links past generations or 'the ancestors' with future descendants.

Philosophers, psychoanalysts and other writers have puzzled over the nature of the ego. It is understood that the conscious ego is only the surface of the personal self. Below this surface, emotions and memories, fantasies and instincts prompt thoughts and actions. The conscious mind easily fills up with apparently unrelated ideas unless it is directed by practised control. Memories intrude into the present and give rise to powerful emotions, although the connection may be below the threshold of consciousness. Writers like Virginia Woolf and James Joyce sometimes put into words the random wandering of the 'stream of consciousness'. They represent the inner life of their characters, with thoughts, impressions, emotions, memories often without logical sequence or even coherent syntax. Concentration is required for creative and coherent thought, and the control of the roving thoughts is an important educational skill, all the more difficult in the context of restless, hyped-up entertainment media.

Many pathological psychiatric conditions, such as some forms of schizophrenia, are disturbances of the 'self'. Sometimes there are several 'selves', or sometimes an inflated identity such as 'Christ' or 'Napoleon' borrowed from history or legend. In cases of amnesia or dementia the self exists only in the present moment and cannot be related to the past and the self disintegrates.

There are times when a new identity is consciously invented, either for the purposes of amusement, drama, crime, espionage, or simply a new beginning. Individuals may disguise themselves by dressing up, using masks, wigs, make-up, and face-paint sometimes for dramatic performance or simply for amusement at a social or sporting event. In disguise, the ego for a time plays at being another self. 'Con men' can be expert at assuming extravagant new identities. On the other hand, those being trained to infiltrate an organization with a false identity have to be carefully and expertly trained so that the false story of self is not detected. Without the corroboration of those that share the same memories, the self can become seduced by its own imaginings and becomes a new self.

The Assertion of Self
Hierarchy and the need for leaders prompts some individuals to make a bid for power and most individuals have an urge to

exercise their willpower and determination. The more open and equal societies allow more individuals to express their individuality, and such self-expression is appreciated as the very essence of freedom. Homes are usually personalized and almost any work area will be made individual if at all possible with some small possessions, photographs, mementoes, and ornaments. Beyond the physical self, the individual expresses itself by its dress and possessions, following group fashion but often with personal idiosyncrasies. This becomes mixed with signals of status. Males may seek to intimidate other males; while females often seek to attract male attention. Individuals of both sexes try to assert themselves directly or indirectly, and have to learn how to negotiate with others who also seek to assert themselves.

Like other animals an individual may seek to leave a mark of its presence. Animals often urinate and spray but these markers depend on smell, which is a weak sense in man. Homo sapiens therefore use visual signs such as graffiti, slogans, or cartoon-type drawings, initials scratched on trees, windows and other surfaces. Most humans are commemorated by some sort of memorial, grave marker or tombstone, and many individuals themselves try to leave something of themselves in art, writing, or more recently in recordings, photos, videos etc.

Above all, individuals seek to be validated by approval, affection and the love of others. An individual's reputation is very significant, and determines its standing in the social group, sometimes extending into the group memory and even legend. This sense of self-worth and acceptance is probably essential to the development of a healthy human psyche. The celebrations of birthdays, and other personally important events allow each individual, in turn, to be given particular recognition by the group. If attention is not affirmative, the individual may become deviant. Any attention is better than none because in the wild an individual that was neglected or isolated was vulnerable. The persona may for its own needs invent situations that demand attention exhibiting Münchausen's syndrome, or Münchausen's syndrome by proxy. These are conditions where an individual self-harms or harms another dependent individual—usually a child—so that they initiate a medical emergency and arouse the concern of others. Secret self-harming seems to be an attempt to numb psychological pain by inflicting physical pain. Pain is also a way of defining the self in opposition to others and may help the individual feel 'alive'. The pain may also release endorphins, so that the pain itself becomes pleasurable.

'Self' Expression and Hero Worship

This need for personal expression can manifest itself in art and performance. Certain individuals have special charisma and talent and become leader-performers, sometimes in these days of the mass media, for huge human populations. Many have an ambition to be famous as a human form of achieving a higher place in the hierarchy. Less confident individuals can be terrified by performing and suffer stage fright, feeling exposed and vulnerable like any social creature isolated from the safety of the pack, herd or shoal. Those that wish for fame and power, but do not have the gifts or personal qualities sometimes instead relate to a chosen celebrity. There have always been heroes and cult figures, but with the modern media the interest in celebrities is like a kind of aggrandized small town gossip fed by the paparazzi. The celebrated personality often eventually finds the adulation tiresome and intrusive. Fans can be quite innocent followers of the famous, but some smitten individuals can become caught up in quite dangerous fantasy relationships.

Some members of the public project themselves on to a celebrity as if finding validation for themselves by association, as well as following a leader. Royalty represents more than mere celebrity, and carries a symbolic significance. Religious leaders such as saints, holy teachers, shamans, and others can become extremely powerful, sometimes for the good of humanity and sometimes otherwise. Any piece of a celebrity's clothing, their handwriting or autograph may be collected like saintly relics. Saintly relics have long been thought to have magical powers. Throughout Catholic Europe, skulls, finger bones, tongues, clothing, possessions, all sorts of fragments from the lives of saints are treasured in churches and museums. Some institutions and individuals collect letters, manuscripts, and realia of the famous. Such scraps and remnants of celebrity, holiness or fame, of no intrinsic value, are treasured for their associations.

The Surrender of Self

Self assertion brings its satisfactions, but it is as much a burden. Protestant individualism has emphasized personal accountability and therefore sinfulness and its consequences. Most individuals carry some guilt, shame, and bad memories, and suffer boredom and loneliness:

> Which way I fly is Hell; myself am Hell;
>
> John Milton, *Paradise Lost*, IV, l. 75.

The Longing for Oblivion

Many of man's happiest experiences seem to be when the conscious mind is by-passed, and the self is absorbed into some other sphere. Man's consciousness of self can be a kind of psychological prison, preventing the animal blending with whatever is beyond and separating it from being one with its natural environment. Freud discussed a death instinct, a longing for oblivion or 'thanatos' (death); something similar is found in many eastern religions as nirvana, anatta, and in Christian terms 'the peace of God which passes all understanding'.

Almost everyone has to face hardship and disappointment as well as times of joy and fulfilment. However, many are permanently disadvantaged. If some have more; more have less. By definition a hierarchy ranks individuals; those at the top are likely to take resources from those below them. The stressed, lonely and unloved are like other animals that are rejected by the group and appear miserable and unfulfilled at the periphery of the pack or herd. The lone wolf is a folkloric figure of sadness and sometimes heroic desperation. Nature is without pity, but perhaps these deprived animals have little awareness of their condition, but humans are very aware of their frustration and rejection, and often seek escape from their tormented egos.

Sleep

The need to escape from the self can become very pressing; there is a longing for peace—for 'peace of mind'. Sleep is the most obvious means of escape. Most animals sleep much of their time but Homo sapiens are awake usually for some sixteen hours a day and are easily bored. Many other animals such as cats have short spells of enormous natural curiosity, but for most of the time they sleep deeply and peacefully. It is almost unimaginable for a cat, dog or other such animal to suffer from insomnia, while Homo sapiens has many wakeful hours to engage that busy, urgent brain which often cannot easily be stilled in restful sleep.

Soothing Touch and Movement

Quite apart from sleep most humans have a great need to relax body and mind and seek ways of achieving this. On the simplest physical level the human animal like the other apes enjoys being groomed—'being pampered'. Massage, hairdressing, and other such services answer this need in modern circumstances. Gentle touch soothes infants, young children and pet animals. The rhythmic movement of cradles, rocking chairs and swings may evoke subconscious memories of being gently rocked within the womb as a foetus, carried by the mother animal as an infant, or even wake an evolutionary memory of swaying in tree branches as a pre-human ape.

Brain Wave Patterns

Certain kinds of electrical activity in the brain are associated with certain states of mind. An escape from the self may be experienced in hypnosis where mental focus with muscle relaxation affects brain action. Other trance-like states, meditation, a medium's sense of possession, and sleep seem to be similar. Mantras (the repetition of a meaningless sound) switch off restless consciousness into meditation and trance. Heightened states of artistic or spiritual inspiration may correlate with particular brain wave patterns.

Brain Chemistry

Brain chemistry also alters consciousness. Fever, fasting, frantic dancing, even some kinds of pain can release endorphins which are experienced as states of ecstasy. To some extent other natural hormones can have a similar effect. Love, tantric sex, fear, anger and other emotional states stir up hormones that act like drugs in the body and can release the self from cerebral control. Shakespeare writes of the 'madman, lover and poet,' similarly experiencing special psychological states. The personality is gripped by other forces and acts almost like an automaton, perhaps directed by the same powerful energies that drove Homo erectus and later the Cro-Magnons.

Where the individual cannot find release, especially from a particularly troubled, frustrated or stressed self, it may learn how to do this artificially and find release in chemically altered states of mind.

Merging into the Group

The need for a pack or herd to act unanimously in times of danger or other excitement programmes Homo sapiens to lose their sense of individuality. If that group 'mind' becomes mindless, as easily happens, terrible violence can result. It is the rampage of the hooligan, the suicidal charge of warriors, the genocidal attack of conquerors, the pack in full cry after prey, the 'tally-ho' of the hunt, human army charges, religious mania, football fans in full cry. Tennyson's 'Charge of the Light Brigade' imagines the cavalrymen's state of mind as they make their suicidal charge. They have lost all autonomy, and without question know they have to 'do or die'—and die they did. Certain drugs in addition dangerously lower the threshold of the group's reason and control. Assassins were originally known as 'hashish eaters'. The female Bacchantes of the ancient world rampaged in a drunken orgy of violence, tearing animals to pieces in their frenzy.

Pop or rock concerts arouse enormous group excitement because of audience participation. The individual soccer fan would be embarrassed to sing alone, but during a match he will happily participate in the song of the football terraces, mysteriously coordinating voice and movements with hundreds of others, to become 'one voice' roaring and singing for an hour and more. This state seems to be enhanced by the bodily movement of holding up the arms, shutting the eyes and swaying in a state of self-surrender, as if reaching upwards to some source of inspiration, like a small child asking to be picked up by a sympathetic adult. Music can inspire an ecstasy of self-forgetfulness. In a secular world, self-surrender at concerts and sports events is almost a replacement for religious ecstasy. In

253

former times mass religious observance would have accessed special areas of psyche, under the influence of shamans and priests. There are still congregations that surrender themselves to spiritual experience. Being part of a group experiencing the same excitation seems to free the spirit from the physical self into an ocean of euphoria. This experience is unforgettable, and for those that experience it, something transforming and transcendent.

The Life of the Spirit
Other Animals

Other animals live for their allotted time and simply feed, sleep and breed. As far as can be ascertained these animals do not suffer existential pain or angst. They cannot envisage their own deaths, and have no sense that their lives should have meaning beyond personal survival and the production of offspring. Homo sapiens, however, usually search for some special purpose for their lives — the product of their own purposeful mind-sets, and awareness of cause and effect.

The Emotional Need for Religious Experience

A sense of supernatural presence seems part of Homo sapiens' fundamental nature. The ability to think symbolically soon peopled the world with supernatural spirits, and developed ways of communicating with them. Spirituality may have given essential reassurance and helped survival when Homo sapiens knew itself to be a vulnerable animal. Social cohesion would have been enhanced by religious practices and ceremonies. The spirits could be reached, pleased or placated by special rituals. Being aware of its powerlessness, the animal perhaps needed to imagine some power or powers that ordered its environment and sanctioned its spiritual and secular leaders. One of the most common and fulfilling religious experiences is thanksgiving. Even chimpanzees have been known to celebrate the coming of rain with dance-like movements. Any link with creative or moral power or any thoughts of life after death develop later, probably as a by-product of the animal's special awareness of death, the mechanism of cause and effect and its own sense of justice. What never seems completely to die in human society is spiritual longing. God will not go away.

For many modern secularized individuals all that remains of religion are the figures of speech inherited from the ages of faith like 'hello' (be hallowed or blessed) and 'goodbye' (God be with you), 'Thank God', 'God bless you', 'My God!', 'God help me!' 'Christ' 'Jesus' etc. However, at times of great crisis almost inevitably the wounded soul seeks the godhead—whatever that is perceived to be. At times of terrible stress even the unbeliever is often driven to look for religious help and comfort and a stricken population often turns to its priest and place of worship because there is no other way to deal with the trauma. After the mass shooting of small children in Dunblane, Scotland, or the murder of two schoolgirls in Soham, England, the communities turned to their churches for solace and commemoration. It has been said there are no atheists in battlefield 'foxholes'. Even in a world of unbelief the religious need is still often felt and expressed. The need is undeniable though the answering reality may be denied.

Wild man's religious feelings are difficult to imagine. Somehow Homo sapiens had to relate to these supernatural powers and keep them friendly. Often like lower status individuals attempting to ingratiate themselves with individuals of higher status, they would offer presents and submission. Quite early on there seems to have been a sense that these powers liked blood and death as presents or offerings. The powers may have seemed like hungry predators to whom a victim must be offered to make them well-disposed towards humans, show them favour or at least allow them to survive.

Relating to the Gods—Sacrifice

Making an offering in exchange for a benefit, expresses a deeply felt intuition of natural justice. It may be seen as a way of repaying the gods for good fortune, a successful hunt, a fertile environment, and general well-being; it may be a way of propitiating the gods for mistakes or misdemeanours. An offering or even a sacrifice is almost a kind of business transaction as if making 'a deal' with the gods. Blood is always highly significant; representing 'life'; the sacrificial victim literally offers its life's blood. Animal sacrifices were common in many religions. The animal might have a special value as a rarity such as a spotless lamb or a white bull. The animal might represent the human community, or a group might select a captive, a slave or even one of themselves as the sacrificial victim.

The Aztecs and other cultures certainly used human sacrifice. Abraham felt he had to sacrifice his son Isaac, but once he had made the commitment, his god relented. Ceremonies and sacrifices with symbols, vestments, firelight, rhythmic movement and music, usually led by a particularly charismatic individual, would synchronize and pattern the group emotion and make the religious experience extremely powerful. The deities might then be persuaded to turn their anger elsewhere, or even show some benevolence.

The Development of Worship

As agriculture developed, the fertility of the land became crucial. Organised religion began to develop with set places of worship and special people to lead the devotions. Even today the weather is extremely important; early man was much more vulnerable.

The seasons, the solstices and equinoxes were of immense significance.

The Symbolism of the Seasons

In its original tropical habitat Homo sapiens would have experienced seasonal changes such as a rainy season rather than summer and winter, but as the human family spread into the northern and southern hemispheres and across the whole planet, the seasons had a different significance. At some point the human imagination interpreted the cycle of the seasons as a metaphor for the rhythms of human life— flower, harvest, death, and re-growth. Trees and plants seem to die back into the earth during the winter where their life is held there safely until the return of warmth and light. The spring and summer seem to recall life back from the earth into leaves and blossoms. A few evergreen trees—in England the holly, ivy, yew, pine and semen-berried mistletoe—were especially significant as promising renewed life. The Green Man is the folkloric personification of the green life of plants. The fairies, such as Oberon and Titania in Shakespeare's *A Midsummer Night's Dream,* personify the mysterious influences that controlled the English natural world. The Greeks and Romans had myths of Hades or Pluto (God of the Underworld), Demeter or Ceres (the mother-goddess of the Earth), Persephone or Proserpine (her daughter, who must live in the underworld for half the year) to explain the changing seasons. The natural world dies in the autumn, the Earth mourns through the winter, and in the spring there is rebirth and new life.

Mortality-- The Greatest Mystery

A unique feature of human mental life is the awareness of individual mortality, surely a side effect of the sense of self. Other animals certainly register fear and pain, but apparently have no awareness that they personally will die. In the words of W.B. Yeats:

> Nor dread nor hope attend
> A dying animal;
> A man awaits his end
> Dreading and hoping all;
> ...
> Man has created death.

W. B. Yeats, 'Death' 1-4, 12.

This puts man's sense of life into a completely different context from that of any other creature. An animal relaxing in the sun with a full belly enjoys the moment without any sense that this will inevitably change. They have no sense that they may be injured or will age and certainly die. The fox fleeing from hounds has an instinct to run and no doubt experiences panic, but beyond that has no anticipation of the pain and death ahead. Humans, on the other hand, are hardly ever able to forget that life is fleeting, and that they and their loved ones will inevitably age and die. It is difficult to face this reality and each individual is tempted to think they are immortal, but there are regular reminders to the contrary as they move through their lives, 'To be or not to be, That is the question....' --the ultimate question, expressed with ultimate succinctness.

Common to primitive and modern man is a need to reverence the dead and beyond that often to imagine their continuing existence in another non-material existence. Elephants seem to mourn their dead, but most other animals seem to accept loss without the same anguish. Since at least the time of the Neanderthals, perhaps more than a hundred thousand years, some hominids have ritualised the disposal of their dead with flowers, with unremembered and unrecorded ceremonies. Humans have an intense awareness that the life force has gone while the body remains inert and decomposing. It was soon understood that the corpse was a threat to health. Out of respect for the once living person, human societies have found various ceremonial ways of disposing of dead bodies. No other animal has this instinct, which may be a by-product of the awareness of the uniqueness of identity, empathy for the deceased, and a consciousness of personal mortality. There is often a need to close the unseeing eyes and cover the face as if confronting death is too disturbing. It is a recognition that the dead have gone beyond meaningful eye-contact and communication. Memory, a sense of passing time, and the awareness that the dead have gone for ever make for the ultimate mystery. Man's power to project from the present to the future, from the death of others to the death of self confronts it with the inevitability of its own end.

Imagination and memory can conjure up the dead, as if they still exist. Millennia before there was any understanding of genetics, Homo sapiens had an intuition that ancestors and descendants participate in each other's immortality. It is as if the genes become conscious, and express themselves in memory and anticipation of future lives. Ancestor worship is a common way of expressing this awareness. The dead are often thought to have supernatural powers and an ability to intervene in mortal affairs. Sometimes the dead are feared, especially if they are known to have been 'unquiet spirits'. This awareness of death may be the root of man's religious sense.

Spiritual Awareness
Beyond the awareness of death, there is often a sense of the numinous, and experiences of mystery, which can seem like a blending of the self with a universal life force. There is no way of knowing if this is an experience shared by other creatures. Before man had machines, the natural world must have seemed full of strange forces and presences—nymphs, tree spirits, an

aura of the numinous in the woods or on the hills, other dimensions of being such as angels, seraphim and cherubim, demons, goblins, and so on—some benign, some malicious and many indifferent. Even now, a spiritual presence or presences can be strongly intuited by sensitive individuals in certain locations.

Joy

Very significant are fleeting states of joy which impinge on many individuals and seem to be intimations of a benign spirit and a higher state of being. Hopkins' poetic language captures this overwhelming exhilaration as he watches a windhover (or kestrel) in flight:

> I caught this morning morning's minion, kingdom
> of daylight's dauphin, dapple-dawn-drawn Falcon, in his riding
> Of the rolling level underneath him steady air, and striding
> High there, how he rung upon the rein of a wimpling wing
> In his ecstasy !
>
> Gerard Manley Hopkins ,'The Windhover', 1-5

Or the poet's joy in spring:

> Nothing is as beautiful as Spring--
>
> ...
>
> What is all this juice and all this joy?
> A strain of the earth's sweet being in the beginning
> In Eden garden–
>
> Gerard Manley Hopkins, 'Spring', 1, 9-11

It can be just one of those heart-stopping moments described in
Edward Thomas' poem 'Adelstrop':

> All I saw was Adelstrop only the name.
> And willow, willow herb, and grass...

The influential philosophy of Plato supposes a pre-existence
where the human spirit is part of another dimension from where
it derives its knowledge of the Ideal. In mortal life there is an
ever unfulfilled longing to return to the Ideal state where the
spirit can transcend its animal nature. Wordsworth describes his
experience as a child when he felt a spiritual joy in nature. These
intuitions faded as he matured, though as an adult he could still
be 'Surprised by joy...'

> ... trailing clouds of glory do we come
> From God, who is our home:
> Heaven lies about us in our infancy!
> Shades of the prison–house begin to close
> Upon the growing Boy
> But He beholds the light, and whence it flows,
> He sees it in his joy...
>
> Wordsworth, *Ode: Intimations of*
> *Immortality*, lines 64-70

Browning writes of 'infinite moments', when he experiences
fleeting states of spiritual promise and awakening. Such
occasional touches stimulate a tantalizing hope and affirm the
spiritual context of human existence. For Browning such
moments were often associated with his marital relationship.
However, his poem, 'Cleon' contemplates the frustration of a
hugely successful Greek polymath who has spiritual intimations
but cannot connect with their source:

> ...there's a world of capability
> For joy, spread round about us, meant for us,
> Inviting us; and still the soul craves all,
> ...
> We struggle—fain to enlarge
> Our bounded physical recipiency,
> Increase our power, supply fresh oil to life,
> Repair the waste of age and sickness. No,
> It skills not: life's inadequate to joy,
> As the soul sees joy, tempting life to take.
>
> Robert Browning, 'Cleon' 239-250

Schiller's *Ode to Joy* so impressed Beethoven that he set part of it to music in the last movement of his ninth symphony:

Freude, schöner Götterfunken,	Joy, beautiful spark of the divine
Tochter aus Elysium,	Daughter of Elysium,
Wir betreten feuertrunken	Inspired by your fire we tread
Himmlische, dein Heiligtum !	Your holy of holies.
Deine Zauber binden wieder,	Your magic binds together
Was die Mode streng geteilt;	What custom has divided
Alle Menschen werden Brüder,	All mankind are brothers
Wo dein sanfter Flügel weilt.	Under thy gentle wings.

...

Schiller celebrates the brotherhood of man, friendship, marital love, and experience of joy by all creatures, worthy and unworthy. As a result he concludes that beyond the material world there must be a loving father spirit

Brüder! über'm Sternezelt	Brothers! Above the starry firmament
Muss ein lieber Vater wohnen	A loving father must dwell.

These experiences of joy are usually associated with the natural world. The noise, crowds and excitement of the modern city are likely to eclipse this sort of euphoria. With the light pollution in cities, modern man cannot see the stars; shoes, metalled roads and modern transport systems mean it is out of touch with the Earth itself. In the words of Hopkins '…the soil/ Is bare now, nor can foot feel, being shod'. The secular nature of modern society makes individuals less sensitive to spiritual experiences. Could it be that binge drinking is a kind of modern city-dwellers' substitute for 'joy'?

The Habit of Tranquillity

Some religious gatherings are noisy and promote the kind of ecstasy often experienced in certain evangelical Christian services. Some very hectic religious ceremonies may lead to glossolalia or talking with tongues, or physical collapse. At the other end of the continuum the surrender of self depends on quietude. In the modern world it is difficult to cultivate a habit of tranquillity. With so much easy entertainment requiring a minimum attention span, and perhaps generating actual attention deficit disorders in young children, every minute is often filled with noise and activity. A gap in this cacophony is experienced as boredom, but sustained quiet is essential to calm jangled brainwaves. Boredom is an important precursor to enlightenment. Peace is experienced when the individual sets itself apart either in a sanctified place or in the quiet of nature, alone or with a like-minded group meditating on what they perceive as God. There may then be a sense of communication with that entity, and silently or together the group may pray, either spontaneously or following a set liturgy.

Relating to the Gods—Prayer

Prayer is a concentration on the spiritual presence and while there may be petitions, it is the openness to the spiritual influence that is the essence of prayer. Over the centuries, there have been religious communities that have devoted themselves to prayer on behalf of the wider community. Some individuals develop special mystical powers, though some visionary states have been diagnosed as perhaps some disturbance of the temporal lobe. The neurotheology of Ellen White, the founder of the Seventh Day Adventists in the early nineteenth century, may in fact, have been right temporal lobe epilepsy. This however, does not necessarily invalidate the experience. It could be argued that this may be the way the spirit world communicates with some human subjects.

Spiritual Experience and Expression

Throughout the millennia there have been multiple experiences of the divine. For the mystics there is that sense of joy and oneness with a benign power, and whatever this power may be, it enriches, calms and inspires. This enormously strong spiritual impulse has over the millennia inspired the greatest architecture, painting, music, and poetry. As soon as architecture was sufficiently developed, Homo sapiens put its greatest efforts into constructing astonishing religious monuments such as Stonehenge rather than into more practical edifices. The instinct prompted huge, exquisite buildings at a time when the ordinary people lived in hovels.

What act of faith prompted the populace to look at an empty field and set about building Salisbury Cathedral? Could it indeed be 'something' external to Homo sapiens, reaching into the material world through the mind of man or is it just a projection from that mind? The greatest European art for centuries depicted the nativity, crucifixion, resurrection or other Christian stories. Handel wept with emotion as he composed *Messiah*, and centuries of faith have inspired transcendent settings of the Christian liturgy. Can all this inspiration simply be wishful thinking? Were some of the greatest geniuses simply seduced by a dream?

The hierarchy and tradition of the established religions are likely to limit and contain extremism. While this can be stifling and restrictive, at their best the established religions accommodate and focus the human intuition for the numinous in traditional formats, backed by centuries of deep thought and spiritual exercises. They can be supremely uplifting, using the great poetic language of the scriptures, often combined with the most inspired music, perhaps performed in buildings that bring together the highest human achievements in architecture and art, and so these apes express their spiritual intuition and 'sing their souls'.

The End Time

Embedded in the muddle and pressures of passing lives, there are prophetic visions of an 'end time' when pain and suffering will cease. Isaiah envisages the suspension of the 'survival of the fittest' mechanism. As a man of his time he would have known animal slaughter and predation as an inescapable part of life. His vision imagines a time when such killing will come to an end. 'They shall not hurt...' neither carnivores like the wolf, leopard, lion, and bear, nor the reptiles and insects that bite and sting. There will be no more killing of prey and eating of flesh, with all the pain and fear this entails. All creatures will live in trust and harmony:

> The wolf also dwell with the lamb, and the leopard shall lie down with the kid: and the calf and the young lion and the fatling together; and a little child shall lead them. And the cow and bear shall feed; their young ones shall lie down together; and the lion shall eat straw like the ox. And the sucking child shall play on the hole of the asp, and the weaned child shall put his hand on the cockatrice' den. They shall not hurt nor destroy in all my holy mountain...

> *Isaiah* 11,6-9.

This is not heaven, but earthly life transformed, envisaged by human sapientia at its most inspired, the ideal towards which earthly life aspires—though biologically unachievable.

Cycles of Faith

There are cycles of faith when the religious impulse becomes dull and distant, and is followed by a renewal of fervour, often in response to a charismatic and inspired individual like Isaiah, Buddha, Jesus, Mohammed, and reformers like Martin Luther or even John Wesley. Unfortunately, there are many 'false prophets' and many gullible seekers for the 'Truth'. The result may be rise of a cult leader like David Koresh or other such cult leader. The established world religions are now likely to be more temperate, cerebral and stable than cults and exciting new revelations. At the beginning of this new millennium, faith is challenged as never before by secularism; science is gradually reducing mystery by research and reason. This must be welcomed. A flight into fundamentalism offers no ultimate reassurance and is likely to lead to terrible conflict. The new age of reason seems to be more than a phase in the cycles of faith so that the life of the spirit has to adapt to this new context.

Religion and Reason

Cause and Effect

The awareness that to achieve a desired effect, a particular cause must be applied has given the human animal an extraordinary control over the forces of nature. This ape can act purposefully. It can envisage a result and perform whatever action is necessary to achieve it. In this it is uses its sapientia—its forward-looking imagination, and its constant urge for improvement.

Other animals can be conditioned to associate one event with another like Pavlov's dogs. David Hume showed the human mind is programmed to think in patterns of cause and effect. This allows it to forecast the consequences of an action. For Homo sapiens the connection between the two events is consciously felt to have an inevitability, the first event 'causing' the second. This is more than a conditioned reflex as the causal connection can be made after one occurrence rather than reinforced by repetition. Repetition serves to test the intuited connection.

Cause and effect is so familiar a mental construct to modern man that it is almost impossible to envisage a mind-set where events follow randomly through time, each day a muddle of occurrences just happening by chance. Many other animals must experience life in this way. For man, cause and effect is so positive that if something happens without an apparent cause it becomes a miracle or a mystery.

The First Cause

As Homo sapiens can act purposefully, it understands itself as an 'effect' of some 'cause', or creative power which has acted purposefully in an act of creation—'a divine watchmaker', 'a first cause'. Every human culture has some sort of creation myth. Such a huge effect as creation must have an unimaginably powerful cause. The movements of the sun, the moon, the stars and the earth must also be caused by some great power or powers. For the whole of mankind's existence, the heavens have been enormously significant. For millennia the sun, moon and stars were the only sources of light, and then latterly only firelight, or the feeble lights of oil lamps, rush lights, tapers, or candles. Unexpected events like a lightning strike or an eclipse must have been terrifying. An animal with an awareness of cause and effect and of purpose, set in an environment so full of strange happenings, must try to explain and understand its place in nature. The easiest explanation is, that just as man can 'cause' an effect, there must be some vast power or supernatural being or beings, 'causing' world events and natural happenings, and having power over all creatures, including man. Someone or something must have the power to bring about abundance; something or someone must be the cause of drought, flood or pestilence.

What 'immortal hand or eye' could 'frame' tigers, lambs and other creatures so surely? Why does the viscous transparent and yellow liquid in an egg turn into a perfectly formed chick in about three weeks? Why does an apple develop from a flower bud? Is there a power that masterminds the life-path of each human creature from cradle to grave? Modern science explains the workings of genetics, but that does not necessarily make an ultimate creative force redundant; that force, whatever it is, has to work in the physical world. The ultimate questions still remain unanswered: why there is 'something' instead of 'nothing' and why are we here?

Faulty Causal Connections

Before the development of rigorous scientific methods, causes were all too easily linked to effects without sufficient proof. Tradition or ignorance mistakenly suggested a particular cause would have a desired effect. Alchemists, healers and magicians through the ages linked certain substances or actions with effects that were in fact quite arbitrary. This gave enormous power to superstitions and magic. It also allowed deliberate or unintentional hoaxes. However erroneous the connections, they confirm the human mind's extraordinary impulse to impose a causal link on its experience.

Even in modern times there are huge sales of useless diets, beauty treatments, and health products. Newspapers and magazines often have columns telling fortunes by the stars and stage magicians really have special abilities, or do they achieve their miraculous feats by some ingenious, rational means? The fascination for the audience is just this question. If modern, scientific man can be so deceived, how much more powerful must magic have been in pre-scientific times?

Scientific Truth (a posteriori) and Spiritual Truth (a priori)

Over the last four hundred years, only a fragment of the time Homo sapiens has existed, science has developed a whole new framework of expertise and understanding. This discipline requires demonstrated and repeatable causal connections. This has brought immense practical benefits and material prosperity so that Homo sapiens has escaped from the stark conditions of its animal existence. Science has exposed many old beliefs as superstitions, and gradually loosened the power of meaningless and sometimes cruel rituals. These are great benefits, and science continues to answer questions that have previously been given religious explanations, often embedded in scripture. The result has been a huge loss of confidence in religion.

Secularism

There have always been sceptics. They are often justified in seeing religion as an evil influence. The scriptures can be the source of inspiration and wisdom, but when they give rise to dogma and fundamentalism they are positively dangerous. 'Faith I live by; dogma I kill for'. At its best religion can give a vision to earthly life and underwrite a virtuous morality. Without religion, any view of life is foreshortened to the here and now, while morality is manmade.

The Pursuit of Happiness

Increasingly the pursuit of happiness, in Western society at least, is considered the aim of mortal life as there is no belief in heaven or even life after death. The pursuit of happiness includes animal comforts, psychological satisfaction and emotional peace. Increasingly western life delivers animal comforts. Anxieties about famine, predation, and general insecurity have been largely removed. However, many modern societies are still often unhappy and discontented, and fail to deliver psychological satisfaction. Homo sapiens' imagination makes contentment difficult and happiness elusive. The hopeful sapientia of the human spirit looks towards improvement, perhaps with materialistic dreams of winning a fortune and enjoying limitless indulgence. Quite apart from individual discontents, there are more general anxieties about pandemics, nuclear war or climate change. It is as if there is a kind of 'worrystat' which keeps many Homo sapiens permanently anxious and beset by existential worries so that there is little emotional peace. Happiness is unachievable for many, and even fortune and indulgence often do not bring happiness.

Different temperaments deal with such anxieties and disappointments in different ways, but one of the greatest sources of consolation is by definition unavailable to non-believers. Some societies passively accept life as it is but such acceptance is a practised state of mind, usually derived from eastern religious philosophies. Whether from tradition or some innate psychological need, there is a suspicion that the aim of human life is something more than simple happiness. It does not follow however, that happiness should be negated, or that false spiritual hopes be used as 'the opium of the people'. Material contentment and open-minded spiritual sensitivity are surely complementary.

The disciplined scientific mind-set has perhaps closed off access to other forms of truth. Throughout human history and pre-history some of humanity's most powerful insights and wisdom have come from special intuitions and spiritual awareness. Because it is difficult to distinguish 'a priori truth' from superstition and misapprehension, there is a tendency simply to discount any knowledge that cannot be scientifically proved. Attempts have been made through the centuries to prove the existence of God, and because these have failed it does not follow that all religious insights are mistaken. Modern man cannot retreat from proven scientific fact; on the other hand, science itself has limitations. Because science has explained so much, it does not follow that it can explain everything. For instance the human mind has qualities that defy easy scientific analysis.

Mysterious Powers of the Mind

The power of suggestion may indeed produce a quasi-magical effect. Luck, morale, being 'in form', curses, faith healing, mediumship, intuition, the 'eureka' experience, the effect of placebos,—are all aspects of hardly understood operation of subconscious mental energies. Causes can be suggested. Placebos seem to be a matter of auto-suggestion. Inconsequential shifts in fortune seem to have a pattern, a balance between hubris and nemesis, or the turns of the 'wheel of fortune'. Luck may be an ability to control negative moods and soften negative events, and then make the best of opportunities with foresight and determination. Morale and being 'in form' are probably related to confidence, and the response to a leader's charisma, and there is obviously also a physical aspect. Being cursed can be an acute awareness of another's disapproval and ill will, while kindly attention has the effect of blessing. Faith healing may be a hopeful response to a healer's personality and own self-belief. Intuition seems to be an opening of the mind to non-cerebral awareness. These explanations attempt to impose cause and effect on human mental events but such simple analyses are not altogether convincing.

Special States of Consciousness

Creative thought often depends on a 'eureka' experience. A solution to a problem or project can produce 'a state of flow', which is experienced as a pleasurable self-forgetfulness. The process of artistic creation has often been described as a kind of trance-like state in which the conscious self is suspended and inspiration seems to come from some unknowable depth of the psyche. Some theories of poetry consider the poet as a vates or seer who is in touch with some transcendent power. The ancients depicted this experience of 'artistic flow' as possession by the Muses. The operation of the subconscious, like spiritual awareness, is beyond intellectual analysis.

Morality

Homo sapiens' moral sense is similarly mysterious. These apes have rich social lives, and their interactions are programmed by strong moral drives. Causation has a moral concomitant; conduct has consequences. A particular behaviour will be rewarded or punished by the response of the group or perhaps by natural results for example, excessive indulgence will lead to sickness. The moral imperative becomes, on the one hand, a code of law, and on the other an internalised moral sense or conscience. It is recognised that kindness, generosity, and moral guidance make life more tolerable for man and most other forms of life. Beyond any rational calculation, deeply embedded in the human psyche is the sense of natural justice.

Most human beings will agree on a general set of moral values at the root of which is a sense of justice. The origin of this very powerful intuition may be biological or a genuine spiritual quality (however that is interpreted), perhaps both. In most societies morality will have begun as a religious ideal. The further development of generosity and empathy has been importantly rooted in the creeds of Christianity and other religions. Most faiths have their own ways of endorsing the spiritual life, establishing compassion, empathy and truth as the ideal, whether it is considered an aspect of a god or rather a spiritual quality arising from within man itself.

The Imagery of Good versus Evil
Spiritual insights have usually been expressed in myth and metaphor, and consolidated in sacred texts and scriptures.

The very words Go(o)d and the (D)evil in the English language seem to suggest 'good' and 'evil'. It is strange that 'Santa' and 'Satan' are almost the same word, with almost opposite meanings. Temptation seems to be like the voice of an evil spirit. Satan is depicted as a speaking serpent able to beguile Eve. In Hebrew folklore Satan is the leader of a group of rebellious angels, Belial, Moloch, Mammon, Beëlzebub—The Lord of the Flies, and so on.

Man's 'original sin' is not so much an action, but his animal nature, 'the devil'. At Christian baptism, the child 'dies' to the old Adam and is washed free from the hold of its animal self:

> ... 'grant that the old Adam in this child may be so buried, that the new man may be raised up in him...sanctify this water to the mystical washing away of sin...grant that this child...may receive the fullness of thy grace..'
>
> *The Book of Common Prayer*

273

The newly baptized ape is thought of as a new animal with special spiritual resources, or grace. These spiritual resources battle with man's animal nature. The prize is goodwill, empathy and at best, agape, the expression of the loving spirit felt by many to be at the heart of creation, and seeded in mankind.

The Christian Image of the Devil

In the imagination of the ages evil characters have been thought of being in league with supernatural forces, the devil, or other personifications of evil. Christianity probably took its image of the devil from the deities the early Christian missionaries discredited. Pan—the god of nature, the fauns, satyrs, and centaurs are half human and half animal; though in their myths are mischievous rather than fiendish. The Devil, like Pan, is human to the waist, but his head has animal horns that go with his goat-like hind quarters, cloven hooves, and tail. Sometimes his animal brown eyes are deepened to blood red. Man is a creature with high cerebral capacities grafted on to a basic animal nature. The Devil is the personification of this animal nature. The genitals, lower digestive system, and the organs felt to generate and register primitive emotions are in the lower part of the body, together with orifices associated with waste, contamination and carnality. The Devil's goat-like hindquarters are enough to suggest an undercurrent of animal instinct driving and corrupting a subtle and intelligent mind. King Lear angrily denounces his cruel daughters as half human and half animal:

'

> Down from the waist they are Centaurs,
>
> Though women all above:
>
> But to the girdle do the gods inherit,
>
> Beneath is all the fiends':
>
> There's hell, there's darkness, there's the sulphurous pit...
>
> Shakespeare, *King Lear*, IV, vi, 127-131.

Lord of the Flies is the title of William Golding's novel which describes the descent of angelic English choirboys into animal savagery. As a teacher, Golding had observed children and knew the cruelty of their animal natures when unrestrained by social pressures. The children's animal nature—the devil, Beëlzebub— escapes and is only caged again when the children are once again under adult control.

Principles and Practicalities

A lamb cannot deter a tiger; a seal cannot confront a killer whale. Bullying gang leaders, psychopathic dictators and all those that exploit others, nourish hate and use violence are driven like animals to become the 'fittest' and survive at the expense of others. To act violently and destructively is exciting and gives primitive pleasure and satisfaction. This is likely to make bullies all the more ruthless and powerful. It is easy to arouse the animal instincts which prompt the group to rid itself of the weak, or scapegoat the 'different'. In addition, there is hierarchical satisfaction in having power over others who are forced to submit. This particularly appeals to bullies. The tyrant becomes the pack leader, his very ruthlessness itself attracting loyalty and encouraging attacks on the weak and vulnerable, and anyone who questions such cruelties.

Over the millennia prophets and saints have called their communities to live according to the law of God as they have perceived it and clashed with their society's accepted cruelties and prejudices. Their moral values often meant challenging political or royal power. This was frequently very costly, provoking cruel persecution for them and their followers.

Prevention

Of course it is better to prevent a cruel leader gaining the ascendancy in the first place. Once the tyrant has power, it may take years to reclaim it with terrible suffering for many individuals. To prevent such abuse, injustice or any other cause for unrest that might give the deviant a chance to stir up discontent to gain power, has to be resolved. It has to be recognised that whatever the power of the humane ideal, rationalization of baser motives is all too plausible. A healthy society has mechanisms to identify the harmful deviant and put pressure on them either to reform, or to deter and intimidate them before it is too late. All this depends on the majority having a coordinated sense of their social mores. If keeping the moral foundations strong is felt to be important, there needs to be a core of dedicated, thoughtful, individuals who do the soul-searching for the community. This is often a church or priesthood, or a secular equivalent such independently minded journalists, lawyers, writers and scholars. These figures need to be accorded status by the rest of the group if they are to lead them successfully, but it is important that power is diffused rather than concentrated. The human need for pageantry needs to be separated from power, otherwise the combination can lead to an acceptance of power with divine or quasi-divine authority. A free press, an uncorrupted legal system, fair and open education, a state figurehead without power, and control of the executive by the populace are the essentials that prevent tyranny.

Confrontation

However unpalatable it is, human beings confronting extreme and embedded brutality sometimes have to adopt brutal strategies themselves, though this has to be recognized as a failure and a falling away from the ideal. It is impossible to stop a land-hungry psychopath, or a bullying gang leader by reason or generosity of spirit, as many saints and martyrs have discovered down the centuries.

Ghandi, and Martin Luther King challenged colonialism and discrimination with passive resistance, but the oppositions they confronted were at least to some extent principled. To confront Genghis Khan with passive resistance might have been very different. How would Jesus have confronted Hitler or Saddam Hussein? He would presumably have been horribly executed again, as indeed many of his Christian followers have been. However, the story does not end there.

Such martyrdom is not necessarily in vain. The victims encourage the others by their moral strength, and furthermore they illustrate the depravity of the man in power and make injustice visible. This may, in turn, eventually rouse intervention, either from within or from outside the society, and unfortunately such intervention may have to be violent. With modern communications the world community becomes quickly aware of atrocities, and for the most part closes ranks against the perpetrators. The lesson of history is that somewhere and somehow the higher human spirit will re-emerge. 'Hope' escapes from Pandora's Box; the great Christian virtues are Faith, Hope and Charity, and these are echoed in the other great religions. Auschwitz was liberated; Apartheid came to an end; the Iron Curtain crumbled. This is the perennial 'resurrection'.

Divine Justice and Human Society
On the mortal plane, justice has to be dispensed by an authority, self-appointed or appointed by the group; beyond mortal existence, divine justice is intuited as monitoring and guiding human behaviour through the voice of conscience. The divine all-seeing eye is imagined to record all the hidden sins and

deceits, undetectable by other humans. This gives religious endorsement to the principles that are good for social cohesion.

In some modern societies the morality is becoming almost completely secular, and it is possible to promote morality in a secular context. Perhaps this has been the ultimate purpose of religion, to seed and enhance Homo sapiens' special spiritual qualities whether or not there is any external power at work. However, there is always a danger that without some religious authority, natural law —'survival of the fittest'—becomes as valid as any other.

The Benign Spirit

For the developed religions the creative power felt to be at the heart of existence is intuited to be moral. This then implies that the divine power must itself be not only just, but benevolent. Justice aims to promote social well-being, well-being depends on good relationships, and these depend on trust, forbearance, and understanding. Therefore a life lived with generosity and compassion meets with divine approval. This is the great insight of Judaism. While other civilizations were worshipping gods of thunder, goddesses of sexual indulgence, or quarrelsome and cruel gods of nature, the Hebrews experienced their one god as a protective, loving spirit, and nearly 3,000 years ago sang, 'The Lord is my shepherd, I shall not want...' Such a hopeful vision has to be taken on trust. Nevertheless, the psalmist, and many poets, philosophers, and creative thinkers in most cultures have expressed an abiding faith in the unseen.

The Habit of Accountability

The great religious leaders teach a habit of accountability, and an openness of mind that accepts and can reflect on moral error. To confess to wrong-doing, the individual has to trust that the confession will be heard by a deity that is loving and forgiving.

Confession is often part of established religious observance. Provision is made for repentance—' We have erred and strayed...', followed by some form of absolution. This counteracts the tendency to protect the ego and deny culpability. It is much more comfortable to take the easier option and remain self-satisfied and unrepentant. A habit of self-awareness and self- criticism is an important part of moral development. In any programme for reform—secular or spiritual—the starting point is always a recognition of what has gone wrong, and the individual's responsibility for this. 'I am X, and I am an alcoholic' for instance, or 'I am violent, I am angry, I am dishonest'. The wrongdoer may make the choice to seek inspiration from the various aids that religions offer, and find positive spiritual strength where he can. It might be the spiritual exercises of the great religions that can bring about change, making alienated individuals feel forgiveness, love and hope from a power beyond the natural. The concept of a loving god, a protective father figure, answers to this anxiety. Of course this may be a projection from the human imagination, but this too is real in its own way.

Almost always in developed cultures this god is now confidently felt to be benevolent, and a source of blessing even in times of tragedy. This, in turn, has most importantly encouraged social reforms and Homo sapiens' slow progress towards more just and more generous societies.

Justice and Life after Death
It would be expected that a just god would reward the virtuous. Unfortunately, the reverse often occurs; suffering and misfortune afflict the good and innocent while lying and cheating allows some corrupt individuals to prosper:

> The race is not to the swift, nor the battle to the strong, neither yet
> bread to the wise, nor yet riches to men of understanding, nor yet
> favour to men of skill; but time and chance happeneth to them all.,
>
> *Ecclesiastes* 9 v.11

Homo sapiens tries to understand why its god-given intuition for fairness seems so at odds with the rewards and misfortunes of living.

This incongruity, combined with mystery, mortality and morality, eventually make for some religious ideologies that project a time of reckoning beyond death when the brave and the just will be rewarded, and the wicked and unjust will either cease to exist, will be reincarnated as a lower life form, or will simply be damned. The question then is what happens beyond death—' the bourne from which no traveller returns...'? The rational mind suspects that there may be nothing; however there is a strong intuition that existence continues in some changed state. There might be a Hell or perhaps a Heaven. Heaven might be something like the best place, at the best time, with the best company, or more abstractly, a blissful blaze of white light and joy, an assumption into the life force itself. Near death experiences are generally of this sort, but might simply be explained by failing brain function. To be rewarded by immortality the individual is expected to respond positively to the intuition of a benign creative power, despite all discouragement.

Why So Much Suffering?

However, the concept of a loving power still seems hopelessly at odds with life experience. Where was such a god when his Chosen People suffered the Holocaust? How can so much pain and suffering in the world be explained? The possible answers are discouraging.

Malevolence

God might simply be malevolent. In *King Lear* the tortured Duke of Gloucester similarly remarks ' As flies to wanton boys, are we to the gods—./ They kill us for their sport.' Similarly, Thomas Hardy concludes his tragic novel, *Tess of the d'Urbervilles,* with the comment that 'the President of the Immortals ...had ended his sport with Tess.'

Indifference

It may be that god is indifferent to man. Many religions reflect the capriciousness of experience by projecting this on to populations of uncaring gods and goddesses that behave like childish human beings. It could be that once the natural world has been set in motion, god leaves it to follow its course. It may be that there was no act of creation and any so-called gods have no interest in the Earth or its creatures.

Divine Justice and General Punishment

With the belief that human morality might be a reflection of the divine, it has been suggested that god is morally perfect and like a strict parent punishes his creature for its failures. While some disasters can be the result of human greed or carelessness, the causes of many natural disasters such as earthquakes often have their origins millions of years before the evolution of Homo sapiens. Sinful man is therefore in no way directly responsible for them, but for all that, such disasters might still be used by an omniscient deity as punishment.

Individual Virtue or Sin

If the good are rewarded with success and happiness and the evil automatically made to suffer, morality would be mechanistically reinforced. This is what human justice attempts to do. However, would goodness then be a free choice with all the development of moral strength such a choice demands? How would different individuals, with their different potential for moral behaviour be fitted into such a system? Would it actually be moral at all?

Individual Miracle or General Principle
Cruel accidents seem to occur randomly. Illness, misfortune and tragedy, strike the innocent and the guilty, the wicked and the good. Why does god allow this? God could suspend the laws of nature or send guardian angels to the rescue. In secular fantasies it is Superman who defies gravity and performs miracles. While this might be a relief to the individual, the whole system would become chaotic. A woman suffering from breast cancer might be miraculously cured, but why her and not another woman? Why not all women? Why have breast cancer at all? Why have illness or death?

The Necessity for Natural Disaster
On a cosmic scale, natural disasters may have a purpose beyond human imagining. The earthquakes, volcanic eruptions, and tidal waves have their origins in the very structure of the planet and its moveable crust. These movements recycle the minerals and elements of the Earth; otherwise there would be stagnation, perhaps a flat swamp over the whole surface of the planet where life or non-life would stagnate. As it is the Earth maintains its equilibrium by re-balancing heat with cold, turbulence with calm, and drought with flood. Hurricanes, tornadoes, frosts, heat waves and cloudbursts, assault living things. The system is not kind to individuals but a material world without such 'rough edges' would exert no pressure for survival, so no evolution.

Then matter occasionally rains in from space bringing new material, and perhaps new life-forms. Large impacts can cause extinctions but from these comes new life; if the dinosaurs had not been exterminated, the mammals would never have evolved as they have. Perhaps in time other mass extinctions will open the way for an advance on mammals and Homo sapiens itself, in a way unimaginable to minds confined to the present. Could there be post-mammalian creatures, with a range of senses and mental abilities and perhaps other unimagined capacities that could supersede man and other mammals?

An Unrevealed Ultimate Purpose
The deity may have a guiding principle looking far beyond Homo sapiens, to a time beyond time, that is unimaginable to a mere creature. There is a hopeful prophecy of an eternity of expanding spirituality:

> And God shall wipe away all tears from their eyes; and there
> shall be no more death, neither sorrow nor crying, neither shall
> there be any more pain; for the former things are passed away.
>
> *Revelation* 21, v.4

However, to reach this ideal existence there may have to be unimaginable ages of painful development. Evolution is not possible without selection. The creative force in the natural world, the 'survival of the fittest', entails enormous individual animal suffering, but it has led to the evolution of man and man has become the vehicle for the expression of empathy and agape in nature. Dostoevsky in *The Brothers Karamazov* asks why a loving god would bother to create such a world of pain and suffering at all. Is it worth all the anguish? Could god's purpose have been otherwise achieved? Why any purpose in the first place?

The Struggling Deity
It could be that there is no 'almighty' but rather a benevolent spirit itself struggling with negative natural forces, recruiting man as an ally in its cosmic struggle with evil.

Acceptance of mystery

There is possibly no answer; there simply has to be an acceptance of the randomness of life experience. The book of *Job* explores the reason for suffering and concludes it is impossible to explain.

No Answer

Increasingly secularized cultures simply conclude there is no divine power at all, and all the happenings of the material world are matters of chance, or mechanical effects of nature. There is no meaning in these events, or pattern of any kind. This is extremely difficult for most humans to accept. Whether from tradition or innate psychological need, when positively confronted with an empty universe, even most secular human beings will say they believe in 'something'.

Essential Humanity
The Higher Purpose of Suffering

The answer that is most compatible with a loving god is the realization that observing pain, misfortune, disappointment, separation, and loss usually arouses love, compassion, empathy and even agape in humans. Without pain or suffering, deceit, violence, or murder, floods or droughts, there would be no necessity for kindness or compassion. Without suffering, wisdom, moral strength and spiritual insight would be less likely to develop.

No Suffering, No Challenge

It is an important life-skill to cope with the inevitable disappointments of living, and some families or even cultures do not equip their young with sufficient resilience. Some individuals can tolerate misfortune; others are less accepting. It is natural to try to protect children from misfortune, but they have to be gently prepared for disappointment and even hardship. Struggling with adversity is a human rite of passage

The great prophets foresee a time when there will be no more suffering, the ultimate vision but perhaps not in the dimensions of space and time as we know it. Such a consummation is contrary to human nature however much it is desired. Milton has difficulty in giving interest to the lives Adam and Eve in the Paradise Garden; in fact the myth illustrates humanity's inability to deny its curiosity and ambition— its defining characteristic, its sapientia, the fruit of the Tree of Knowledge. Human nature is not satisfied with unchanging contentment. The prospect of good news for ever is like a story without a villain; a journey with no where to go and there is no need for hope or improvement. Without distress, ill-health, crime or natural catastrophe there would be no danger to challenge the young and no need for the old to impart wisdom. It would be a world of Stepford Wives— a lobotomized planet.

Compassion and Empathy in Response to Suffering

Those that suffer offer an opportunity for compassion and so in a sense suffering is a gift from those that suffer to those that can come to their aid. Beggars in the past were often understood as giving opportunities for charity and the achievement of grace. Without the constant struggle to overcome the trials of mortal existence, there would be no challenge for those that have to endure misfortune or those that seek to help them, and ultimately there would be no need for empathy.

The Challenge of the Victim

Programmed for excitement and the exercise of its cruel animal instincts, Homo sapiens themselves generate plenty of challenges for compassion and empathy, quite apart from accidents of nature. The hungry, naked, disabled, and ill challenge the comfortable. It is all too easy to fail the challenge and respond with denial, sophistry or self-righteousness. The story of the Good Samaritan tells how a victim who 'fell among thieves' challenges the others that travel on the road. They are given a chance to feel empathy and even express agape for the wounded fellow traveller but none of them want to be involved. They simply cross over to the other side of the road, and go on their way. Unexpectedly, a Samaritan—one of a people considered inferior by the Jews—responds with wonderful generosity. The parable shows not only the unexpected goodness of the Samaritan but also the importance of victims on life's road.

What happened to those in the Good Samaritan story that 'passed by'? In worldly terms they saved themselves expense, time and contact with an undesirable stranger, but in terms of humanity they were failures. The Samaritan's response was correspondingly costly but on such behaviour ultimately the survival of humanity depends.

From time to time most human beings are helpless or become victims, and reach out to others for help; the weak and humbled victim may, in turn, be the strong and confident rescuer and vice-versa. 'The Wheel of Fortune' turns; Homo sapiens have enough imagination to know this, and giving help in one circumstance becomes almost a kind of species-specific insurance that help will be given to the helper when it is needed. The very pattern of life illustrates this from the dependency of an infant cared for by parents, to those infants in adulthood caring for ageing parents, even if modern life makes these relationships less personal. Beyond this almost innately calculated reciprocal altruism are feelings of concern, kindliness and fellow feeling. The more compassionate spirits feel empathy. If empathy and agape are the expression of the immanent spirit or in secular terms what is noblest in the heart of man they give meaning to the life of Homo sapiens. Otherwise it seems suffering has no purpose. Morality floats in a vacuum of meaninglessness, and each individual might as well seek its own interests like most other animals. However, this ultimately undermines the special qualities that have allowed Homo sapiens, at its best, to rise above its brutish nature to become humane. The future of mankind and the planet itself may well depend on the humanity of humanity.

Freewill

If it is recognised that goodwill, kindliness and compassion should always be the choice as opposed to suspicion, selfishness and malice, the world would be transformed. The mechanism that controls the choice has to become conscious and practised. There could be training sessions where the options are made explicit, and their effects are projected. With open-eyed awareness, the damage of negative reactions could be compared with the beneficial effects of a positive, controlled response. Of course, in many ways, this is not new, but part of most programmes of socialization. However, the whole system could be de-mystified and anchored to specific psychological and imaginative strategies. Cognitive behavioural therapy or 'talking' therapies can change negative attitudes to more positive ones and so help depression. The same sort of strategy could be applied morally, a whole 'road map' of thought patterns accessed by familiar linguistic routes that promote goodwill and understanding. This, in essence, is the function of prayer, a keying in to a sense of the benign spirit for the strength to choose the kinder, more positive option. This is the point where freewill operates.

Soul—Great and Small

The creative, loving spirit is perhaps extending compassion into creation. This empathetic energy has embedded itself in the only surviving hominid and over the millennia has gradually guided the ape towards becoming itself an expression of the benevolent spirit. In this way the animal world is linked with the spiritual, and the expression of divine compassion and love in man becomes the crown of creation. It may indeed be that this is itself the godhead. The great soul of the universe calls out to its human embodiment, and as the human soul expands it enriches its physical environment, including the other Homo sapiens it encounters. After death, the soul unites with its source; the more developed the human soul, the more it contributes to the universal soul. The human life that has been devoted animal instincts and pleasures, leaves no spiritual 'substance':

> What of soul was left, I wonder, when the kissing had to stop?
> Robert Browning, 'A Toccata of Galuppi's', l.42.

Not Fallen but Rising

Homo sapiens has been described as 'a little lower than the angels'. According to the biblical account the creature was created perfect, but exiled from Paradise for its disobedience. It has therefore been considered a fallen creature. However, it is possible to suggest an alternative view where Homo sapiens is not falling, but rising. It is indeed an animal with the selfishness and aggression needed to survive as an animal, but it also has an 'unanimal' capacity for compassion, empathy and even agape. It is a creature rising above its animal self, never yet perfect but with the growing potential for perfection.

Conclusion

The ideal of human altruism reaching beyond the self, the group, the tribe, the nation, the race, the species to encompass the whole planet together with its wonderfully diverse natural life is slowly growing. There are times when this seems in doubt. It is easy to lose historical perspective and forget the cruelties to which man and beast were routinely subjected even in recent centuries. Human society may become more and more secularized, but the principles of justice, integrity, and altruism have been deeply and permanently embedded. In the words of a famous popular song 'All you need is love'.

Confronting evil, therefore, has to be pragmatic with the great ideal in mind. The ideal is exemplified by the great religious teachers, but most ordinary individuals in ordinary situations have to compromise. They are not all called upon to be martyrs or to live as beggars without worldly goods. It is rather that ordinary followers live as generously and honestly as they can. Nelson Mandela, after twenty six years of imprisonment, promoted reconciliation rather than revenge, once he achieved political power, largely under the influence of Archbishop Tutu. This is an example of how understanding and forgiveness can defuse danger and potential violence, and prevent further cycles of revenge and atrocity. If ever the poisonous effect of such cycles was demonstrated, ironically it is in the Holy Land, where peace was once preached so convincingly by a young Jew.

Quo Vadis ?
A Purpose for the Planet?

Whatever the unborn and dead may know, they cannot know the
beauty, the marvel of being alive in the flesh...

The magnificent here and now of life in the flesh is ours...

I am part of the sun as my eye is part of me...

I am part of the earth my feet know perfectly...

My blood is part of the sea

My soul is an organic part of the great human soul, as my spirit is
part of my nation. There is nothing of me that is alone and absolute
except my mind and we shall find that the mind has no existence by
itself, it is only the glitter of the sun on the surface of the waters.

D.H. Lawrence, *Apocalypse and The Writings on Revelation.*

Earth is of no importance in the vastness of space and time; it is
just a scrap of debris thrown out by apocalyptic cosmic events.
The life it supports is just a freak permutation of elements that
have allowed a cellular flowering that has led to Homo sapiens.
Homo sapiens itself is just a recently evolved mammal destined
become extinct like all other living species. There is no purpose
or intention in anything—just chance and blind fate. In terms of
sheer reason, this is the incontrovertible truth.

An Anthropic Principle?

However, there are other perceptions of truth. Some thinkers
perceive an anthropic principle guiding the Earth to become
hospitable to Homo sapiens. The laws of nature seem to be set
very precisely to allow this animal's evolution. Gravity,
temperature, atmosphere, time-scale and sequence could all have
been different. This marvellous coherence almost suggests the
universe knew that Homo sapiens was coming. Pure generative
power evolves a web of space-time that leads from particles to

people. Not only is the Earth or Gaia, hospitable to man, there is something in man's mind that seeks 'the other'. It is as if there is a spiritual principle finding expression in animal material; a spiritual force which has infiltrated itself into the physical universe to make the moral darkness speak. The aggregate soul of man is like a spiritual 'periscope' peeping out above the sea of animal stuff to envision a 'new heaven and a new earth.' Is this soul stuff perhaps 'god'?

Homo sapiens' Escape from Nature

Homo sapiens is no longer entirely dependent on the chances of the natural world. Predators, diseases, parasites, inclement weather, genetic defects, injuries, and age once kept the human population in balance with its environment, and shaped its development. Homo sapiens is no longer just a link in the food chain, over-breeding to provide a proportion of its numbers as food for predators. The animal's ability to cooperate, feel empathy, and use the concepts of cause and effect purposefully has allowed the weak, old and disabled to survive, and individuals in general to live far beyond their natural span. Faulty genes still cause the least fit to die early of cancers, drug addiction, cystic fibrosis and so on, but even faulty genes may soon be weeded out. Moreover, in the future it may be possible for Homo sapiens to mastermind its own evolution either by cloning or by other as yet unimagined technologies. The need to control such developments with high moral standards hardly needs comment. The control of population is increasingly becoming a huge moral and practical issue.

Gaia's Resistance

Gaia is the home of an inventive creature that has however begun to abuse it. After billions of years of biological interrelationships, the natural world is suddenly at the mercy of one of its creatures. Two hundred years of rampant of capitalism and industrialization has generated huge material stresses and Gaia is beginning to respond with resentment or even fury at its ill-treatment. It is as if Gaia is not an impersonal object but a consciousness with its own sense of justice. Previously it has seemed that man could use the natural world and its resources at will. This generation realises that the environment is not endlessly exploitable, and that man's continued assault could lead to a collapse of the ecosystem:

> ...We, life's pride and cared-for crown,
>
> Have lost that cheer and charm of earth's past prime:
> Our make and making break, are breaking down
> To man's last dust, drain fast towards man's first slime.

> Gerard Manley Hopkins, ' 'The Sea and the Skylark'

There have always been natural extinctions but now man can destroy itself. No other creature since the beginning of time has faced such a possibility. The imagination of ordinary Homo sapiens cannot visualise the catastrophe that might be ahead, but Byron has the poetic imagination to envisage the dead planet:

> The world was void,
> The populous and powerful was a lump,
> Seasonless, herbless, treeless, manless, lifeless,
> A lump of death—chaos of hard clay.
> The rivers, lakes, and ocean all stood still,
> And nothing stirr'd within their silent depths;
> Ships sailorless lay rotting on the sea,
> And their masts fell down piecemeal: as they dropp'd
> They slept on the abyss without a surge—
> The waves were dead; the tides were in their grave,
> The moon, their mistress, had expired before;

The winds were withered in the stagnant air,
And the clouds perish'd; Darkness had no need
Of aid from them—She was the Universe.

Byron, 'Darkness'

Perhaps the Apocalypse or Armageddon will be a handing on such a ruined world to our grandchildren and their grandchildren and succeeding generations. The planet still has billions of years of existence, with or without Homo sapiens and the other creatures that at present share life here. If Homo sapiens become extinct, provided the Earth remains hospitable to some kind of life, there is time for a whole new evolutionary cycle, from amoeba to ape, or whatever conditions dictate. Gaia can survive without man, but man cannot survive without Gaia. In fact the rest of the world would welcome Homo sapiens' extinction.

The Natural World at the Mercy of Man

Homo sapiens shares a planet with a huge range of other wonderful and irreplaceable creatures. Stars have guided wild night-flying birds along certain migration routes for millions of years. Over the last century they have had to fly between the stars and the great wens of disorientating light from Homo sapiens' cities. Loggerhead turtles now struggle among the deckchairs and beach furniture to breed where they have bred for millennia. The ancient tree canopies of the great rain forests are being destroyed and cannot be regenerated if the process goes too far. Aquifers that have taken thousands of years to fill are being drained in decades. Rubbish that takes thousands of years to degrade is buried in landfill sites. The oceans are disturbed by mechanical noise so that whales and dolphins are disorientated, and poisoning, over-fishing, and dredging ruin the marine environment. The albatross is being drowned in thousands on long fishing lines. Like the Ancient Mariner, who on a reckless impulse broke his bond with nature, modern Western man is

293

literally and metaphorically killing its 'albatross'—the beauty
and fecundity of the natural world:

> O if we but knew what we do
> When we delve or hew--
> Hack and rack the growing green!
>
> ...
>
> After-comers cannot guess the beauty been.
>
> Gerard Manley Hopkins, 'Binsey Poplars' 10-12, 20

All over the planet the natural processes attempt to continue in
the face of Homo sapiens' destructive behaviour, but there is no
time for evolution to help them survive. Man is largely
indifferent to this in the face of its own perceived needs for more
space, more water, more economic growth, and more energy.
This is compounded by the projected huge increase in the human
population.

The Fatal Impulse

The very hopefulness that makes man reach for a better life, its
sapientia, spurs on commerce, consumption and materialism to a
dangerous exploitation of the physical environment. Homo
sapiens has an insatiable appetite for comfort and self-
indulgence, and is using fossil fuels, water, land and other
resources recklessly. Democratic freedom, while promoting
justice and equality, also tends to encourage short-term mass
consumption. Electoral popularity does not accord well with
denial and control. As populations and prosperity grow, more
people will claim their share of resources. What was once
rationed by poverty, is made widely available by prosperity, for
example mass travel and increasing migration. Even if
technology can, to some extent, make substitute materials,
resources are likely to be limited. As resources diminish, if man
does not share and reduce its demands, greed and cruelty may

ravage the planet to bring about the destruction of all living things.

For the Indulgence of the Few, All Suffer

Until recently only a small proportion of the world's human population had the power to disrupt and damage the world's natural processes; this potential is rapidly being widely dispersed and the result is unimaginable. There has to be a limit to growth, to economic growth and population growth. It is possible that the rich world has already doomed itself together with the rest of the human population to irrevocable disaster. To be the poor third world and watch helplessly as the self-indulgent first world destroys the planet, must arouse indignation, fear and enormous frustration. The rich, powerful populations are just beginning to be aware of the unfair stresses they impose on the poor and helpless who share the planet. They will suffer the consequences of the first world's destructive activities, having enjoyed none of the benefits. Pacific islands are already sinking beneath the ocean; their populations are in no way responsible for the global warming that is destroying their age-old culture and gentle lifestyle. Like the poor, the planet's other creatures struggle to fulfil their biological functions. Perhaps the present generation would be more circumspect if they personally knew they would be reincarnated in the ruined world of 2100, trapped in their own over-heated mess.

A Resurrected Hope

The Jesuit poet, Gerard Manley Hopkins depicts the satanic forces of Homo sapiens' animal nature damaging and polluting the natural world. However, as the Earth moves into darkness, there is the glimmering of a new dawn. Hopkins imagines the benign spirit of the Holy Ghost 'brooding' the globe of the Earth with a tender warmth, generating fresh, new life.

Generations have trod, have trod, have trod;
And all is seared with trade; bleared, smeared with toil;
And wears man's smudge and shares man's smell: the soil
Is bare now, nor can foot feel, being shod.

And for all this, nature is never spent;
There lives the dearest freshness deep down things;
And though the last lights off the black West went
Oh, morning, at the brown brink eastward, springs—
Because the Holy Ghost over the bent
World broods with warm breast and with ah! Bright wings.

Gerard Manley Hopkins, 'God's Grandeur'

Hopkins as a Christian priest has confidence that there is a benign spiritual power that cares for its creation like a devoted parent, never finally rejecting it, despite its waywardness. Modern secular man has no such certainty, but must generate its own hope and reassurance.

The Childhood of Man

Homo sapiens like other ape species could survive for several million years; so far it has existed less than two hundred thousand. It is a challenge to imagine a million years of human history, and so contextualize the past and present. Are we perhaps just living through the birth-pangs and early childhood of the species? The benign spirit intuited as the creative force may be similarly not so much 'almighty' as 'becoming'.

Hope for the Future

This super ape has foresight, wisdom, and astonishing powers of relationship. It may use its imaginative power to sift the myths of religions and history for a fuller understanding of its nature. Science and technology can contribute vital knowledge and new resources. Above all the spirit of cooperation guided by empathy and agape that is in embedded in every emotionally healthy Homo sapiens, must be nurtured and prized above all other things.

The hope is that prosperity will bring sensitivity, and education and the global media a greater understanding, of the world's interconnectedness. Perhaps material satiety will lead to a spiritual hunger, which, in turn, will encourage contentment with less material indulgence. It may be possible that technological advances will come to the rescue. Material success has to be detached from hierarchical assertion, and the effects of over-indulgence fully recognized. Above all, if Homo sapiens accepts its animal nature and its dangers, more effort can be made to control, switch off or redirect these powerful energies. Conscious techniques can be developed to resist the otherwise unconscious drives that once protected a vulnerable African ape. Language in the form of particular ciphers, prayers, wise sayings or whatever can be practised, and applied at times of individual stress. The dynamics of group situations must similarly be understood, and means found to direct their energies always for the betterment of society. The old territorial and hierarchical squabbles should never be settled by war. No ideology or religion justifies conflicts that ruin millions of lives or worse. The ape that not so long ago roamed the savannah in tribal groups of some 100 individuals, will soon have to relate to 9,000,000,000 of its species. To extend empathy so far is the greatest challenge of its existence.

The Essential Loving Spirit

At its best, Homo sapiens have an amazing capacity for imagination and empathy. It is a creature that has transformed its planet with hopefulness and visions of betterment. Communication, one of its greatest gifts, is now globalized and instantaneous. The great religions teach that there is an all-powerful and all-loving god and this loving power at the heart of the universe expresses itself in an ape on this especially hospitable planet, Gaia or Earth. For many a positive belief in that external power and the special providence of Gaia may have gone, but the hope for humanity still remains a loving spirit.

It is not so much that paradise has been lost because of man's sin, but rather that slowly and painfully, humanity is rising above its animal self to create a first Eden. To accomplish this, it must fulfil a new vision of life on Earth. This vision could be on the brink of fulfilment. The twenty-first century will decide.

> Everyone suddenly burst out singing;
> And I was filled with such delight
> As prisoned birds must find in freedom,
> Winging wildly across the white
> Orchards and dark-green fields; on—on—and
> out of sight.
>
> Everyone's voice was suddenly lifted;
> And beauty came like the setting sun;
> My heart was shaken with tears; and horror
> Drifted away...O, but Everyone
> Was a bird; and the song was wordless; the singing
> will never be done.
>
> Siegfried Sassoon, 'Everyone Sang'.